WESTMINSTER ABBEY
ITS WORSHIP AND
ORNAMENTS

JOHN OF ISLIP, ABBOT OF WESTMINSTER

ALCUIN CLUB COLLECTIONS
No. XXXVIII

WESTMINSTER ABBEY
ITS WORSHIP AND ORNAMENTS

By

JOCELYN PERKINS
C.V.O., M.A., D.C.L., D.D., F.S.A.
SACRIST OF WESTMINSTER ABBEY

VOLUME III

GEOFFREY CUMBERLEGE
OXFORD UNIVERSITY PRESS
LONDON
1952

Oxford University Press, Amen House, London E.C.4

GLASGOW NEW YORK TORONTO MELBOURNE WELLINGTON

BOMBAY CALCUTTA MADRAS CAPE TOWN

Geoffrey Cumberlege, Publisher to the University

PRINTED IN GREAT BRITAIN

CONTENTS

VIII. THE ELEVEN EASTERN CHAPELS

A. *The Chapels of the North Transept*

1. ST. ANDREW 1
2. ST. MICHAEL, ST. MARTIN, AND ALL SAINTS . 3
3. ST. JOHN THE EVANGELIST . . . 4

B. *The Chapels of the North Ambulatory*

1. THE CHANTRY CHAPEL OF JOHN OF ISLIP . . 7
   WITH (i) THE JESUS ALTAR ABOVE . . . 7
   (ii) THE JESUS ALTAR BELOW . . . 7
2. ST. JOHN BAPTIST AND OUR LADY OF THE PUE . 12
3. ST. PAUL 18

C. *The Chapels of the South Ambulatory*

1. ST. NICHOLAS 19
2. ST. EDMUND AND ST. THOMAS OF CANTERBURY . 19
3. ST. BENEDICT 21

D. *The Chapels of the South Transept* . 22

1. ST. BLAISE 24
2. ST. FAITH 27

IX. THE FURNITURE

1. THE PULPITS 33
2. THE FONT 41
3. THE LITANY STOOLS 43
4. THE LECTERNS 45
5. THE GATES 48
6. THE FLOORS 51

X. THE ORNAMENTA

1. THE SIXTEENTH- AND SEVENTEENTH-CENTURY PLATE 55
2. THE VERGES AND MACES 66

3. THE ANCIENT FABRICS 68

    (i) FRONTALS 68

    (ii) COPES 74

    (iii) TAPESTRIES 83

XI. WORSHIP AND ORDER, 1560–1950

1. THE ELIZABETHAN CHAPTER AND THE WORK OF RECONSTRUCTION 87

2. PROGRESS AND DEVELOPMENT UNDER THE EARLY STUARTS 95

3. PURITANISM RAMPANT 102

4. THE REBUILDING OF THE WASTE PLACES . . 112

5. THE END OF THE GOOD DAYS . . . 139

6. DRABNESS AND DULLNESS 141

7. THE STIRRINGS OF NEW LIFE . . . 151

8. A BRIGHTER DAY 155

9. A HALF-CENTURY OF ADVANCE . . . 165

10. THE ABBEY UNDER FIRE 193

APPENDIXES

I. THE INVENTORY OF THE ORNAMENTS IN ST. EDWARD'S CHAPEL IN NOVEMBER 1520 . . . 203

II. THE INVENTORY OF DEAN NEILE . . . 205

III. THE INVENTORY OF 1661 214

IV. THE INVENTORY OF 1750 216

V. A LETTER FROM DEAN GABRIEL GOODMAN TO LORD TREASURER BURGHLEY 217

VI. PARTICULARS OF MONEYS EXPENDED BY THE DEAN AND CHAPTER IN 1660 AND 1661 . . 221

VII. THE WAX CHANDLER'S BILL FOR 1690 . . 222

VIII. THE SURVEYORS OF WESTMINSTER ABBEY . . 223

INDEX TO VOLUMES I–III

INDEX TO VOLUMES I–III . . . 225

ILLUSTRATIONS

1. JOHN OF ISLIP, ABBOT OF WESTMINSTER   *Frontispiece*

Photographed (quarter size) from the Obituary Roll of John of Islip in the Library of the Dean and Chapter of Westminster, by R. B. Fleming.

The Abbot is shown in monastic garb. Above, three albed angels bear shields showing (1) the cross and martlets of St. Edward the Confessor, (2) the cross-keys of St. Peter with the ring of St. Edward, and (3) the Royal Arms of the House of Tudor. Below, surmounted by a mitre, are the Abbot's personal arms, and those of the medieval monastery. On a band beneath the three lower angels are the words *Inquire pacem et persequere eam*, the Abbot's 'reason'. The central figure is bordered by an interlacing trellis of two slipped stems from which spring flowers bearing the names of the grace or virtue with which each is associated:

Dexter	*Sinister*
Honeysuckle—Fortitude	Marigold—Prudence
Violet—Counsel	Borage—Justice
Lily of the Valley—Intellect	Daisy—Temperance
Corncockle—Wisdom	Gilliflower—Constancy
Columbine—Fear of the Lord	Pink—Faith
Fleur-de-lis—Science	Pansy—Hope
Lily—Piety	Rose—Love

2. THE SCREEN OF THE CHAPEL OF ST. ANDREW   *facing page* 2

Eighteenth-century drawing in the Library of the Dean and Chapter of Westminster.

Photograph by R. B. Fleming.

3. THE CHANTRY CHAPEL OF JOHN OF ISLIP   *facing page* 8

Photographed (quarter size) from the Obituary Roll of John of Islip in the Library of the Dean and Chapter of Westminster, by R. B. Fleming.

The artist omits part of the south side of the chantry chapel, so showing the internal arrangements during the short interval between the burial of the Abbot in 1532 and the revolutionary conditions heralded by the Dissolution in 1540. The east wall has a tryptych with a Crucifixion: the decoration above it has long disappeared, and is not recorded.

The altar (the 'Jesus altar below') has a frontal and frontlet. Against the north wall seems to be a smaller altar, which Weever conjectured to be that of St. Erasmus. The Abbot's grave in the centre is marked by a tester on four Renaissance pillars, over a cadaver.

On the left the artist shows Abbot Estney's tomb, and a part of the screen which separated the chapel of St. John the Evangelist from the ambulatory, and was destroyed to make room for the cenotaph of General Wolfe. The demi-figure in a medallion in the upper part of the chantry's western wall no longer exists. It probably disappeared at the same time.

N.B. Other drawings from the Islip Roll have already been reproduced (vol. i, frontispiece; and facing p. 50).

4. THE JESUS CHAPEL IN THE ISLIP CHANTRY TODAY   *facing page* 9

Photograph by R. B. Fleming.

The north wall of the lower stage of Islip's Chantry contains a four-light window, the thank-offering of the present Dean (the Very Rev. Alan C. Don) for the preservation of the Abbey and the Church of St. Margaret during the Second World War; the glass is by Mr. Hugh Easton and was dedicated on 13 March 1949 in memory of Abbot Islip and of Paul de Labillière, sometime Dean.

The kneeling Abbot, in Benedictine habit, holds a model of the buildings added by him to the Deanery; over him is a diamond pane of medieval glass bearing his rebus, and below are the words of his 'reason'. A cherub on the left bears a model of the Abbey, and above are the arms of Dean de Labillière who held office throughout the war.

On the right is St. Margaret of Antioch. A cherub holds a model of St. Margaret's church (rebuilt largely by Islip) and above are the arms of Dean Don, its Rector from 1940 to 1945.

The altar frontal is of Pointe Hongroise, and the ornaments are of silver.

5. THE MURAL PAINTINGS IN THE CHAPEL OF ST. BLAISE   *facing page* 30

Photograph by R. B. Fleming.

These remarkable pictures of the Incredulity of St. Thomas and of St. Christopher bearing the Christ Child have been discovered only in the last few years, having been hidden for several generations by a large monument.

6. THE EAST END OF THE CHAPEL OF ST. FAITH   *facing page* 31

Photograph by R. B. Fleming.

This picture shows an attempt of the thirteenth-century builders to reproduce a normal east end in Pre-Reformation times. Above the Altar is a low reredos on the central panel of which is depicted the Crucifixion with the figures of Our Lady and St. John the Evangelist on either side. The great figure of St. Faith rises above, taking the place of and intended to suggest a stained-glass window.

The Altar is vested in an interesting early-eighteenth-century fabric of rich crimson velvet (see pp. 69, 70).

7. THE CANDLESTICKS OF THE HIGH ALTAR   *facing page* 60

Photograph by A. F. Brown.

8. THE ELIZABETHAN AND THE SPANISH CHALICES   *facing page* 61

Photograph by A. F. Brown.

For the Elizabethan Chalice see pp. 63, 64.

The Spanish Chalice, another memorial gift, is a fine specimen of late-sixteenth-century silver repoussé work, with a charming design of strap work and cherubs' heads. The various marks indicate that it was manufactured in the Salamanca Mint.

On the lower portion of the base is an inscription in Spanish to the following effect:

> The Gift of Antonio de Orveta and
> His Wife of Lima in the Year 1600

9A. SEVENTEENTH-CENTURY FRONTAL OF CLOTH OF GOLD AND CLOTH
OF SILVER   *facing page* 70

Photograph by R. B. Fleming.

9B. SEVENTEENTH-CENTURY FRONTAL OF CRIMSON VELVET
                                                         facing page 70

Photograph by R. B. Fleming.

10. THE FUNERAL ARRAY OF THE HIGH ALTAR   *facing page* 71

Photograph by William E. Gray.

The design of the black frontal and dorsal is based on a description of one of the Pre-Reformation frontals in the Suppression Inventory: 'a black fronte with escutcheons for Abbots' dyrges'. It was decided for this purpose to utilize the splendid array of Benefactors' shields (the oldest architectural heraldry in the world) almost all of which still grace the north and south choir aisles.

From left to right they are as follows:

Top Row

Henry III, King of England. Alexander, King of Scotland. Raymond, Count of Provence. Roger de Quincy, Count of Winchester. Henry de Lacy, Count of Lincoln. Richard, Count of Cornwall.

Middle Row

Frederick II, Holy Roman Emperor. St. Edward the King, Confessor. Louis IX, King of France.

Lower Row

Richard de Clare, Count of Gloucester. Roger Bigod, Count of Norfolk. Simon de Montfort, Count of Leicester. John, Count of Warrenne and Surrey. Humphrey de Bohun, Count of Hereford and Essex. Richard, Count of Rothsay.

This fine work was designed by Mr. W. H. Randoll Blacking and executed by the Royal School of Needlework.

11. THE PROCESSION OF THE REGALIA AT THE CORONATION OF
GEORGE IV   *facing page* 80

From the History of the Coronation of George IV by Sir George Nayler, Garter King of Arms.

Charles Wild, Del^t: M. Dubourg, Sculp^t.

Photograph by R. B. Fleming.

An outdoor Procession from Westminster Hall to the Abbey formed for generations a prominent feature in the great solemnity of the Coronation. It was omitted at the Coronation of William IV to the regret of many, and this precedent has been followed on the four subsequent occasions.

It was the custom for the Regalia (which had been brought from the Tower to the Abbey on the previous afternoon) to be carried at an early hour on Coronation Day by the Dean and Prebendaries (attended by the whole Collegiate body), through the north transept door, to Westminster Hall.

The illustration shows George IV seated at a large table beneath a richly upholstered throne at the south end of the Hall. The Abbey Procession has just entered the building and Dean Ireland is advancing at the head of the Prebendaries to deliver the Crown of St. Edward into the hands of the King. The Dean is wearing a blue velvet cope with a heavy gold fringe, quite unlike anything now possessed by the Abbey. Probably it was made for the occasion. Nothing is known of its existence today. Eleven of the twelve Prebendaries of Westminster were present, the absentee being the Right Rev. Dr. William Carey, a former headmaster and a munificent benefactor to Westminster School. He had been appointed in the previous year to the Bishopric of Exeter, though he retained his Stall at the Abbey for another ten years. He had doubtless elected to take his place among his episcopal brethren on the north side of the Sanctuary.

The six senior Prebendaries at that time were the Rev. C. Fynes Clinton, D.C.L., the Rev. Thomas Causton, D.D., the Rev. H. H. Edwards, M.A., the Rev. Lord Henry Fitzroy, M.A., Rev. Joseph Allen, M.A. (destined in later years to occupy the sees of Bristol and Ely), and the Rev. Frederick Blomberg, M.A. It is these, presumably, who are about to follow the Dean, bearing respectively the Orb, the Rod with the Dove, the Sceptre with the Cross, the Staff of St. Edward, the Bible, and the Paten and Chalice. All six are similarly attired in the plain cloth of gold copes, one of which has, however, disappeared since 1821.

The remaining five Prebendaries find no place in Charles Wild's picture, viz. Rev. W. H. E. Bentinck, M.A., Rev. William Short, D.D., Rev. James Webber, D.D. (later Dean of Ripon), Rev. William Tournay, D.D., and the Rev. Andrew Bell, D.D., LL.D., a great educational reformer—'the eminent founder of the Madras system of education'.

Doubtless they wore the copes of crimson and purple velvet.

The Regalia having been delivered up to the King, the Heralds would then set about the marshalling of the Procession, which included the entire body of Peers, Peeresses, Bishops, Judges, the Dean and Chapter, Heralds, Gentlemen-at-Arms, and many others.

12. THE ABBEY CHOIR AT THE CORONATION OF JAMES II.
I. Collins et Nic Yeates fc. *facing page* 81
Photograph by R. B. Fleming.

Representations of those who took part in the Coronation of James II have been depicted in a remarkable series of plates in the monumental history of that ceremony by Francis Sandford, Lancaster Herald. Here, four Choristers and eight Lay Vicars represent the Abbey Choir in the Procession from Westminster Hall to the Abbey. They wear cassocks and the long surplices of the Anglican tradition.

13. THE STONYHURST COPE *facing page* 90

This superb fabric is made of cloth of gold with the design raised in crimson velvet.

The Crown of England lying on a portcullis is the outstanding feature and occurs three times. The remaining space is occupied with red and white Tudor roses and some elaborate foliage work. There is a border of SSS.

In accordance with the will of Henry VII this cope and its companions were made at Florence and presented by him to Westminster Abbey, doubtless for use in his Chapel.

'The whole suit of vestments and copes of cloth of gold tissue wrought with our badges of red roses and portcullises which we of late at all proper cost and charge caused to be bought and provided at Florence in Italy; that is to say the whole vestments for the Priest, the Deacon and the Sub-Deacon and twenty nine copes of the same cloth and work.'

(Will of Henry VII, 1509)

There is a tradition that this cope was acquired at some unknown date by the Jesuit College (English) at St. Omer, which migrated to Stonyhurst in 1794.

The Hood and Orphrey embroidered with a representation of the Annunciation and Saints beneath canopies are said to be English work, much restored.

'For breadth and beauty of pattern and for the labour that must have been bestowed upon it, the cope stands unrivalled as a work of the loom in the sixteenth century.'

At Stonyhurst College is preserved also a chasuble of strikingly similar material, but restored and doubtless reduced. Is it one of 'the whole suit of vestments' mentioned above in the royal will? Nothing is known of the dalmatic and tunicle.

N.B. I am greatly indebted for this information to the Rev. H. Chadwick, S.J., Librarian of Stonyhurst College.

14. THE BLUE SILK COPE OF DEAN SPRAT *facing page* 166

Photograph by A. F. Brown.

This cope, said to be of French origin, was the personal property of Dean Sprat and was given to the Dean and Chapter by his widow in 1713. The wearer in this picture is the Rev. Lord John Thynne at the Coronation of Queen Victoria when, though Sub-Dean, he was Dean *de facto*. He had been made Sub-Dean of Lincoln at an early age, but was installed at Westminster in 1831, just before the Coronation of William IV. His connexion with the Abbey was fruitful, potent, and continuous to his death. An unconscious reformer before the age of Church Reform, yet a staunch adherent to ancient usage, he directed his zeal to the removal of abuses, the raising of the standard and scope of the services, and the enrichment of the fabric. Twice over and for long periods he acted as Dean *de facto*, and though offered the Deanery by Sir Robert Peel on the departure of Samuel Wilberforce to Oxford in 1845, he never desired to be other than second officer in the Church of Westminster. Nothing was more remarkable than the chivalry with which he handed over to two Deans the powers that he himself had wielded. For half a century he was part of the Abbey, 'like one of its own massive pillars'.

15. THE CLERGY OFFICIATING AT THE THANKSGIVING SERVICE FOR THE GOLDEN JUBILEE OF QUEEN VICTORIA, 20 JUNE 1887

facing page 167

This photograph was taken in the College Garden of the Abbey after the great ceremony. Dean Bradley occupies the centre of the picture, wearing Dean Sprat's cope of blue silk. Archbishop Benson (Canterbury) and Archbishop Thomson (York) are in purple velvet copes. Dr. Temple, Bishop of London, wears the robes of a Peer, possibly because all the available copes of the Abbey were in use. The Sub-Dean (Canon Prothero) and Dr. Duck-worth, being the two senior Canons, have been assigned the copes of crimson velvet, while the rest of the Chapter (viz. Canons Farrar, Furse, Rowsell, and Westcott) appear in the plain cloth of gold fabrics. The five Minor Canons are wearing Choir habit.

16. THE BANNER OF OUR LADY — *facing page* 182
Photograph by R. B. Fleming.

This magnificent Banner, designed by Sir J. Ninian Comper, displays modern English embroidery at its best. The groundwork consists of silk brocade, divided into alternate panels of blue and murrey. On Our Lady's right stands St. Peter grasping two keys, one of gold and the other of silver; on her left is the Founder of the Abbey, St. Edward the Confessor. The latter is represented as a young man, full of health and vigour, in remarkable contrast with the bearded, white-haired figure of medieval art.

The back of the Banner consists of a groundwork of blue silk, embroidered with the so-called arms of St. Edward the Confessor and the following words by Mr. John Drinkwater, in gold:

They died that freedom still should live.
In life, O friends as proudly give.

The Banner forms a Memorial from the relatives and friends of members of the Girls' Friendly Society to those who gave their lives in the First World War. The work was carried out at the Royal School of Needlework. The dedication took place on 4 November 1922.

17. A BODY OF SERVERS — *facing page* 183
'Illustrated' copyright photograph.

The Brotherhood of St. Edward the Confessor was formed in 1929—a guild of servers, confined to former Choristers of the Abbey, who officiate as indicated in the picture.

The group stands before the Altar of the Holy Cross. The Cross-bearer wears the Abbey's fine blue tunicle, and the Officiant wears one of the crimson velvet copes designed for the Coronation of Edward VII.

PART VIII

THE ELEVEN EASTERN CHAPELS

(a) The Chapels of the North Transept

PARTITIONS of wood or stone extended from the east end of the stalls from pier to pier of the lantern, forming the choir into a great inner chapel. They were pierced by doorways entitled the *ostia presbyterii*. One of these led by a descent of three steps into the north transept, where a scene of spacious beauty met the eye—the floor space then devoid of chairs, or pews, or the gigantic piles of commemorative masonry of today.

The eastern aisle was occupied by a range of chapels separated by richly designed screens, and furnished in the most sumptuous manner. A few traces still survive of this medieval splendour which, coupled with some stray remarks of older historians, suggest a wonderful ensemble. John Carter's righteous indignation is fully intelligible:

'We see nearly the whole space and the site of these several altars occupied with monuments face to face and back to back striving which should have the greatest portion of elbow-room, and setting at nought the old idea that the statue of the deceased should front the east.'[1]

1. THE CHAPEL OF SAINT ANDREW

In the northern bay was the Chapel of St. Andrew, smaller than its companions, by reason of a doorway in the eastern wall. It has been conjectured that this doorway opened upon a covered pathway to the Palace, for the convenience of the Royal Family when visiting the Abbey on less important occasions.[2]

---

[1] *Gentleman's Magazine*, 1799, p. 669.
[2] Frederick Bond, *Westminster Abbey*, p. 92.

B

The Purbeck marble shafts on the west side have retained their brilliant sheen, for until comparatively recent times they were protected by an elaborate screen provided, with other furniture, by James Palmer, Clerk to Edward III, and renovated by Abbot Kirton[1] at a cost of £10. According to Keepe, it was 'richly adorned with curious carvings and other imagery work of birds, flowers, cherubim, devices, mottoes, and coats of arms of many of the chief nobility painted thereon, all done by the command and at the charge and cost of Edward Kirton, Abbot of Westminster'.[2]

Dart, writing about forty years later, states that the screen was 'one of the beautifullest pieces of ancient work that I have seen; for it was not long since removed—when some marks of the painting and gilding still remained'.[3]

The Dean and Chapter possess a picture of this screen dated February 1722 which shows that these writers were using no exaggerated language. It consisted of stone tracery divided into twelve lights with a central doorway, the spandrels adorned with two crowned figures holding inscribed scrolls. Above was an inscription with a *rose-en-soleil*, its centre inscribed with the Sacred Monogram. The pinnacled frieze with its clusters of angels, shields, trees, scrolls, gilt eagles, and black ravens could hardly have been richer. The wanton destruction of this screen was a grievous disaster. A vague statement has been inserted on the drawing that it was removed during the preparations for a Coronation in the eighteenth century, presumably that of George II on October 11th, 1727. Probably this inscription is incorrect and the explanation must be sought in the huge monument erected on this site by James Gibbs to the memory of John Holles, Duke of Newcastle. The artist, who is said to have 'staked his immortality' on his

[1] Abbot of Westminster 1440–62. Pearce, *Monks of Westminster*, p. 130.
[2] Keepe, *Monumenta Westmonasteriensia*, p. 170; John Crull, *The Antiquities of St. Peter's, Westminster*, vol. i, p. 221.
[3] Dart, *Westmonasterium*, vol. i, p. 40.

THE SCREEN OF THE CHAPEL OF ST. ANDREW

design, secured the approbation of the Chapter, but the screen received its death sentence. The Duke died in 1711, but the monument was not erected till twelve years later, that is to say, shortly after the drawing was made. Whatever the explanation, the loss of the screen was deplorable.

2. THE CHAPEL OF SAINT MICHAEL, SAINT MARTIN, AND ALL SAINTS

The next chapel bears the composite dedication of St. Michael, St. Martin, and All Saints. It retains one substantial fragment of former magnificence, a mutilated portion of an elaborate reredos of the fifteenth century. Half of it was evidently destroyed when Roubilliac's famous monument of Lady Nightingale was erected. The remainder was revealed only when it was found necessary to reconstruct the huge cenotaph of Sarah, Duchess of Somerset, which had become ruinous. The reredos consists of three canopied niches with ribbed vaults, together with pinnacles and buttresses. Beneath, though largely hidden, are remains of the panelling at the back of the former altar. The dimensions of the reredos agree with the groove of the wall where the altar once stood, but it cannot definitely be affirmed that it belonged to this particular chapel. The altar was the gift of Roger Cretton and John Savery.[1]

It is a wonder that even these pitiful remnants should have survived when the neglect which this group of chapels have suffered is borne in mind. Keepe states that during the closing decades of the seventeenth century the monuments in these three chapels were 'almost covered by the scaffolds placed here, being made use of at present for the lower Convocation house for the Deans, Prebends and

---

[1] Stanley, *Historical Memorials of Westminster Abbey*, 3rd edition, p. 610; Pearce, *Monks of Westminster*, p. 121.

Doctors, and that of King Henry VII is for Archbishop and Bishops when the Parliament sits at Westminster'.[1]

3. THE CHAPEL OF SAINT JOHN THE EVANGELIST

The third chapel was dedicated to St. John the Evangelist, a Saint ever dear to the Confessor's heart. It was a square sided double-bayed building, originally the largest chapel in the church except the Lady Chapel. It was divided into two portions by an open arch forming a miniature nave and chancel and surrounded by screens of great beauty. Shortly before the close of the monastic period it underwent almost complete reconstruction at the hands of Abbot John of Islip, who reduced its area by one-half. One remnant of its medieval glory has fortunately survived in its western screen though little trace of the original colouring survives.

The story of the restoration of this screen is remarkable. During the seventeenth and eighteenth centuries it was by degrees imbedded in a collection of monuments, six on its western side and three on its eastern, an immense wall of marble serving as a background for these pious memorials. During the early years of Dean Stanley's decanate the marble wall was removed, when the lower portion of the western screen and the doorway by which access was gained to the Chapel were revealed. Realizing that the screen agreed in every detail with that in the Chapel of St. Nicholas, Gilbert Scott at once gave orders for its complete restoration, or, it would be more correct to say, rebuilding. Unfortunately, the doorway was subsequently utilized for the monument of Sir John Franklin. This much-restored relic of the past consists of three bays, each of four cinque-foiled lights and a doorway in the centre with a four-centred head.

[1] Keepe, *Monumenta Westmonasteriensia*, p. 172. See vol. ii, pp. xiii and xiv, also illustration facing p. 166.

The southern screen of the Chapel must have been a real gem, for it was 'made and adorned with several coats of arms by John Estney, Abbot, painted and gilt with gold who lies on the south his effigies engraved in brass'.[1] An illustration in the Islip Roll gives some idea of the general appearance of the Abbot's tomb and this southern screen prior to their demolition by the rude hand of the eighteenth century.[2]

There now appears upon the scene a Dean the results of whose regrettable exploits in this part of the Abbey can never be removed. Zachary Pearce was born with a silver spoon in his mouth. He inherited wealth, he married wealth, he received wealth, and he derived practical benefit from a wealth of powerful friends, among them the learned but highly unorthodox Consort of George II. He became a Queen's Scholar in 1704 and was elected from the School to Trinity College, Cambridge. Fortune quickly smiled upon him, for at the early age of thirty-four he was preferred to the important benefice of St. Martin-in-the-Fields, thanks to the powerful influence of Lord Chancellor Parker. Nineteen years later he received the Deanery of Winchester, followed by the Bishopric of Bangor, and in 1755 the Deanery of Westminster then held *in commendam* with the Bishopric of Rochester.

Pearce was in some ways a favourable example of the Walpole-Newcastle type of Bishop. He was an excellent classical scholar, Cicero and Longinus being his favourite authors. He took part in the Deist Controversy, roundly accusing Conyers Middleton of infidelity. His work on the latter author ran into no less than nine editions. He took a genuine interest in his remote Diocese of which he made a tour almost every year. He always promoted Welsh clergy when he could, thus setting a worthy example to some of his brethren. But there is not much more to be said

[1] Keepe, *Monumenta Westmonasteriensia*, p. 164.
[2] See illustration facing p. 8.

in his favour. He was but slenderly equipped with gifts of administration. The criticism of one of his Prebendaries at Winchester, when there was some possibility of his chief being promoted to the See of London (for which, to do him justice, Pearce had no ambitions whatever), could hardly have been more scathing.[1]

Pearce's administration at the Abbey was disastrous. Although an Old Westminster, he never seems to have taken root in the Deanery. Like most of his contemporaries, he was incapable of appreciating the Gothic beauty of the church, but one might well have expected that a man of his literary ability would have acquired sufficient historical appreciation to preserve him from some of his unfortunate errors. During his decanate there was celebrated the Bicentenary of the Foundation of the Collegiate Church by Queen Elizabeth in 1560. It fell to Pearce's lot to preach the sermon on this historic occasion, but it displayed little grasp of the significance of Queen Elizabeth in the history either of the Abbey or the country.

Almost on the same day the body of General Wolfe was laid in his father's grave at Greenwich. The authorities were obviously bound to respect the urgent request of his bereaved mother, but it will always be a matter for regret that one of the Makers of Canada was not laid to rest in the Abbey, there to sleep with 'king and statesman, chief and sage'. The task of designing a suitable memorial full worthy of the 'little red haired corporal' was placed in the hands of the sculptor Joseph Wilton, at that time rising to fame. The vast proportions of the monument, one of the largest in the Abbey, indicates the burst of national enthusiasm evoked by Wolfe's heroic exploit, but it provided the unfortunate Dean with a tough, practical problem with which he was ill-equipped to deal. At this point Horace Walpole made his appearance. He has told the discreditable story in characteristic fashion and he has managed to

[1] See vol. i, p. 133.

confine Pearce in a literary pillory from which he will never emerge.[1]

After two centuries we are amazed that it should have been possible to consider seriously the iniquitous proposal to remove the Tomb of Aymer de Valence. Fortunately it still remains to delight our eyes, but its continued existence has been made possible only by the sacrifice of a lesser but still priceless gem. The scapegoat was the southern screen of St. John's Chapel, together with the fine tombs of Abbot Estney and Sir John Harpedon, which still survive in a somewhat battered condition. Of the remainder of the furniture provided for this Chapel by the bounty of William Sonwell[2] not a vestige remains. Such was the result of the Dean's concession of 'ten feet' to Wilton and others!

(b) The Chapels of the North Ambulatory

1. THE CHANTRY CHAPEL OF JOHN OF ISLIP

'The last efflorescence of monastic architecture co-incided with its imminent downfall.'[3] In this picturesque sentence Dean Stanley has summed up the significance of the Chantry Chapel of Abbot John of Islip. It forms, together with the lower portions of the western towers, the last piece of constructive work before the great crash. Of the pre-Reformation Abbots Islip alone achieved the distinction of being interred in a chapel of rare beauty, linked in perpetuity with his name.

This 'good old father', whose motto was 'seek peace and ensue it', was a dynamic personality. The building of Henry VII's Chapel, and St. Margaret's Church, the completion of the nave, and the extensive additions to the Abbot's House, could scarcely have been carried through successfully had the Church of Westminster not been

---

[1] See vol. i, p. 83.
[2] Pearce, *Monks of Westminster*, p. 124.
[3] Stanley, *Historical Memorials of Westminster Abbey*, p. 336.

blessed with a chief endowed with those gifts which make for vigorous leadership.

In the erection of his chantry chapel, Islip gave signal proof of these qualities. The Norman Abbots had been content with a humble resting-place in the cloister, where they lie beneath simple incised slabs. Under the Tudors there uprises this commanding figure who erected for himself a building intended to serve as a mausoleum and chantry chapel, thus emulating King Harry of Monmouth himself. It represented a striking new development and the manner of its execution was on a par with the conception. The story is told by a picture in the Islip Roll. The Abbot was not the man to do things by halves. He chose the large double-bayed chapel of St. John the Evangelist for the furtherance of his ambitious scheme, boldly reducing its area by one-half. He cut off the eastern portion by means of a wall which he adorned with a medallion bearing the head of Our Lord. In the space thus acquired he built his chantry chapel, dividing it by means of a floor into an upper and a lower chapel, each furnished with an altar at which Masses were directed to be constantly said for the repose of the Abbot's soul.[1]

The south front consists of two stories divided by a moulded cornice enriched by various carved devices, including the Abbot's name, his arms, and his rebus (an eye and a man with a hand breaking off a slip from a tree). The two eastern bays of the lower story are pierced with a fine window of five cinquefoiled lights; the western bay is filled in its head with blind but similar tracery, and a doorway beneath. The upper story is a mass of sculptured panelling, alternating with a series of seven cinquefoiled niches.

The great feature of the Lower Chapel is the elaborate fan-vaulted roof, the moulded ribs of which unite in an eight-pointed star. The cells are filled with carved devices, viz. Islip's arms and rebus, with his name in large charac-

---

[1] Stanley, *Historical Memorials of Westminster Abbey*, pp. 335 and 336.

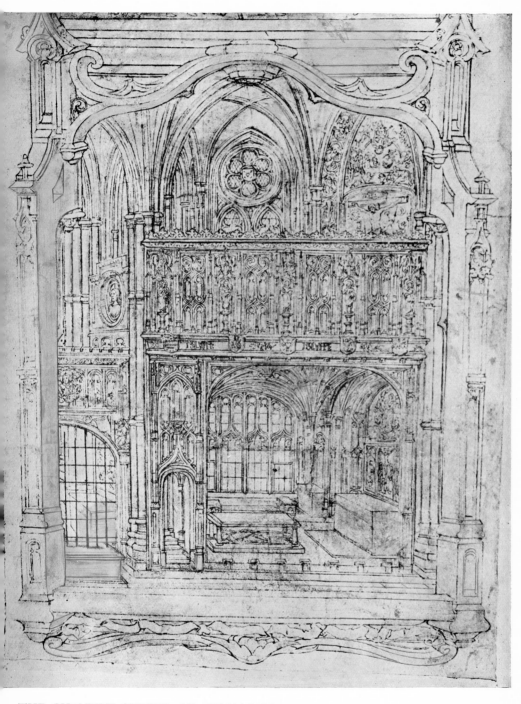

THE CHANTRY CHAPEL OF ABBOT ISLIP AND THE JESUS ALTAR BELOW

THE JESUS CHAPEL IN THE ISLIP CHANTRY TODAY

ters. The north wall is pierced by a large window containing four cinquefoiled ogee lights with tracery in a four-centred head. The western wall is covered with window-tracery panelling, consisting of ten ogee cinquefoiled lights with vertical tracery in a four-centred head.

The Upper Chapel was provided with an organ and it was here that the Jesus Anthem was sung after Compline on Friday evenings. At one or both of these two chapels the *Missa Nominis Jesu* was said or sung every Friday throughout the year. Such forms of devotion—Jesus Masses and Jesus Anthems—became exceedingly popular during the fourteenth and fifteenth centuries, not only at Westminster but also at Worcester, Norwich, Durham, and elsewhere.[1] As time went on, the Chantry came to be known as the 'Jesus Altar above' and the 'Jesus Altar below'.

The Islip Roll indicates that the eastern walls of both Upper and Lower Chapels were richly painted. The latter contained a large Crucifixion with the Doom above.[2] None of this decorative work exists today, except that in the Upper Chapel, on the side walls of the eastern recess, there are the remains of two large figures of kings, standing on pedestals beneath canopies painted in monochrome.

Islip was buried in a large vault beneath the Lower Chapel. The place was marked by two slabs of marble surmounted by a tester of black marble resting upon fluted bronze columns of Renaissance design with acanthus capitals and moulded bands at half their height. This tester still remains and it is possible that it forms another specimen of the genius of Pietro Torrigiano.

The Islip Chantry Chapel has suffered greater degradation than almost any other part of the Abbey. The

---

[1] Rev. J. T. Fowler, *Rites of Durham*, pp. 220–2.

[2] John Weaver described this decoration as 'the picture of Our Saviour Christ hanging on the cross seeming to call to give good counsel unto mankind in certain rimes with Abbot Islip holding up his hands in prayer beneath'. *Ancient Funerall Monuments*, p. 488.

destruction of its two altars was the first ignominy, followed in the reign of James I by the intrusion of a massive but uninteresting tomb of Sir Christopher Hatton which usurped the place of one of them. Worse was to come, for which Zachary Pearce was partly, if not wholly, responsible.

This Dean never lacked influential friends; prominent among them was the celebrated statesman, William Pulteney, 'the greatest leader of Opposition that the House of Commons had ever seen',[1] as Sir Robert Walpole learned to his cost. Pulteney and Pearce were both of them Old Westminsters; they probably overlapped, for barely six years separated them. When Pearce entered upon his long incumbency of the Church of St. Martin-in-the-Fields, Pulteney evidently became a member of his congregation, for the registers record the burial in one of its vaults of an infant son in 1726, a daughter aged fifteen in 1741, and his wife Anna Maria in 1758. By this time Pearce had been Dean of Westminster for two years, largely through the powerful influence of his friend, now become Earl of Bath.

Doubtless it was the memories associated with his school-days and his close friendship with the Dean which determined Pulteney, when verging upon four-score years he lost his eldest surviving son, to provide for his own burial in the Abbey. He was allowed to invade the sepulchre of the great Islip and constitute a new vault therein, for himself and his family. On April 20th, 1763, the remains of the Countess and the two children were transferred from St. Martin's to this new resting-place.[2] They were joined on the following day by the son who had died at Madrid twelve weeks before at the early age of thirty-two from a fever contracted while serving with

[1] Macaulay, *Critical and Historical Essays*, ii, pp. 153, 154.
[2] J. L. Chester, *The Marriage, Baptismal and Burial Registers of the Collegiate Church of Westminster*, pp. 402, 404.

the Grenadier Guards in the Peninsula. Finally, the Earl
of Bath was allowed to add an enormous ledger of black
marble, on which he recorded the deaths of his wife and
children.[1]

In the following year he died himself and was buried by
Pearce at dead of night amid scenes of indescribable dis-
order. In the general confusion 'a dreadful conflict' ensued.[2]
Spectators standing on the tomb of Edward I tore down its
tester and used the woodwork as well as their swords in
defence! It must have been a terrible experience for the
old Dean to witness such a close to the friendship of a life-
time.

In order to facilitate the carrying of coffins into the
Chapel, the Abbey authorities actually permitted the
destruction of one of the beautiful bays of the south front
and the substitution of a coarsely carved wooden door.
The date of this outrage is uncertain, but suspicion inevitably falls upon the decanate of Zachary Pearce. After
such happenings, it is hardly surprising to learn that at
a later date this beautiful place was converted into 'the
rubbish hole of the church', while its screen was 'backed
up with deal boards'.[3] So completely was it barred off that
most people were actually unaware of its existence, which
was 'for no other reason but that it is the memorial of
Islip'. John Carter, most downright of men, might well
exclaim, 'Why this relick of the venerable Islip on which a
greater degree of ornament has been bestowed than fell to
the lot of most of these small chapels, should have been in
particular seized upon for a receptacle of dirt and rubbish
cannot well be conceived'.[4]

Fortunately the wheel has come full circle during recent
years. During the early forties the Chapel received a care-

[1] His own death and titles are recorded at the foot of the ledger in characters
of different lettering.
[2] *Gentleman's Magazine*, 1799, part ii, p. 859.
[3] Ibid., p. 734.
[4] *Gentleman's Magazine*, 1812, p. 339.

ful scientific cleansing, with the result that the sculpture now appears in all its original beauty. The destroyed bay has been made good and the ugly wooden door has disappeared. The altar has been set up once more and provided with suitable furnishings, and the Holy Mysteries are now celebrated here every week.

These welcome developments were happily linked with the Wilberforce family, three of whom in successive generations have been associated with the Abbey—William Wilberforce, the great philanthropist buried in the north transept; Samuel Wilberforce, the famous Bishop of Oxford and Winchester, who for a short time was Dean of Westminster; and Basil Wilberforce, for upwards of twenty years Canon of Westminster and Rector of the Church of St. John. Their names have been recorded on a marble tablet.

This work of renovation has been crowned by the filling of the large window with stained glass, the gift of the Very Reverend Dean Don, carried out by Mr. Hugh Easton.

2. THE CHAPELS OF SAINT JOHN BAPTIST AND OUR LADY OF THE PUE

The radiating chapel next eastward is dedicated to St. John Baptist. It is filled with tombs of varying dates, many of great historical interest. Like its neighbours, it was protected by a screen, with an entrance in the centre. Unfortunately the screen was swept away in order to provide space for the three fine tombs of Abbot George Fascet, Thomas Ruthall Bishop of Durham, and Abbot William of Colchester. Not a trace of the reredos (the gift of two monks, John London and John Northampton[1]) or the other pre-Reformation furniture, has survived, save a double locker in the north bay of thirteenth-century date.

The Chapels of Abbot Islip and St. John Baptist are divided from each other by an immense buttress of such

[1] Pearce, *The Monks of Westminster*, pp. 112 and 115.

thickness that it was found possible to scoop out an alcove to serve as a small chapel consisting of two bays of irregular form, the walls and ceiling of which were decorated with exceptionally brilliant painting. In this small chapel, the white hart of Richard II appears on the eastern wall, an indication that this development took place during the last quarter of the fourteenth century. The Assumption of the Blessed Virgin is depicted in the central boss of the vault. The remains of a painted aureole, its rays evidently designed to emanate from the head of a statue supported by a bracket on the north wall, suggest that here stood the Chapel of Our Lady of the Pue, or, as it was sometimes termed, Saint Mary the Little. A hole in the vault indicates the existence of a chain, supporting a lamp in front of the statue.

It is natural to connect this little chapel with the Dame Mary of St. Pol, Countess of Pembroke and founder of the College of that name in the University of Cambridge. She was the third wife of Aymer de Valence, whose stately tomb occupies a prominent position in the Presbytery. According to one tradition, her marriage was coupled with the tragic murder of her husband on their wedding-day. The Countess at some unknown date presented to this Chapel an alabaster image of the Blessed Virgin and also provided for the decoration of the roof. On her death in 1377 she bestowed further benefactions,[1] including an endowment for the support of a chantry priest attached to a chapel near her husband's tomb. The Virgin's symbol of the painted stars on the roof of this Chapel, the carving of the Assumption, and the close proximity of Aymer's tomb, speak for themselves. Before very long further offerings began to find their way 'ad ymaginem beate marie vocate le pewe'.

It has been suggested by Dean Armitage Robinson that

[1] These included a gold cross set with emeralds, images of St. Peter and St. Andrew, a gold chalice, and two tapestries.

this is the chapel alluded to by Froissart when describing
the historical visit paid to the Abbey by Richard II, before
he went forth to meet Wat Tyler at Smithfield in 1381
'imploring help where human counsel was altogether
useless'.

'In this church there is a statue of Our Lady in a small chapel,
that has many virtues and performs great miracles, in which
the Kings of England have much faith. The King made his
devotions, and paid his offering to this shrine.'[1]

In 1523 this Chapel underwent rough handling, for in
that year the fine tomb of Bishop Ruthall made its appearance. The Abbey authorities regarded the latter as so
important that they even blocked up the entrance to the
Chapel of Saint John Baptist. Drastic measures became
necessary, and the Chapel of Our Lady of the Pue suffered.
This small two-bayed building was deprived of a portion of its north-eastern corner, and converted into a
passage-way. The statue of Our Lady with its lamp may
conceivably have remained, but the altar inevitably disappeared. It was an inglorious end.[2] The original doors
have been preserved, and still display considerable traces
of their original gay decoration; indeed this little chapel,
despite its losses, still forms one of the gems of the Abbey.
The outer doorway has shafted jambs with a cinquefoiled
and subcusped arch in a square head with foliated spandrels, terminating in figures of angels supporting shields
of St. Edward the Confessor and France Ancient and England quarterly. A quantity of vermilion painting with
diapering of black lines on white has survived neglect and
the passage of time. The doors are in two folds, divided
into five panels with cinquefoiled heads and foliated spandrels. The iron *chevaux-de-frise* still remains, and likewise the grate at the head of the doorways. Both the outer
and the inner bays display a great quantity of elaborate

[1] *Proceedings of the British Academy*, 1907, vol. iii, pp. 15–17; J. A. Robinson,
An Unrecognised Westminster Chronicler, p. 7.
[2] Francis Bond, *Westminster Abbey*, pp. 252, 253.

colour decoration of a brocade pattern with blue centres, on some of which are white fleurs-de-lis. The gorged white hart on the east wall is still distinct. The lesser bosses of the vaulting consist of roses and heads of angels, while the ribs are decorated with barber's-pole bands and rosettes. The walls are covered with pear-shaped decorations, on each of which is a fleur-de-lis. On the north side is a richly painted niche with a cinquefoiled and subcusped head beneath which is the outline of a figure with long painted radiations round its head. The general ensemble is most beautiful; and it is a matter for congratulation that this glorious work has survived. It helps us to realize the brilliant appearance of the interior of the Abbey in Pre-Reformation times.

Immediately above the entrance to the Chapel of Our Lady of the Pue are painted the words *Sanctus Erasmus*. This inscription has been responsible for creating more than one problem, not yet entirely solved.

Elizabeth Wydville,[1] Queen Consort of Edward IV, could claim a more intimate association with the Abbey than any other member of the Royal Family, before or after. It fell to the lot of this hapless lady, twice over during her storm-tossed career, to have personal experience of its inner life as a 'sanctuary woman'. In the great political crisis which arose half-way through her husband's reign, she 'took Westminster', that is to say, she fled here for refuge, together with her three little girls and Lady Scrope. She was welcomed by Abbot Millyng who provided the party with a daily allowance of 'half a loaf and two muttons'. In the midst of all this turmoil she gave birth on November 4th, 1470, to her eldest son, the unfortunate Edward V. Born in the Sanctuary 'like any poor woman's child', and attended by the Sanctuary nurse, the little Prince was baptized in the Abbey by the Sub-Prior, with Abbot Millyng, the Prior, and Lady Scrope as his god-parents. This en-

---

[1] Agnes Strickland, *Queens of England*, vol. iii, passages in pp. 328–77.

forced sojourn of the much-tried Queen Consort within
the precinct of the Abbey lasted several months before it
terminated with the triumphal entry of her husband into
London.

Edward IV and his wife had good reasons, then, for
showing their affection to the great church which had
thrown open its gates to this defenceless group of women
and children. Abbot Millyng was immediately promoted
to the Bishopric of Hereford. The King granted a handsome contribution of fourscore oaks towards the building
of the nave, while in 1486 the Queen herself made an
important addition to the thirteenth-century Lady Chapel,
known as the Chapel of St. Erasmus, and endowed it by
Royal Charter with property in Westminster. It probably
stood at the west end on the south side. Its span of life,
however, was brief, for it was demolished with the Lady
Chapel when Henry VII and Abbot Islip embarked
upon their vast undertakings at the east end of the
Abbey.[1]

Obviously such sweeping changes could hardly be carried through without compensation. The memory of
Elizabeth Wydville's bounty would be far too fresh in the
minds of men. Moreover, her eldest daughter was now
seated upon the throne. The complete suppression of the
Chapel of St. Erasmus was unthinkable, though the form
of the compensation offered is not very clear. It has been
suggested by the late Mr. J. T. Micklethwaite that the
Chapel of Our Lady of the Pue underwent some kind of
enlargement in order that it might accommodate the altar
of St. Erasmus.

Others again have affirmed that the whole chapel was
henceforth appropriated to St. Erasmus and that the altar
of Our Lady of the Pue was re-erected in St. John Baptist's Chapel, or possibly that a new double dedication was

---

[1] R. B. Rackham, *The Nave of Westminster*, p. 33.

bestowed upon the old altar in that building.[1] There is
some reason for thinking that at a later date an altar in the
Islip Chapel (for there were undoubtedly two in the lower
story) was dedicated to St. Erasmus; in fact, Weaver
actually speaks of 'the Chapel of Erasmus where he (Islip)
lies buried'.[2] Opinions are likely to differ indefinitely.

The beautiful panel or niche over the doorway, beneath
which is inscribed the Saint's name, must always have been
closely associated with St. Erasmus. It forms one of the
most attractive pieces of sculpture in the Abbey, and fully
deserves John Carter's rapturous eulogy.

'If ever the chisel of our ancient artists had brought their
art to its summit of perfection, if ever excess knew its utmost
bounds, the recess over the chapel is a most striking proof of
their genius and their extraordinary skill.'[3]

It has generally been supposed that this lovely piece of
work which once enclosed a statue of St. Erasmus was
brought here from Elizabeth Wydville's chapel and reset
in this new position by Abbot Islip. The niche, which is of
exceptional breadth, is of painted alabaster, with a triple
canopy of tabernacle work of the most elaborate description, surmounted by carved cresting. Its base, enriched
with *roses-en-soleil* and quatrefoils, is enclosed in squares.
It is flanked by scrolls, pierced with daggers, and by
several carved and painted badges of Abbot Islip, whose
name is repeated twice. Beneath is the fifteenth-century
inscription, *Sanctus Erasmus*. Whether the inscription
refers to the Chapel or merely to the niche and the statue
it once contained remains a problem.[4]

Carter continues in his characteristic fashion 'Well could
I lament away an age for the irreparable loss this recess has

[1] Francis Bond, *Westminster Abbey*, p. 254.
[2] John Weaver, *Funeral Monuments*, p. 488.
[3] *Gentleman's Magazine*, 1799, p. 734.
[4] Professor Lethaby ultimately came to take the view that the panel 'is a work
of Abbot Islip's time', and that 'his initials beside it were carved by the artist who
made the panel'. *Westminster Abbey Re-examined*, p. 297.

cruelly sustained, by cutting away parts of its work for the purpose of introducing a despicable performance of some low-hoveled cutter of monumental memorials'.[1] It is only fair to say that the latter object no longer disfigures the niche.

3. THE CHAPEL OF SAINT PAUL

The Chapel of St. Paul has suffered no less than its neighbours. The picture of the Dedication of the Abbey given to this Chapel by John Sutton disappeared long ago.[2] The magnificent fifteenth-century screen of freestone remains in part, though badly injured. It consisted originally of five bays. Almost the whole of that portion which lies to the west of the doorway was destroyed in the eighteenth century to make room for the monument of the first Earl of Bath.

Fortunately the charming doors with their cinquefoiled panels have survived. The doorway is flanked by panelled buttresses with a four-centred arch in a square head with foliated spandrels. Above are four open cinquefoiled lights, surmounted by a moulded and embattled cornice. The splendid tomb of Ludovic Robessart, Lord Bouchier, has been incorporated with the eastern portion and lies outside the scope of this volume. It must suffice to say that 'the whole was brilliantly coloured and gilded including the big heraldic beasts and the banners they bear'.[3]

Things have changed since John Carter indignantly exclaimed, 'this monument is an incitement to emulation, it only waits the fiat—we want its room. Perhaps the statue of some overgrown nabob or some harpy fattened on the widow's and orphan's tears may soon be elevated on its overthrown glories, conquered by interest and innovation.'[4]

---

[1] *Gentleman's Magazine*, 1799, p. 734.
[2] Pearce, *Monks of Westminster*, pp. 54–5.
[3] Lethaby, *Westminster Abbey and the King's Craftsmen*, p. 32.
[4] *Gentleman's Magazine*, 1799, p. 734.

The safety of the surviving portion of the screen can fortunately be assured.

(c) The Chapels of the South Ambulatory

1. THE CHAPEL OF SAINT NICHOLAS

The fate of the Chapel of St. Nicholas resembles that of St. Paul. Every trace of the altar adorned by William Bromle[1] and other furniture (except a double locker) has disappeared. Fortunately the fine fifteenth-century screen has survived virtually intact, likewise the oaken door hung in two folds with cinquefoiled panels. The former is of stone and divided into six bays, one of which forms the doorway. The side bays are divided into three ranges of cinquefoiled headed panels, the two ranges being open. Above is a moulded and embattled cornice with a series of shields with roses, vine leaves, and heads of lions. Two of these bear the initials W. and A., referring possibly to Abbot Colchester. Over the doorway is a four-centred arch, its spandrels decorated with a pelican and a falcon.

2. THE CHAPEL OF SAINT EDMUND AND SAINT THOMAS OF CANTERBURY

This Chapel occupied a position of special dignity. It enjoyed a royal endowment which, in addition to its support of certain charities for the benefit of the poor, provided a fee of three shillings and fourpence to any priest who said Mass here on the Feasts of the Nativity and the Translations of St. Edmund and St. Thomas.[2] Interment therein, a great privilege, came to be designated burial 'entre les royals'.

The Chapel has suffered terribly. The sculptured reredos has disappeared, while the clumsy and unsightly top rail of the screen recalls a gruesome disaster.

[1] Pearce, *Monks of Westminster*, pp. 100–1.
[2] H. F. Westlake, *Westminster Abbey*, vol. ii, p. 411.

Shortly before Christmas 1776 a well-known figure passed away, Elizabeth Percy, Duchess of Northumberland, the sole heiress of Charles, Duke of Somerset, and the first of her name to be interred in the Northumberland vault in the adjoining chapel. The deceased Duchess earnestly desired that her obsequies should be characterized by simplicity rather than pomp, and that her funeral should be 'as private as her rank may admit'. Accordingly the service was fixed to take place at an extremely late hour. But the Abbey authorities were sadly at fault in their preparations. The arrangements made to secure good order and decorum proved wholly inadequate. The general public poured in, creating utter confusion in the dim, mysterious Abbey lighted only with candles and torches. Unfortunately, a considerable number managed to secure, as they supposed, a highly favourable position for viewing the spectacle, on the screen of St. Edmund's Chapel.

The full procession, ending with the Dean and the distinguished mourners, had just reached the Chapel of St. Nicholas with the open Northumberland vault, when suddenly the heavy wooden screen collapsed. In one moment the whole structure, said to have weighed no less than three tons, lay on the floor in fragments, with spectators pinned beneath. The performance of the Burial Service was impossible. Dean Thomas hastily retired, while efforts were made to release the unhappy sufferers. Two hours and a half after the body had entered the Abbey the delayed funeral rites were performed; but it must have been a strangely unedifying ceremony, conducted between one and two in the morning to the accompaniment of cries of 'Murder!' from sufferers still to be rescued.[1] No one was actually killed, but the number of broken arms and legs was considerable.

Those portions of the screen which remained intact were

[1] *Annual Register*, vol. xix, p. 197, and *Gentleman's Magazine*, 1776, p. 576.

again set up, but the upper portion was scrapped, and the unsightly toprail, 'a bold modern cornice', substituted. The reason given by John Carter for this niggardly treatment does not reflect favourably upon the Abbey authorities: 'It was indeed set up, that is so much of it as was not damaged', but 'the rest of the work from an apprehension that it would be attended with some expense to repair was thrown aside'.[1]

Unfortunately the screen was not the only sufferer. The superb alabaster canopy over the tomb of Prince John of Eltham was involved in the general ruin. It was a glorious mass of tabernacle work, resembling the splendid canopy over the tomb of the Prince's hapless father, Edward II, in Gloucester Cathedral.

The disaster made a tremendous impression. It sealed the fate of torch-light burials in the Abbey. The funeral of Lady Charlotte Percy five years later was the last save those of 'royal personages'. The times were fast-changing and the custom soon became obsolete.[2]

The two English martyrs to whom this Chapel is jointly dedicated were for centuries regarded with deep veneration. The Chapel came to occupy a place in general esteem second only to that of St. Edward the Confessor: hence the large number of personages of royal descent who have found here a last resting-place.

3. THE CHAPEL OF SAINT BENEDICT

It was more than natural for monks following the Rule of St. Benedict to set apart a chapel in honour of their illustrious founder. Among the treasures prized by the Convent was the alleged head of the Saint, the gift in 1355 of Edward III.

The screen of this Chapel has disappeared, but a glimpse appears in the background of one of the large pictures in

---

[1] *Gentleman's Magazine*, 1799, p. 773.
[2] *Gentleman's Magazine*, 1817, p. 341.

Sandford's *History of the Coronation of James II*. It was wantonly destroyed in order to make room for the monument of John Dryden, which, before it was reduced to comparatively modest dimensions (an improvement largely due to the Sub-Dean Lord John Thynne), must have been a deplorable eyesore. The bust and pedestal stood in an arched recess which formed the centre of a huge marble screen decorated with pilasters of the Ionic Order and terminating in a pediment. It extended from pillar to pillar, and concealed every trace of the Chapel from view.[1]

Much of the original pavement consisting of stone squares and flagstones has survived, notably the footpace of the altar. The slip tiles of the latter with their designs of foliage and shields of arms are most attractive. The painting at the altar, the gift of John Murrimouth,[2] the Abbey recluse of the period, has long given place to the immense monument of Frances, Countess of Hertford.

(d) The Chapels of the South Transept

The south transept presents a very different appearance from its northern companion, for the eastern aisle has for good reasons always been devoid of either chapel or altar.

In designing this great royal church, the requirements of the Sovereign and the Court then residing in the Palace of St. Stephen, over against the east end, were borne closely in mind. A royal entrance at the distant west end would have been the reverse of convenient during medieval times. The building operations which continued for generations would have made passage through the nave extremely difficult.

Hence, on great occasions of ceremony, the Sovereign was wont to enter through the north portal, the most ornate of the entrances to the church. After being escorted by the

---

[1] Crull, *The Antiquities of St. Peter's, Westminster*, vol. ii, illustration facing p. 29.
[2] Pearce, *Monks of Westminster*, p. 95.

Abbey authorities down the north choir aisle as far as the entrance to the Sacristy,[1] he would then turn southward, and passing eastward through the doorway of the *pulpitum* into the choir, be conducted to the Royal Pew (*Cawagium Regis*). The latter was probably situated on the south side of the Presbytery, where it is still the custom to place the Royal Box at the Coronation. At the end of the service the Sovereign would return by a different route, described by Dart as leading to the Old Palace, viz. 'the low arched door in the south-east angle of the south transept'.

Old customs die hard at the Abbey, and for many generations after their departure from the Palace of St. Stephen, the Sovereigns of England continued to use the portal of the north transept as their state entrance. It was the practice of Queen Elizabeth, for instance, to repair to the Abbey, there to perform her devotions on her way to the opening of Parliament. Five such visits are officially recorded in the Chapter Book, and this list is probably not exhaustive. The ceremonial has been described in full detail, and it is definitely stated that the Queen was conducted along the time-honoured royal route described above. Even at a date so comparatively recent as 1760 the body of George II was received by the Dean and Chapter, not at the west door as might have been expected, but at the north transept.[2]

Thus, the curious difference between the planning of the south transept and the north becomes intelligible. It was essential to secure a clear passage-way from the Presbytery to this door specially cut in the south-east corner and communicating directly with the Palace. Hence the erection of a series of chapels in the eastern aisle of the south transept was impracticable.

[1] This doorway has long been known locally as the Demons' Door.
[2] Francis Bond, *Westminster Abbey*, pp. 71, 72 *passim*.

1. THE CHAPEL OF SAINT BLAISE

But the south transept was not devoid of altars. One such existed bearing the dedication of St. Blaise, the patron saint of Woolcombers, though not a trace survives today. For upwards of a century all knowledge of its existence disappeared. Only within comparatively recent times has its curious history been revealed.

The Chapel of St. Blaise, according to Dart, originally consisted of an enclosure, square in plan, and surrounded on three sides with stone walls or screens. The eastern screen stood several feet east of the place where is now the modern wall, which provides a back to the monuments of Matthew Prior, Shakespeare, and others.[1] The western enclosure was pierced with a doorway in the centre and skirted the passage leading into St. Faith's Chapel. On the south it was bounded by the wall of the transept.

In the document entitled the 'Cartulary of Westminster' quoted by Dean Stanley, it is stated that Prior Richard de Merston spent one hundred marks on the altar of St. Blaise and its appurtenances.[2] Moreover, this Chapel was closely associated with the famous name of Abbot Nicholas Litlyngton, who was buried here in 1386 beneath a plain marble slab. Apparently some traces of his tomb still remained when Widmore[3] was writing his history during the first half of the eighteenth century. Dart, again, when enumerating the Benefactors of the Abbey, speaks of 'his chapel' in connexion with the great Abbot. Hence we can assume that it was equipped with splendid furniture and that its screens were at least as ornate as those which have escaped destruction. Striking confirmation of the magnificence of the Chapel has been revealed within the last few years by the discovery of the two majestic paintings of the

[1] Dart, *Westmonasterium*, vol. i, p. 64.
[2] Stanley, *Historical Memorials of Westminster Abbey*, 3rd edition, p. 608; and Pearce, *Monks of Westminster*, p. 96.
[3] Richard Widmore, *History of the Church of St. Peter, Westminster*, p. 107.

Incredulity of St. Thomas the Apostle and St. Christopher on what was once its south wall.

Professor Tristram has claimed that the emergence of these two great figures which, hidden away behind monuments, had passed out of the mind of man, 'must rank among the most important discoveries of recent years'. The figure of St. Christopher, over nine feet high, is clothed in a tunic. The general colour scheme is purple, blue, and yellow, on a light green background. Purple and green predominate in its companion on a vermilion background diapered with crimson fleur-de-lis.

The two figures are outstanding examples of the work of the Westminster School of painters in the latter part of the thirteenth century. They may even be the work of Master Walter, the King's painter, one of the most famous English craftsmen of his day.[1] It is possible that these figures formed part of a series adorning the whole south transept. They clearly added immense dignity to the grave of Nicholas Litlyngton.

At some date unknown, but subsequent to the Dissolution, the Dean and Chapter decided that this Chapel, stripped by now of most of its glory, might well be adapted to form a choir vestry. Accordingly they extended its area westward to the wall now covered with the monuments of Handel and others, enclosing it with wainscot partitions.

The first allusion to the Chapel in this, its Post-Reformation character, occurs in the pages of Keepe whose history was written in 1682. His words suggest that its use as a vestry had become an established custom by that time. 'In the South Cross where the Dial and Clock stand and the place made use of at present as a Revestre, was formerly a Chappel dedicated to St. Blase in which Chappel Nicholas Litlyngton Abbot of Westminster was buried in the year 1386, after he had governed the Monastery twenty five

[1] E. W. Tristram, *The Times*, Dec. 5th, 1936.

B 1254   E

years.'[1] Dart speaks in greater detail and complained of this 'scandalous blot on the beauty of this part of the Church'.[2] Thus the existence of the medieval chapel was still remembered in the early decades of the eighteenth century, when further changes took place.

In 1721 there died a distinguished Old Westminster, the poet Matthew Prior. It was decided to commemorate him with a monument of exceptional importance, including a bust by Coysevox presented to him, when at Versailles on a diplomatic mission, by Louis XIV. The inscription was composed by Dr. Freind, the Headmaster, 'in honour of one who had done so great honour to the school'. The monument was designed by James Gibbs and placed in the hands of the sculptor Rysbrack for execution, the immense sum of £500 having been bequeathed by Prior for 'this last piece of human vanity'. Down came the eastern screen of the Chapel of St. Blaise and part of that on the north. An ugly wall was erected from pillar to pillar to serve as a background for the huge monument. It seriously reduced the original area of the Chapel, though it came in useful, later on, for the memorials of Shakespeare and others.

The Dean and Chapter, a few years later, decided to transfer the Choir Vestry to the adjoining Chapel of Saint Faith, at the same time destroying the remaining vestiges of the Chapel of St. Blaise, save for a few tiles which disappeared in the following century. The following Chapter Order dated December 18th, 1735, is fully explicit:

'That the Screen by the Clock be taken down (the Floor made good) and the Materials thereof be used in Wainscotting the Dining Hall: And that the Chapel now behind the Screen be fitted up for a Vestry.'[3]

The wainscoting still survives, converted into panelling

[1] Keepe, *Monumenta Westmonasteriensia*, p. 52.
[2] Dart, *Westmonasterium*, vol. i, p. 41.
[3] J. Armitage Robinson, *The Abbot's House at Westminster*, p. 78.

for the walls of the Abbot's Dining Hall; but the Chapel of St. Blaise has entirely disappeared.

All this time the circular staircase known as the Night Stair, which communicated directly with the Dormitory, had survived in the south-western corner of the transept. For some reason this position suggested itself as highly suitable for Roubilliac's monument of the great Duke of Argyll and Greenwich, who died in 1743. The Night Stair was doomed and before long perished. Another short flight of steps remains here, but this mounts over the now blocked-up doorway that once opened on to the head of the Night Stair (from the bridge across the west end of St. Faith's Chapel) and forms part of the continuous arcade passage-way round the eastern limb of the church. Even these were hidden from view by an unsightly and useless wall of ashlar above and around the top of the Monument.[1]

From this time forward the Chapel of St. Blaise naturally faded into oblivion, and the Abbey historians have constantly confounded it with that of St. Faith. That the two existed, independent of each other, never seems to have occurred even to so able an antiquarian as Brayley. Not for many years was the Chapel of St. Blaise once more accorded a definite place in Westminster history.

2. THE CHAPEL OF SAINT FAITH

At the southern termination of the great transept in the space between the Abbey Church and the Chapter House, not infrequently termed the slype in monastic foundations, stands the Chapel of St. Faith. This simple building, in which the builders have confined the decoration to a minimum, displays a sharp contrast with the lofty Abbey. It has even been likened to the Catacombs of Rome. A simple brass recording that the body of the Right Rev.

---

[1] This wall was removed by Sir Gilbert Scott in 1863, revealing the short staircase and two beautiful detached groups of clustered marble pillars. *R.I.B.A. Proceedings*, vol. vi, New Series, p. 136.

Charles Pettit McIlvaine, Bishop of Iowa, rested here for
a few days in Easter week, 1873, on its way from Europe
to America is the one and only memorial.

During Pre-Reformation days this building was usually
styled the Revestry. 'Idem revestiarius altare beatae Fidis
parare et hornare tenetur.'[1] The title indicates that the
Chapel was in former centuries used as a sacristy. Its
dimensions, however, are so restricted that it would have
been impossible to house within its walls the vast treasures
of plate and fabrics possessed by the Church of Westminster. The principal Sacristy stood on the north side of
the nave. Its foundations still survive beneath the turf, also
the doorway which gave access to the nave.[2]

Hence it has been conjectured, not unreasonably, that
the Chapel of St. Faith was reserved for the special use of
the Lord Abbot when it fell to his lot to sing the High
Mass. In the western portion his vestments could con-
veniently be placed, while the presence of a step and a
double piscina indicate clearly enough that the eastern
portion formed a chapel.

That St. Faith's Chapel was regarded during the Middle
Ages as a building of some importance may be inferred
from the gruesome description of the entrance doorway
given by Dart. The building was 'formerly enclosed within
three doors, the inner the middle which is very thick lined
with skin-like parchment and driven full of nails. These
skins, they by tradition tell us, were some skins of the
Danes tanned and given here as a memorial of our delivery
from them.'[3]

The building formerly graced by the presence of the
mitred Abbot and the adjoining Chapel of St. Blaise now
came to be occupied by humbler folk, such as the Lay-
vicars and Choristers. Their surplices continued for long

---

[1] *Customary of the Benedictine Monasteries of Saint Augustine Canterbury and
St. Peter Westminster*, vol. ii, p. 59.

[2] See p. 23, note 1.   [3] Dart, *Westmonasterium*, vol. i, p. 64.

years to hang here in this 'dark vestry', together with a melancholy relic of former glories, a piece of furniture on which copes were once suspended. An additional chamber, too, seems to have been constructed in the upper portion of the Chapel at the west end, in order, presumably, to provide extra accommodation. With its cumbersome wooden staircase it must have been a terrible disfigurement.

At the beginning of the nineteenth century, or perhaps a little earlier, the surplices of the Choir were removed to a chamber beneath the organ, and a degraded chapter opened in the history of St. Faith's Chapel. When Sir Gilbert Scott entered upon the office of Surveyor in 1849, he found the place a lumber room, 'used for the reception of all sorts of odds and ends to its great disfigurement and injury'.[1] Here, among other debris, lay an 'ancient oaken pulpit with diminutive sounding board'; and an immense quantity of precious ironwork removed at the time of George IV's Coronation from the tombs which it was fashioned to protect. Even the magnificent thirteenth-century grille attached to the tomb of Queen Eleanor of Castile, said to be the finest specimen of wrought ironwork in England, lay neglected here for well-nigh a generation![2]

The new Surveyor did not neglect the opportunity and the grille was soon replaced. In the ironwork of Henry V's Chantry, however, he found a more serious problem. A considerable portion had disappeared, while the remainder lay scattered about the floor in a hundred pieces! The reverent and loving care which rescued these remarkable fragments must always be remembered in Scott's favour. He strove to improve the general condition of St. Faith's Chapel, for, as far as possible, he cleared it out and re-arranged it and he also designed the excellent door into the south transept. In striving to make good the

[1] Scott, *Gleanings from Westminster Abbey*, p. 49.
[2] See vol. ii, pp. 138–40.

thirteenth-century pavement with new encaustic tiles, and grinding the glazing off the old, he was less successful.[1]

In 1895 the Sacred Mysteries were once more cele-brated in St. Faith's Chapel with the establishment of a Thursday Celebration. The forces of conservatism were, however, still predominant, and the more progressively minded members of the Collegiate body had to rest content with a makeshift state of things. The necessary furnishings were meagrely carried out with the aid of various odds and ends. A new altar, it is true, was provided; but, despite the fact that the length of its medieval predecessor was clearly indicated on the eastern wall, it was made far too short. The authorities considered it essential to provide for any celebrant who might desire to use the north-end position.

The little chapel, despite its unworthy furniture, soon justified itself. It proved an unspeakable boon to hundreds and thousands of people eager to find a quiet place in the overcrowded Abbey in which to say their prayers in peace.

During subsequent years its general appearance has been greatly improved. The ineffective altar has been extended to the original length, and provided with frontals based upon the Colour Sequence peculiar to Westminster Abbey. Simple communicants' kneelers, together with desks, and seats of oak for the clergy have been constructed. A silver lamp now hangs before the altar, and handsome Persian carpets have been added. The lighting and seating arrangements have been altered and the place is no longer disfigured by rush-bottomed chairs. Lastly, two fine pieces of tapestry have been suspended from the walls. One represents the expulsion of Hagar and Ishmael, while the other consists of two panels of the 'vase and arcade' type.

The outstanding feature in the Chapel of St. Faith is the remarkable oil-painting which adorns the greater portion of the eastern wall.

[1] Scott, *Personal and Professional Recollections*, p. 153.

THE MURAL PAINTINGS IN THE CHAPEL OF ST. BLAISE
IN THE SOUTH TRANSEPT

THE EAST END OF THE CHAPEL OF ST. FAITH

Immediately above the altar rises a plain pointed arch, richly ornamented, about eighteen inches in depth, the soffits of which have been painted in red and white zigzags. Beneath is the painting of a female figure, representing the Saint to whom the Chapel is dedicated. The figure, which is more than life-size, stands upon a pedestal within a niche, formed by means of two pillars painted deep red, and surmounted by an angular canopy of light blue edged with yellow. It is arrayed in an outer mantle of rose colour, lined with fur, thrown over an inner robe of blue. The hair flows from the coroneted head in ringlets. The right hand is clasping a book which crosses the breast. From the thumb of the left hand, attached to a ring, hangs the iron bed upon which St. Faith, according to tradition, suffered martyrdom.

This piece of English primitive art has been aptly described as 'a very tall, austere figure, the attitude graceful and sternly appealing'.[1] Its gentle dignity and the elegant folds of the draperies are most attractive.

Beneath the figure is a low panel-like painting suggestive of a reredos. It consists of an oblong compartment, divided up into a number of yellow lozenges within squares. The central lozenge contains a picture of the Crucifixion, with the customary figures of the Blessed Virgin and St. John the Evangelist in robes of green and purple. The other lozenges are blank. The painting, notably the lower portion, recalls the half-ruined *retabulum* which formerly adorned the High Altar.

On the left-hand jamb of the recessed arch is a small panel on which is painted the kneeling figure of a Benedictine monk. From the lips of this figure proceeds an inscription of two lines in Lombardic lettering extending obliquely upwards:

X *Me: quem: culpa: gravis: premit: erige: Virgo: salutis:*
X *Fac: mihi: placatum: Christum: deleasque: reatum.*

[1] Noppen, *Westminster Abbey*, p. 62.

The general appearance of the kneeling figure, coupled with the character of the inscription, suggests an act of penitence. Whether this be the case or not, it is reasonable to assume that one who was both painter and donor is here represented.

The picture has suffered badly from both time and ill usage. It is a wonder that even the smallest fragment has survived to our own day. In spite of every disadvantage, it is a most attractive work of art, and never fails to inspire enthusiasm. Professor Lethaby has described it as the 'most remarkable Gothic wall painting now remaining to us', and 'the most romantic work of art in London'.[1]

The picture dates, almost certainly, from that decade of the thirteenth century in which Henry III's new choir was completed. The City of Westminster must have been at that time one of the art centres of the world. The King's enthusiasm for beautiful things of every description attracted a large number of the leading artists in Europe. To these was the welcome task assigned of assisting in Henry's numerous and magnificent undertakings. Such names as William of Florence, John of St. Omer, Peter of Hispania, and William of Westminster possess an obvious significance. Among the monks serving in the Abbey at that time was one William, whom Henry III was wont to style 'his beloved painter'. Is it possible that the 'beloved painter' is here portrayed?

[1] Lethaby, *Westminster and the King's Craftsmen*, p. 260.

PART IX

THE FURNITURE

1. THE PULPITS

NOT the least interesting among the Abbey treasures is the venerable oak Pulpit of somewhat curious outline which stands in the nave. Its linenfold panelling clearly indicates a sixteenth-century origin.

The Pulpit is hexagonal in shape, with moulded posts, rails, and cornice. Its six panels are filled with two ranges of carving beautifully executed. It rests upon a stem of double trumpet form with moulded rails and necking, perhaps of later date. The sounding-board, also hexagonal, is connected with the Pulpit by a linenfold panelled standard. A pendant hangs at each angle, separating the depressed arches.

The somewhat top-heavy appearance of the structure is a weak point. It has given rise to a slightly irreverent nickname 'the wine glass'; but the Pulpit is none the less an attractive work of art. Cranmer is said to have occupied it when he delivered the sermon at those two strangely contrasted occasions, the Coronation and the Funeral of his royal godson, Edward VI. The tradition is not supported by documentary evidence, but it is probably accurate, for the Pulpit must have been added to the furniture of the Abbey well before 1547.

During the seventeenth century there appeared a rival structure, though the old Pulpit probably continued in use. Hollar's interesting picture of the east end of the Abbey at the Coronation of Charles II indicates distinctly a Pulpit standing on the north side of the Presbytery near the seats of the Bishops, the shape and general appearance of which suggest the same rostrum as that occupied by Cranmer in 1547.[1]

[1] See vol. i, illustration facing p. 60.

It is far from easy to determine the subsequent history of the Tudor Pulpit, for the older Abbey historians consistently ignore it. An early print of the interior of Henry VII's Chapel, dating from the end of the eighteenth century, shows it in a prominent position on the north side of the altar, and in a later print executed by B. Blück, dated 1811, its position is unchanged.[1] Probably this arrangement had been in existence for a number of years.

Sermons were by no means uncommon events in Henry VII's Chapel in Restoration times when this building was frequently used for the Consecration of Bishops. Five were consecrated on October 28th, 1660, a ceremony which Pepys vainly endeavoured to behold,[2] while a few weeks later, on the following Advent Sunday, John Cosin and six colleagues were elevated to the episcopate. The sermon delivered on the latter occasion attracted considerable public attention. The preacher was William Sancroft, then Dean of St. Paul's, and it was generally regarded as one of his happiest efforts.

It must be concluded, therefore, that after its removal from the choir, the Pulpit was set up in the dignified surroundings of Henry VII's Chapel and remained there for many generations. History, however, repeated itself on an eventful day in June 1911. The Pulpit was temporarily placed against the north-west pillar of the lantern for the Coronation of King George V and Queen Mary when the Sermon was delivered by Archbishop Lang, at that time occupying the northern Primacy. Thus the tradition associated with Cranmer and other prelates has been maintained during our own century. Since then the Pulpit has undergone a further translation, and today forms an interesting feature in the nave.

2. The fine oak Pulpit which stands today in the choir

[1] See R. Ackermann's *History of the Abbey Church of St. Peter's, Westminster,* vol. ii, illustration between pp. 134 and 135.

[2] *Diary of Samuel Pepys,* vol. i, p. 269

appeared during the first decade of the seventeenth century. It is hexagonal in shape, with pairs of enriched pilasters at the angles and a cornice of quadrant section with heads. Each of its six faces is adorned with an oval panel surrounded with a carved wreath and shaped key blocks and a lower panel with conventional foliage. The sounding-board, with its richly panelled soffit and cornice, adds greatly to the general effect.

Dean Stanley has conjectured in his picturesque fashion that this Pulpit formerly 'resounded with the passionate appeals of Baxter, Howe, and Owen, at other times of Heylin, Williams, South, and Barrow'.[1] In the absence of information to the contrary, it may be assumed that it continued in permanent use down to the time of Keene's drastic reconstruction of the choir in 1775. This fine piece of Jacobean work was then relegated to the triforium, as if it were a piece of lumber!

This Pulpit has enjoyed a longer period of regular service than any other among those possessed by Westminster Abbey. The preachers who have occupied it have been remarkable alike for their variety and for the length of their discourses! Even in an age like that of the Commonwealth, when the frequent hearing of immense sermons formed part of the general routine of life, it was found necessary to curb the enthusiasm of some of those who occupied this Pulpit, judging by an entry in the Journal of Guilon Goddard:

'Ordered (18 Thursday 1656) that the lecturers who preach the morning lecture in the Abbey at Westminster, be desired to begin their sermon at seven of the clock, and to end at eight of the clock.'[2]

Later, in the same century, the gigantic sermons of Isaac Barrow proved more than human nature could stand; and on one occasion the unhappy preacher suffered the

[1] Stanley, *Historical Memorials of Westminster Abbey*, p. 531.
[2] C. F. Richardson, *English Preachers and English Preaching*, p. 113.

indignity of being silenced by means of the organ which was brought into play by the obstreperous Vergers![1]

To Dean Ryle must be accorded the credit of having rescued this historical ornament after several generations of neglect. It was first placed in the nave where, in spite of an incongruous modern pedestal, it looked well; but in 1935 it was promoted. A new pedestal and standard in keeping with the bowl and sounding-board were designed by the late Sir Walter Tapper. The salient features of the carving were emphasized by gilding, and this beautiful structure now adorns the choir with splendid effect.

3. The third Pulpit (in a chronological sense) formed part of the iniquitous scheme for the refurnishing of the choir inaugurated by Dean Thomas during the eighteenth century. For some reason the Dean and Chapter not only ejected the seventeenth-century structure but also altered the time-honoured position, for, in certain prints by Blück and Le Keux published during the early nineteenth century, the Pulpit stands beside the north-west pillar of the lantern.[2]

Keene's Pulpit is by no means devoid of merit. Hexagonal in shape it rests upon a single-clustered column, and is divided into six panels richly inlaid with dark wood, decorated with an oval compartment of twelve leaves, with a rose for centre-piece. Each angle is emphasized by a small pillar, the two front pillars terminating in well-executed heads of cherubs. It is surmounted by a sounding-board consisting of an ogee canopy. The latter, supported by a palm tree, is decorated with pinnacles and terminates in a finial. As in the case of the stalls, the designer had no hesitation in employing cast iron for the pinnacles and the finial.[3]

At the Coronation of George IV in 1822 a hexagonal Pulpit (minus a sounding-board, however) was placed

[1] Stanley, *Historical Memorials of Westminster Abbey*, pp. 448, 449; O. H. Osmond, *Isaac Barrow, His Life and Times*, p. 169.

[2] See vol. i, illustration facing p. 86. *The History and Antiquities of the Abbey Church of St. Peter, Westminster*, by J. P. Neale and E. W. Brayley, vol. ii, illustration facing p. 38.　　　　[3] See vol. i, illustration facing p. 86.

against the north-east pillar of the lantern. Its panels were covered with plain crimson velvet, that in the centre being distinguished by a representation of the Sacred Monogram, surrounded by an embroidered 'glory'.[1] The shape and general appearance of this Pulpit, as represented in a magnificent coloured picture by Stephanoff in Sir George Nayler's *History of the Coronation of George IV*, suggests that it was Keene's structure which was specially upholstered in this manner.[2]

This Pulpit is still in existence, though the Westminster period of its story was remarkably brief, covering less than half a century. It may be seen today in the fascinating little church of St. Peter and St. Paul, Trottiscliffe, near Maidstone.

It would seem that the Dean and Chapter decided not to re-erect this Pulpit after the prolonged interval of two and a half years during which the Abbey was closed to the public by reason of the Coronation of George IV. The first steps were being taken at this time towards a complete remodelling of the east end under the auspices of the younger Wyatt and Bernasconi, and a new Pulpit evidently formed part of the scheme. This decision was regrettable, for Keene's structure had already become historic. Many people were alive who could remember the moving discourse delivered from it by the famous Bishop Horsley (subsequently Dean of Westminster). Preaching before the House of Lords a few days after the abominable murder of Louis XVI in January 1793, when London was throbbing with excitement and horror, the eloquence and personality of this famous Bishop so wrought upon the minds of his hearers that they one and all sprang to their feet and remained standing until his majestic peroration reached its close![3]

---

[1] Robert Huish, *Coronation of George IV*, p. 111.
[2] See vol. ii: illustration facing p. 90.
[3] H. H. Jebb, *A Great Bishop*, pp. 108–10.

The story of its highly irregular removal from the Abbey has been told by the Rev. C. W. Shepherd, who, as Vicar of Trottiscliffe from 1875 to 1920, must often have occupied the Pulpit during a later generation.

'Mr. James Lys Seager of the Millbank Distillery lived in this parish (at Trottiscliffe Court) at the beginning of last century. At a certain chop-house to which he went for lunch he made the acquaintance of the architect (Benjamin Deane Wyatt) who was engaged at the Abbey making alterations at the time of the Coronation of George IV. He asked Seager if he wanted a pulpit—because he said he wanted to get rid of one out of the Abbey. Seager hesitated a little but a day or two afterwards accepted the offer and sent and fetched the pulpit away and brought it here.

'The Dean and Chapter of that day were highly indignant, and small wonder, in that they had not been consulted in the matter; but as the pulpit was gone, contented themselves with expostulations.

'The sounding-board over the pulpit did not come for some long time afterwards as they refused to part with it but Seager, after a while, procured it.'[1]

Once established in Trottiscliffe Church, the Pulpit appears to have given immense pleasure to the parishioners, who hastily endeavoured to regularize these unorthodox proceedings. A tablet was erected in the porch of the church to commemorate its arrival. Inscribed thereon are the following words, evidently intended to propitiate the aggrieved Dean and Chapter:

'This Church was beautified in Octr the year of Our Lord One thousand eight hundred and twenty-four, and the pulpit was a gift of the Dean and Chapter of Westminster and presented to the sd parish by Jas: Seager Esq.
                                   C. Shrubsole   Churchwarden
                                   Wm Smith   Overseer'

4. In 1826 a new Surveyor, Edward Blore, arrived at the Abbey and in the following July he submitted a design

---

[1] Letter by Rev. C. W. Shepherd, Rector of Trottiscliffe, dated Nov. 20th, 1911.

for a new oak Pulpit, a poor specimen of the 'imitation Gothic' then becoming fashionable and which he did much to popularize. Fortunately the Westminster period of its existence lasted barely a quarter of a century. It can be seen today in the beautiful Church of St. Peter and St. Paul, Shoreham, a Kentish village not far from Trottiscliffe.

The Vicarage of Shoreham, for many years in the gift of the Dean and Chapter of Westminster, was held in the middle of the nineteenth century *in commendam* with a stall at the Abbey and the Church of St. Philip, Waterloo Place (now destroyed), by the Rev. Edward Repton. This connexion proved to be of substantial benefit to Shoreham, for in 1848 Repton secured the old choir organ, together with its case, the work of Christopher Schrider, and followed up this achievement three years later with Blore's Pulpit.

5. To the latter there succeeded in 1851 the familiar grey marble structure, one of the earliest of the traces left upon the Abbey by Sir Gilbert Scott during his long tenure of the office of Surveyor. A slight improvement upon its predecessor, it harmonized fairly well with its surroundings; but it was an uninspired piece of work. No one will regret its translation to the Cathedral Church of All Saints, Bendigo, in Australia, save for the fact of its association with such famous names as Trench, Stanley, Kingsley, Farrar, Robinson, Ryle, Boyd-Carpenter, Gore, Wilberforce, and Henson.

6. A word still remains to be said about the immense structure which happily disappeared in 1902.

The startling innovation (for such it was considered at the time) of a regular Sunday evening service in the nave was first introduced during the decanate of Dean Trench in 1858.[1] Regarded at the outset as an experiment, it

---

[1] A series of similar Services had taken place during the summer of the Great Exhibition of 1851.

before long became a regular feature of the worship of the Abbey, and the need for a permanent nave Pulpit speedily manifested itself.

During 1862 a huge structure of magnesia limestone from the Mansfield Woodhouse quarry and grey Derbyshire marble arose against one of the north pillars of the nave. Designed by Scott,[1] the greater part of the cost was provided by Sir Walter James. An inscription was added recording the circumstances of its erection:

'This pulpit is presented to the Dean and Chapter of Westminster by a few friends in grateful commemoration of the opening of the nave for public worship and preaching. Jan. 1858.'

The Pulpit was temporarily removed for the Coronation of King Edward VII in order to increase the all-too-limited seating accommodation. Ultimately the Dean and Chapter decided that it should not be re-erected after the ceremony. Their decision was at once inevitable and regrettable. The Pulpit had been occupied by nearly all the great Anglican preachers and divines of whatever school of thought during the second half of the nineteenth century. On the other hand, no considerations of sentiment could outweigh the incongruity caused by the presence of this cumbersome specimen of 'Victorian Gothic' in one of the most beautiful interiors of Christendom. No word of regret, no voice of protest was raised when the Pulpit, long regarded as an eyesore, failed to reappear, and the Westminster period of its story terminated. Soon after it was presented by the Dean and Chapter to the Cathedral of St. Anne, Belfast, where in the more appropriate surroundings of an entirely new building, its demerits were likely to be less in evidence.

[1] Scott, *Personal and Professional Recollections*, p. 154.

2. THE FONT

The records of the Abbey state that the Font was 'newly set up' in the western aisle of the north transept in the second bay from the entrance, shortly after the Restoration. Of its position anterior to that time no evidence exists.

An interesting entry records that on April 18th, 1663, two young men were 'baptized by the Dean publicly in the font then newly set up'.[1] One of them, Paul Thorndyke, twenty years of age and born in New England, was a nephew of Herbert Thorndyke, the famous Cambridge theologian who, two years before, had been preferred to one of the stalls in the Abbey. The other, Duell Pead, was a King's Scholar, aged sixteen. The Baptism of these two adults which took place according to the rite provided in the Prayer Book of 1662 for Persons of Riper Years, speaks for itself. It recalls the troubled years through which the Church of England had recently passed and the obstacles which had surrounded the due administration of the Sacraments.

The Font remained here, raised upon a flight of steps, until there arrived a gigantic specimen of the work of Joseph Nollekens, one of the leading sculptors of the second half of the eighteenth century, viz. the monument erected to the memory of the three captains, William Bayne, William Blair, and Lord Robert Manners, who fell on the ninth and thirteenth days of April 1782 in the encounter between Sir George Rodney and the French Admiral De Grasse in the West Indies. The monument was erected, but devoid of any inscription. No one troubled to make good the defect until seven years had slipped away. It had remained hidden from the public gaze all this long time. The Font was now squeezed out of the position which it had occupied for upwards of a century, and a few

[1] J. L. Chester, *The Marriage, Baptismal and Burial Registers of the Collegiate Church of Westminster*, pp. 67, 68.

years later was found by John Carter lying on the floor beneath the north-west tower.

'Entering through the door of aforesaid partitioned part, now used as a singing room, we noticed turned topsy-turvy on the pavement, the mutilated elegant font that till lately stood in the north transept, but its room being wanted for a modern monument, it was forced to resign its appropriate situation, as have some of the finest ancient memorials in this church on the like occasions.'[1]

Malcolm has confirmed Carter's protest, for he has stated that 'it now lays reversed in the belfry for want of its pedestal and part of its shafts'.[2]

Some years later a new place was found for this mal-treated ornament, on the opposite side of the nave beneath the south-west tower, where its octagonal basin was set up upon a modern pedestal and base[3] so arranged that the officiating minister had to stand facing west! Known today as the Chapel of St. George, this small space had been screened off from the remainder of the nave by Abbot Islip and for a long time served as the Consistory Court. By the year 1819 it had come to be known as the 'Early Prayers Chapel'.

An entry in the Precentor's Book states that in July 1819 there was here baptized the son of Thomas Newly Reeve who had married the daughter of John Catling the second Verger, to which entry the Precentor, the Rev. Dr. Dakins, added the following interesting comment: 'The Font being restored to the Church, the Dean gave permission for the above solemnity.'

Upon this dark and inconvenient enclosure the title of Baptistery was now bestowed, and the Font remained here until 1871, when it was removed by Dean Stanley to the west end of Henry VII's Chapel. The battered octagonal

---

[1] *Gentleman's Magazine*, 1799, p. 668.
[2] Malcolm, *Londinium Redivivum*, vol. i, p. 92.
[3] J. P. Neale and E. W. Brayley, *The History and Antiquities of the Abbey Church of St. Peter, Westminster*, p. 22.

basin, with its ornamentation of blank uncut shields, sculptured sides, and quatrefoils, underwent extensive renovation, costing £89, at the hands of Sir Gilbert Scott, who was also responsible for the design of the existing font cover. The latter consists of an octagonal base, moulded and embattled with carved panels at the angles, with an ogee-shaped top, terminating in a carved finial representing a pelican in her piety. This work was executed by Messrs. Farmer and Brindley in 1872 at a cost of £60.

Although the general character and appearance of the Font remain unchanged, it is to be feared that but a slender portion of the original structure has survived, save the bowl. It scarcely deserves a place in the furniture of so great a church as Westminster Abbey.

3. THE LITANY STOOLS

The Abbey long enjoyed a unique and unenviable prominence among the great churches of England in the absence of any special place or desk for the recitation of the Litany. This defect was the more remarkable in that the Dean and Chapter from the Restoration onwards took exceptional care to ensure that their church was properly equipped with this piece of furniture. Thus a bill amounting to the sum of £4. 6s. 0d. forwarded to the Dean and Chapter in the year 1674 by one John Stead contains among other items 'a Litany Cloth of purple bayse':[1] which hanging some eight years later was replaced by another.[2] Again, in 1710 orders were given that a new Litany Desk be made 'for ye use of ye Choir', while in the following year payment was authorized of a bill amounting to 10s. 9d. for 'making the cover to the Litany Desk'.[3] Again, in 1757 as was customary at the installation of a new Dean the sum of £43. 4s. 2d. was expended upon

---

[1] W.A.M. 337281.   [2] W.A.M. 33716.
[3] W.A.M. 33743.

hangings for the Dean's throne, the Sub-Dean's Stall, the Litany Desk, &c.[1]

The interesting early-eighteenth-century oil painting[2] shows a Litany Stool of considerable dimensions standing in the middle of the choir; but in later pictures no such ornament exists.

The various Coronation Orders, too, increase the mystery of its disappearance. The Rubric in one Order after another lays down that the Litany at these great solemnities is to be sung by two Bishops kneeling side by side. Obviously a piece of furniture of some kind must either have been in existence already or provided by the Office of Woods and Forests, upon which Department down to 1832 devolved the responsibility for making the preparations for a Coronation; but the authorities are all silent. We can only conclude that the Litany Stool was either destroyed or given away without any record at one of the reconstructions of the choir in 1775 and 1848. The disappearance of a piece of Restoration furniture is a grievous loss.

After an interval of sixty-four years the time arrived for the Coronation of King Edward VII and Queen Alexandra and, as provision had to be made for the due observance of the Rubric, a new Litany Desk of massive proportions was specially designed by the Surveyor, the late Mr. J. T. Micklethwaite, for permanent use. It was used for the first time at the postponed Coronation on August 9th, 1902, when the Bishops of Bath and Wells (Kennion) and Oxford (Francis Paget) chanted the Litany therefrom as of old. At the following Coronation this duty was fulfilled by the same pair of Bishops.

In accordance with ancient custom, a magnificent blue Persian carpet was also provided to cover the Litany Stool.

[1] W.A.M. 33788.
[2] See vol. i: illustration facing p. 64.

4. THE LECTERNS

In Pre-Reformation times the Lecterns formed prominent objects in Westminster Abbey. One of them, used at the reading of the Gospel, is distinctly indicated in the Islip Roll, on the north side of the High Altar.[1] Its companion, according to the Customary of Abbot Ware, stood at the west end of the choir. The latter must have been of sufficient dimensions to accommodate two Cantors standing side by side, in front of an open folio.

The first is described in the Suppression Inventory of 1540 as 'a fayre lecturne of latten be the high altar', though for some unexplained reason the second finds no place in this document. Both Lecterns survived the crash of the Dissolution though it was but a brief respite. The besom of destruction soon got to work again with the Accession of Edward VI in 1547 and their doom was sealed. The evidence of the Chapter Book is only too clear:

'Also yt is lykewyse determined that the two lecterns of latten and candelstycks of latten wythe angells of copper and gylte, and all other brasse latten, belle metell and brasse shall be solde by Mr. Heynes, Treasurer, by cause they be monyments of idolatery and superstycion, and the monye thereof comyng to be receyvyd by the sayd Treasurer for makyng of the lybrary (in the northe parte of the Cloyster) and bying of books.'[2]

Simon Heynes had formerly been President of Queens' College, Cambridge. He emerged into the limelight during the interminable discussions within the walls of his University regarding the marriage of Henry VIII and Katherine of Aragon. He joined in attesting Cranmer's instrument of divorce at Dunstable, after which he exchanged the secluded career of a Cambridge don for the larger life of the world outside. Royal favour was not lacking. In return

[1] See vol. i: illustration facing p. 50.
[2] Chapter Book quoted by Robinson & James, *The Manuscripts of Westminster Abbey*, p. 13.

for his welcome services a Canonry at Windsor and the Deanery of Exeter were conferred upon him. Later on, when Henry once more found himself involved in matrimonial complications, Heynes, by this time become a bridegroom himself, was available to play an important part in carrying through the divorce of the King from Anne of Cleves on July 9th, 1540. Before the year was out, a further token of royal favour fell to the lot of this obliging ecclesiastic. On December 19th he was installed as Prebendary of the First Stall in the new Collegiate Church of St. Peter in Westminster, which now took the place of the medieval monastery dissolved in the early weeks of that year. Thus, Heynes found himself occupying the second highest position in the Abbey, ranking in seniority next to the Dean. The results were disastrous.[1]

What then was the fate of the two Lecterns? It is possible that one of them found a home in North Italy, where it has been carefully preserved to this day with jealous care. In an article on Genoese documents in English History which appeared many years ago in the *Antiquary*, there occurs the following paragraph:

'In the possession of the Marquis Persano, who owns a fine villa on the Riviera di Ponenti, some twenty miles from Genoa, are some magnificent choir books. They are superbly bound in silver, and illuminated in the most elaborate fashion. The family tradition is that they were given by Henry VIII to the Genoese Ambassador, Giovanni di Persano, and formerly belonged to our National Abbey. I have examined these gorgeous volumes, and I must confess they are worthy of the historical establishment to which in all probability they really belonged.'[2]

The writer of the article is silent on the subject, but the Persano family also possess a magnificent eagle Lectern of bronze, supposed to have been fashioned partly in the thirteenth and partly in the fourteenth centuries. This, like

[1] Strype, *Ecclesiastical Memorials*, i, part 2, p. 350.
[2] *The Antiquary*, vol. v, 1882, p. 257.

the service books, is attributed by family tradition to a gift of the English Sovereign to this same Giovanni di Persano. It is to be hoped that some further light may be thrown on this highly interesting subject.

The Deans and Chapters of many cathedral and collegiate churches were ultimately led to make good some of the damage inflicted during the rough handling of the sixteenth century, not least in the provision of Lecterns. A number of eagle Lecterns, originally used for the singing of the Gospel, were henceforth employed for the reading of the Lessons, while new ones were fashioned elsewhere. The Abbey, however, has been singularly unfortunate. There is no evidence, either pictorial or documentary, which suggests the existence of any Lectern at all during the seventeenth and eighteenth centuries. It is known, too, that in the early years of Queen Victoria's reign the slovenly custom prevailed at Westminster, and likewise at Canterbury and Wells, of reading the Lessons from a stall.[1]

In an account of the Consecration in 1847 of Robert Gray as Bishop of Cape Town and of three other Bishops for the Church overseas, an allusion is made to an 'eagle' used at the reading of the Lessons:[2] three hundred years since the misdeeds of Simon Heynes.

A second allusion to a Lectern occurs a year later in a letter written by the Sub-Dean, Lord John Thynne, to the Surveyor, Edward Blore.[3] A few years after the refurnishing of the choir in 1848, the Dean and Chapter decided to provide a Lectern, going to Windsor for their inspiration.[4] They could hardly have selected a finer model than the great brass in the midst of the Chapel with the Bible in two volumes. This 'brazen deske with God's Holy Worde thereon' first mentioned in 1552 is of the 'coped' form; that is to say it is made with two flat sloping sides on

[1] John Jebb, *The Choral Service of the United Church of England and Ireland*, p. 201.
[2] *The Guardian*, June 29th, 1847.
[3] Edward Blore; Papers in the Abbey Muniment Room.   [4] Chapter Book.

which the two Testaments are accommodated. It consists of a massive gadrooned pillar, divided half-way by means of an anulet and resting upon a broad hexagonal base.[1]

The Windsor Lectern is a magnificent structure; but its counterpart in the Abbey fell sadly short of its model. Never did it properly harmonize with its surroundings, whether standing in the centre of the lantern with its back to the altar (the original arrangement) or, as recently, standing against the south-eastern pillar. Its supersession in 1949 by the fine oak structure erected by our Baptist brethren in memory of the famous missionary William Carey is a real boon.

5. THE GATES

The eighteenth century has left many traces upon the interior of Westminster Abbey which merit little praise; but one exception must assuredly be made. Whatever its demerits, that century stands without a rival in the magnificence of its wrought-iron work.

Westminster Abbey possesses nothing designed upon a scale so sumptuous as the metal screens which encircle the apsidal portions of the choirs of Bayeux, or St. Ouen at Rouen, or the glorious entrance to the choir at Evreux, or the noble gates at the entrance to the north and south choir aisles which enshrine the memory of Jean Tijou in St. Paul's Cathedral; but it possesses several fine specimens of wrought-iron work of eighteenth-century make which occupy an important place in this great museum of artistic treasure.

1. The earliest is a pair of gates separating the north and south arms of the cross from the two choir aisles. Experts have assigned to them a date at the commencement of the eighteenth century. Although not of great dimensions, they are most attractive with their elaborate scrolls and acanthus leaf decoration, varied by quaint

[1] W. H. St. John Hope, *Windsor Castle*, p. 446.

masks. They must almost certainly have formed part of the great scheme of development when Wren erected the Classical Altar-Piece. An early-nineteenth-century print shows a low dwarf screen of precisely similar design in front of the High Altar[1] which was removed by Sir Gilbert Scott. The latter, with the aid of Messrs. Skidmore, erected an unsatisfactory substitute strongly suggestive of the Great Exhibition of 1851, which has since found its way to the Cathedral Church of Christ in the City of Victoria, British Columbia. The original screen must then have been cut up by the Surveyor and fashioned into these two sets of gates!

2. The workmanship in the fine pair of gates beneath the choir screen is similar to that in the choir aisles. They give the impression of being the work of the same artist or set of artists, and have been attributed to Huntingdon Brown of Nottingham. Probably they date from the third or fourth decade of the eighteenth century, for, although Dart speaks of 'a pair of handsome gates grated with iron and gilt' in this position,[2] the latter bear no resemblance whatever to those with which we are familiar today, if we may judge by the fine print by J. Cole in that volume.[3] It seems reasonable, therefore, to assume that the existing gates[4] formed part of the general rearrangement in 1730 when the organ was transferred from its seventeenth-century position in the north choir aisle to the centre of the pulpitum.

It must not be forgotten that the original gates of the pulpitum were of wood, and to judge by one of the illustrations in Sandford's *History of the Coronation of James*, they were a fine piece of work.[5] The reason for their removal is difficult to understand.

[1] See vol. i: illustration facing p. 100.
[2] Dart, *Westmonasterium*, vol. i, p. 9.
[3] See vol. ii: illustration facing p. 8.
[4] See vol. ii: illustration facing p. 10.
[5] See vol. i: illustration facing p. 126.

The present gates suffered outrageous mutilation during the early decades of the nineteenth century. The wrought iron work in the lunette or upper portion above the cross-bar, which was in existence in the year 1800,[1] disappeared. A picture of the screen as restored by Blore, dated 1828, displays a curtain in place of the metal-work. This outrage probably occurred in the reign of George IV when the Abbey Chapter seemed to have been carried away by an obsession. Down to that time many of the tombs and monuments had been protected by iron railings. Some perhaps were not of great artistic value; but included in this great mass of ironwork were some of the treasures of England, among them the beautiful grate around the tomb of Queen Elizabeth. Such considerations, however, counted for little. They were ruthlessly scrapped and sold for so much a pound. Fortunately the precious grille attached to the tomb of Queen Eleanor of Castile, with the gates of Henry VII's Chapel, and the closure surrounding that monarch's tomb escaped this fate. Probably, then, the mutilation of the gates of the screen took place at the same time, though the exact reason is unknown.[2] These gates have in recent years been carefully gilded and the empty space in the lunette made good with remarkable success.

3. The arrival of the next pair of wrought-iron gates is carefully set forth in the following entry in the Chapter Book dated December 18th, 1733, as follows:

'That two new Iron Gates (according to a draught laid before the Chapter by Mr. James) be made and set up at the entrance to the tombs on each side of the choir.'[3]

It was high time that this improvement took place, for hitherto the entrances to the ambulatory were 'enclosed

[1] See vol. ii: illustration facing p. 12.
[2] See vol. ii: illustration facing p. 17.
[3] Probably John James of Greenwich, the architect of St. George's Church, Hanover Square, who succeeded Hawksmoor in the office of Surveyor of the Abbey on the death of the latter in 1736.

with folding hatches of wood where persons attend to explain and show the tombs'. These gates, though they can
scarcely be said to rival their companions, are excellent
specimens of their kind. They consist of a number of plain
uprights with spear-head cappings. Their standards are
decorated with scroll ornament and plate foliage, and they
are surmounted by cresting similar in character.

The inadequate wooden doorways found a new home in
St. Margaret's Church, but no trace of them exists today.

4. The entrances to the north and south choir aisles
standing parallel with the choir screen were not equipped
with gates of their own until a later date and lack the interest attached to their predecessors. In general character they
closely resemble James's work in the north and south am-
bulatories, though less elaborate in their details. A Chapter
Order of May 24th of the year 1764 informs us that the
manufacturer bore the name of Wood and that he received
a payment of £76. 8s. 0d. for making the two gates 'now
put up in the north and south aisles of the Abbey in a line
with the choir gates'.

6. THE FLOORS

'As York is supreme in glass so Westminster may be
regarded in medieval tiled pavements.' Such are the opening words of a valuable monograph, entitled *The Inlaid
Tiles of Westminster Abbey*, written many years ago by a
former resident of the Precincts.[1]

No less than eight floors paved with tiles of thirteenth-
and fourteenth-century date are to be seen at Westminster
Abbey. One of them, that of the Chapter House, may fairly
claim to be the finest floor in England. It can receive only
a bare mention here, together with the tiles which have
survived in the Muniment Room, the Chapel of the Pyx,

[1] Paper read before the Archaeological Institute on Oct. 4th, 1910, and
published in the *Archaeological Journal* for 1912 by the Rev. P. B. Clayton,
M.A., F.S.A.

the Chapel of St. Catherine, and the Refectory, for all of these lie outside the scope of these volumes.

In two of the chapels of the interior, however, specimens of this beautiful department of medieval craftsmanship have survived in considerable quantities.

In the chapel of St. Benedict the steps on the eastern side are still intact, though the place of the altar which formerly rested upon them has been occupied for upwards of three hundred years by the immense tomb and wall monument of Frances, wife of Edward Seymour, Earl of Hertford. The altar-pace is covered by 230 slip tiles of the four-inch type. The 'restoration' with the aid of tiles of modern manufacture, which has been applied to this surface, has fortunately been merciful and the medieval character and flavour have been but little impaired. The patterns with which the tiles are stamped consist of foliage and shields of arms. Among the latter are included the three chevronnels of Clare, a double-headed eagle, the leopards of England, and the double cross of the Knights Templars. The second and fourth of these devices seem to point to a thirteenth-century origin. The double-headed eagle, for instance, may refer to either the Emperor Frederick II, who married the sister of Henry III, or to Richard, Earl of Cornwall, younger brother of the latter and a candidate for the Imperial Crown. The presence, too, of the cross patriaché of the Knights Templars would seem to suggest a date anterior to 1312, in which year that Order was dissolved.

The entire floor surface of the Chapel of St. Faith must have been paved with slip tiles of thirteenth-century date. Terrible damage was unfortunately inflicted by our nineteenth-century predecessors, and the western portion of the pavement gives today a dull and uninteresting impression. The nature and method of the damage has been described by Henry Poole, the Abbey Mason who carried it out, in his interesting notes of various events during the year 1865: 'Taking up the pavement of the Slype and making good with new encaustic tiles made to assimilate with the old ones by grinding off the glazing.'[1] The eastern portion of the chapel displays a far more satisfactory appearance, for a number of old tiles of the four-inch type remain, though in a much worn condition. They clearly date from the thirteenth century.

Probably the floors of all the chapels were originally paved in this sumptuous fashion, but only fragments have survived. Apart from the inevitable process of wear and tear, which may have necessitated repaving upon a considerable scale, the advent of innumerable tombs and monuments has everywhere wrought havoc. Thus, these fragments can be dismissed in a very few words.

In the Chapel of St. John Baptist about forty large tiles remain in front of the tomb of Lord Hunsdon; a similar patch in the north ambulatory in front of the Bourchier tomb, and still smaller quantities near the tombs of Aymer de Valence and Simon Langham. In St. Edward's Chapel, too, some four-inch tiles have been inserted between the bases of the pillars and the royal tombs of Henry III and Eleanor of Castile.

Recently, however, an exquisite treasure has been revealed. In 1940, a temporary altar was erected (under circumstances described later) on the site of the medieval Altar of the Holy Cross. Subsequently it was decided to make it permanent, and on Low Sunday, 1944, it was solemnly dedicated by the Dean under the ancient title. Experiments indicated that, given the proper treatment, the surrounding pavement could be restored to its original beauty. An immense amount both of time and labour were expended and today this vast expanse, though interrupted by modern slabs and brasses, is a delight to behold. This lovely fawn-coloured pavement, together with the practically perfect floor of the 'incomparable' Chapter

---

[1] *R.I.B.A. Proceedings*, vol. vi, New Series, p. 169.

House, confer upon the Church of Westminster a distinction possessed by few (if any) of its companions in either England or France.

Before leaving this subject a word must be said about the paving of the nave generally. A glance at the two early-eighteenth-century illustrations[1] shows that the original floor was laid out so as to facilitate the dignified movement of a Procession. Probably it was the work of Abbot Islip. Every trace was swept away in the nineteenth century together with a number of ledgers inscribed with epitaphs and shields of arms which might have been of great historical value today.

[1] See vol. i: illustrations facing p. 8 and p. 10.

PART X

THE ORNAMENTA

1. THE SIXTEENTH- AND SEVENTEENTH-CENTURY PLATE

THE Restoration Chapter at once proceeded to make provision for the orderly administration of the Sacraments, and the rendering of Divine Service. One of the new Prebendaries, Dr. Walter Jones, Sub-Dean of the Chapel Royal, was appointed to represent his colleagues in the negotiations with the silversmith, of whom a new set of Communion plate was ordered. Before the New Year opened much had been done to repair the grievous losses of the past.

The Abbey Muniment Room contains a remarkable document,[1] endorsed with the words 'An Inventory of the Plate and other utensills for the use of the Church of Westminster remaining in the hands of the Sacrist, Jan. 30th, 1661.'

A second copy also exists, though displaying some variations, and is entitled: 'A Particular of Plate and other utensills for ye Altar etc. as are in ye Sacrist's Custody January 30, 1661.' It bears the endorsement 'Mr. [Anthony] Tingles. Note of Church Goods in his Custody.'

The Inventory contains a list of the new Plate procured by the Dean and Chapter during these short months: 'Imprimis: 9 pieces of gilt viz one bason; 2 flagons; 2 chalices; 2 pattens and two covers for ye chalices.'

At least six items out of the nine pieces can be readily identified: viz. the flagons and the two chalices, together with the covers of the latter. All are of silver gilt. The chalices are 10 inches in height, 5 in diameter at the lip and 79 ounces in weight. The flagons are 12 inches in

---

[1] W.A.M. 44026 A and B; see Appendix III.

height, 5¾ inches in diameter at the lip, 9¾ inches at the foot, and 170 ounces in weight. They bear the London Hall Mark for 1660–1, together with the maker's mark R.A. over a mullet between two pellets, upon a heart-shaped shield. Unfortunately, it is impossible to discover the name of the silversmith, the records at Goldsmiths' Hall of the names of makers prior to 1696 having been either lost or destroyed. Maker and designer alike must have been men of rare gifts. Destitute of decoration these noble treasures depend for their effect solely upon the beauty of their proportions and the severity of their design.

The remaining three pieces, viz. two patens and one bason, can also be identified, but not quite so definitely.

Two of these are standing patens, devoid of marks, but closely resembling in character and design the two paten covers. Seeing that the latter can definitely be assigned to 1661, it is reasonable to assume that this pair date from the same year. They are 8½ inches in diameter and weigh 38 ounces.

The last piece is the bason, also of silver gilt, the history of which will probably always remain in doubt.

Among the 'decent basons' possessed by the Abbey there are two alms-dishes, almost entirely plain, which at first sight appear to be a pair. A small shield engraved with the cross patence and martlets, regarded as the arms of St. Edward the Confessor, is the sole ornamentation. One of them bears the mark of a maker unknown, viz. the letter R above a pellet, together with the London hall-mark for 1684–5. Its companion, though in general appearance a facsimile, indicates a different maker; viz. the letters R.L. over a fleur-de-lis; but its other marks are undecipherable. Evidence as to its date is entirely lacking.

There is small justification for the usual assumption that the dishes form a pair. Apart from the discrepancy in the makers' marks, expert examination has detected a slight variation in the make indicating that the provenance of the second is other than London. Again, one of the customary five martlets is lacking on the engraved centre-piece. We may assume then that one of these alms-dishes is identical with the bason mentioned in the Inventory of 1661, while the other clearly dates from 1684. The dishes are each 19 inches in diameter, and together weigh 162 ounces.

A document in the Muniment Room entitled 'Particulars of moneys expended by the Dean and Chapter in 1660 and 1661 amounting to £24,763. 15. 4'[1] contains an item of £41 spent upon Communion Plate and a Silver Verge. It would have been hardly possible to procure all these nine pieces for so relatively small a sum, even after allowing for the change in the value of money. Some possibly were personal gifts; but no record exists to this effect.

Ten years later the gift of a second pair of chalices and covers made a notable addition to the Abbey ornamenta. In shape and size they closely resemble the earlier pair; but they are adorned with a wealth of rich repoussé work of cherubs, acanthus, and other leaves. Their united weight is 90 ounces and they measure $5\frac{1}{2}$ inches in diameter at the lip and 6 at the foot. They bear no date-mark; but the following inscription on the under-surface of one of the two invests them with special interest: 'Donum Johannis Sudbary Theologiae D[octo]ris Ecclesiae Dunelm Decani Hujus Olim Prebendarius 1671'.

John Sudbury was one of the eight prebendaries installed in the Abbey after the Restoration. At the end of a year and a half he was promoted to the Deanery of Durham. That he had a sincere affection for the Abbey is undoubted. Like Lancelot Andrewes, he did not forget the 'monastery of the west'. The date, however, of his noble gift is somewhat puzzling. Had he made this presentation in January 1662 on saying farewell to Westminster or had his gift been a testamentary bequest, his

---

[1] W.A.M. 44024.

action would have been fully intelligible. A gift made, however, many years after his departure midway between that event and his death, is less easy to explain. No light is thrown upon the subject in the slight and unsatisfactory Memoir written by Thomas Zouch or by the other scanty records of Sudbury's career.

The year 1684 forms an outstanding landmark. It witnessed the arrival of several remarkable additions, viz. the plain alms-dish already described; a pair of richly decorated flagons, and a large and elaborately worked alms-dish, all of silver gilt. Whether they were due to private generosity, or purchased out of the revenues of the Dean and Chapter, it is impossible to say. No evidence has so far come to light. The two flagons weigh 156 ounces and are 13 inches in height. They closely resemble the 1661 pair in shape, while their decoration is similar to that of Sudbury's chalices: viz. cherub-heads, acanthus leaves, and floral sprays repoussé in high-relief. They bear the London hall-mark for 1684–5 together with the maker's mark R in capital script over a pellet.

The great alms-dish, which bears similar marks, is the largest piece of plate possessed by the Abbey, being 25 inches in diameter and weighing 129 ounces. It is highly effective, though artistically it hardly equals its companions.

Six or seven years later, another generous offering of peculiar interest was made to the High Altar. In 1690 there died one Sarah Hughes, long a resident within the Abbey precincts. She was housekeeper to the Rev. Dr. Knipe, a prominent figure at the time when the seventeenth century was passing into the eighteenth. Under-Master to the famous Busby, he followed him as Headmaster, while in 1707, a prebendal stall also fell to his lot. Sarah Hughes became one of our pious benefactresses, and found a last resting-place in the west walk of the Great Cloister. In her Will she bequeathed her clothes to her sister, and a sum of money amounting to about £80 to her mistress Mrs. Knipe, and Dr. Pelling, a member of the Chapter. The Executors were directed to expend the money on plate for the use of the Abbey Church and the Dean and Chapter quickly took action. The story is carried a stage farther in the Treasurer's Accounts for the next year, 1691:

> 'Bought of John Thursby 11th of June 1691 A Pair of Large Wrought Silver Candelsticks Guilt wt. 210 oz 10dwts at 9s. 7d. per ounce.
> Comes to £100.17.3
> Cases for the Candlesticks £3.0.0
> _____
> £103.17.3
> Received of Dr. Birch by the hands of Mr. John Needham.'[1]

The silversmith's bill is also in existence among the Abbey muniments, viz. 'Mr. John Thursby for a pair of candlesticks, £103'.[2]

The cost having reached a higher figure than the amount of Sarah Hughes's legacy, it became necessary to supplement the latter, viz. 'Ordered that nineteen pounds of the money received from Mr. Thomas Langley of Mathon[3] and now remainynge in Mr. Needham's hands be allowed towards the buyinge of Candlesticks for the Altar'.

These candlesticks were for generations surrounded with mystery. A cartouche on each base had been stamped with the words 'Sarah Hughes', presumably the name of the donor, but all knowledge of the personality of the latter had completely faded away. Suddenly the mystery was solved. Some years ago a letter was found in the Abbey Muniment Room evidently written by one of the Knipe family stating that 'dear old faithful Sarah had died' and

---

[1] Dr. Peter Birch had become Prebendary two years before. John Needham was the Receiver-General.
[2] W.A.M. 44363.
[3] A parish near Malvern where the Dean and Chapter formerly possessed considerable estates and which is still in their patronage.

had left money in trust for 'the buying of candlesticks for the High Altar in the Abbey'.

These magnificent candlesticks are 32 inches in height and weigh 224 ounces. They have triangular widespread bases, stems of a baluster pattern with a large pyriform central knop. They are elaborately adorned with repoussé work consisting of bands of cherubs and floral festoons, closely resembling the decorations on the chalices of 1671. A cartouche on the triangular-shaped base of each candlestick is pounced with the name of the donor, Sarah Hughes. The candlesticks are among the finest of the Abbey's ornamenta and suit their position on the High Altar perfectly.

For upwards of two centuries Sarah Hughes's splendid gifts made but an occasional appearance. They were reserved for use on 'Sacrament Sundays', that is to say, about once a month, when the entire plate possessed by the Abbey was employed to grace the High Altar in accordance with time-honoured custom. A pair of brass candlesticks, the work in 1856 of a firm named Potter, costing £18. 16s. 0d., took their place on week-days. Since the arrival in 1899 of the present Altar Cross, designed on somewhat similar lines, the silver-gilt candlesticks have remained continuously upon the High Altar.

The Victorian pair now serve as standards in the Chapel of My Lady Margaret.

The silver-gilt plate possessed by the Dean and Chapter having by his time assumed considerable proportions, the Dean and Chapter in 1691 thought right to spend the sum of twenty shillings in providing a 'Chest for ye Communion Plate'.

About twenty years later they purchased a delicately perforated straining spoon of the higher standard of silver. It is described in the Treasurer's Accounts as 'a polished spoon, pierced and gilt'.

Such then was 'the great group', to quote the words of

THE SEVENTEENTH-CENTURY CANDLESTICKS OF THE HIGH ALTAR

Mr. W. W. Watts.[1] Many generations were destined to come and go before the arrival of any similar treasures.

In addition to the '9 pieces of guilte Plate', the Inventory of 1661 contains a reference to '4 brasse candlesticks for ye Altar, and 3 brass branches for ye Altar and Quire'. We learn, too, that in 1661 Antony Tingle was paid thirty shillings for scouring three pairs of hangings and repairing 4 candlesticks and branches.[2]

The identification of the 'branches' presents no difficulty. The Inventory clearly refers to the three chandeliers which hang today in the eastern portion of the Presbytery.

It is possible that the 'brasse candlesticks' mean the fine pair of copper gilt standards which have stood in front of the High Altar from some date unknown. The evidence furnished by the candlesticks themselves affords the sole clue to their date and several experts have agreed that the beautifully wrought bases and the lower portions of the stems suggest an early Stuart or even Elizabethan origin. Hence, it may almost be assumed that they form part of the Inventory of 1661 and are identical with two of the '4 brasse candlesticks'. They stand today 51 inches in height, with circular moulded bases, richly gadrooned, resting on three dogs with beaded collars. Both the upper and the lower stems are also gadrooned, being united by means of a big collar with a cord at the centre and embossed with twisted rays. The upper stems terminate in candle-dishes, 9 inches in diameter with embossed gadroons and cords to match the bases. The pair of standard candlesticks and the pair which formed Sarah Hughes's benefaction are doubtless those referred to in a mid-eighteenth-century Inventory under the heading 'the four candlesticks at the altar'.[3]

The standard candlesticks afford a striking illustration of the vandalism perpetrated by former generations. Early

---

[1] W. W. Watts, *Old English Silver*, pp. 130, 131, 133.
[2] W.A.M. 33693.   [3] W.A.M. 6613.

in 1911 a well-known expert, on making a chance examination, revealed a number of solderings and other unsuspected marks. Not one member of the Abbey Staff was aware of their existence. It was clear, however, that, at some distant time and for some cause unknown, the Abbey authorities had actually caused this fine pair of candlesticks to be mutilated and deprived of nearly half their length.

These facts having been unexpectedly discovered, the Dean and Chapter lost no time in repairing the injury. An upper stem was added which brought the candlesticks back to their original height and they appeared for the first time in this rejuvenated form at the Coronation of King George V and Queen Mary in 1911.

Certain other documents dating from Restoration times survive in the Abbey Muniment Room which display problems equally difficult of solution. Thus, we learn that in 1674 Thomas Plucknett, Clerk of the Works, was paid 'for two new candlesticks and charges in going and coming by water XXV. 9'.[1] Again, in the following year, there was 'paid by the hands of Mr. Goss the remainder of the price of two sylver candlesticks for the use of the Church, £15. 14. 6.'[2] Of these two 'sylver candlesticks' there is today no trace. It is known that Dean Atterbury was permitted by the Chapter to melt down some of their plate, and a rose-water dish and ewer of great beauty were the result. Possibly this may explain the disappearance of the silver candlesticks.

The administration of the Dean and Chapter of Westminster during the eighteenth and early nineteenth centuries provided a large target for the criticisms of subsequent generations; but there is every reason for thinking that they realized the value of their plate and lavished all possible care upon it. Experts can see that the great Altar candlesticks, for instance, have periodically received a

[1] W.A.M. 33728.   [2] W.A.M. 33731.

fresh coat of gilding while documents in the Muniment
Room and the Chapter Books tell the same tale. Thus, in
1699, the sum of £10. 15s. 0d. was paid in 'washing and
gilding' the Communion plate.[1] In 1706 Mr. Batterby
(the Receiver-General) was ordered to have the plate
belonging to the church mended and cleaned. In 1712
two Altar candlesticks were mended. In 1754 there was
spent £2. 14s. 0d. in 'mending and cleaning the Communion plate':[2] and two years later another £2 'in repairing
and cleaning the great Gilt Candlesticks, and in mending
one of the Virges'.[3] The years 1789, 1791, and 1816
were marked by similar expenditure, the bill from Messrs.
Baker and Baylis amounting to £3. 15s. 0d.[4] In 1842 and
1848 the Altar candlesticks were again repaired, this time
by Messrs. Garrard.

Two ancient pieces of sacramental plate came into the
hands of the Dean and Chapter during quite recent years,
after a most remarkable history. They are described as a
Communion Cup and Cover, of silver, $8\frac{1}{2}$ inches in height,
$4\frac{1}{2}$ inches in diameter and $19\frac{1}{2}$ ounces in weight, and are
typically Elizabethan in character. Save for one band of
incised ornamentation, cup and cover alike are devoid of
decoration. The latter bears the interesting date 1571, together with the maker's mark, H.W. They were dedicated
for use in the Abbey on the morning of Whitsunday
(May 19th, 1918) in the presence of their Majesties King
George V and Queen Mary. The following extract from
the sermon delivered on this occasion by the late Dean
Ryle speaks for itself:

'I am dedicating this morning a chalice and paten for use
in all coming years in Westminster Abbey. They were made
in 1571, and after a strange chapter of accidents, they were
forty years ago, rescued from the mud of the Isis and have now
been presented to the Abbey. They will be the oldest pieces of

[1] W.A.M. 33731.   [2] W.A.M. 33787.
[3] W.A.M. 33785.   [4] W.A.M. 33820.

Communion plate in the keeping of the Dean and Chapter. They are to be called the "Cyril Dupe" chalice and paten in memory of a young officer who fell on March 21, aged nineteen years and four months. His guardian in making this presentation to commemorate him, quotes from the last letter he wrote:

> "until England falls on her knees before God and acknowledges His omnipotence—until England does that, we shall never win".

This dear lad is but one of thousands moved by the Spirit of God to do his best. Where the Spirit of God is there is no stationariness. The Whitsun message makes us look up and we see the Spirit of God moving above the chaos of the world struggle.'

A few words must be said regarding the ancient and beautiful custom of decking the High Altar with golden plate on all great Festivals and Sundays (those in Lent excepted). The practice has continued uninterruptedly from the Restoration onwards as evidenced by Hollar's print of the Coronation of Charles II[1] and other representations of the interior of the Abbey. It is, moreover, a matter of common knowledge among ecclesiologists that this feature of the modern Westminster use has its roots deep in Pre-Reformation practice. In 1449 Sir W. Bruges 'bequeathed to St. George's Church Stamford for their solemne festdayes to stand upon the high awter ij grete basyns of sylver'.[2] Again, in 1537, at the baptism of the future Edward VI at Hampton Court, 'the high altar was richly garnished with Stuffe and Plate'.[3] In the Church of Spain, too, the custom still prevails to some extent.[4]

Down to the middle of the nineteenth century when 'ritualists' played havoc with many ancient practices which had survived generations of neglect, on the plea that they were Hanoverian, the Abbey was by no means alone in

[1] See vol. i: illustration facing p. 60.
[2] Nicholl's *Illustrations of the Manners and Expences of Antient Times in England*.
[3] Leland's *Collectanea*, vol. ii, 671.
[4] *Transactions of St. Paul's Ecclesiological Society*, vol. iv, pp. 122–5.

thus adhering to the practice of our forefathers. It is regrettable that a beautiful and interesting custom should have
been scrapped elsewhere.

A visit to Westminster Abbey on the morning of some
Sunday or Great Festival or, above all, at the Coronation,
will reveal the effectiveness of golden plate as an altar
decoration. On the latter occasion it is customary to re-
inforce the treasures of the Abbey with the entire sacramental plate, viz. chalices, patens, flagons, alms-dishes, and
candlesticks belonging to the Royal Chapels in St. James's
Palace, Buckingham Palace, and Marlborough House.
The latter is piled up along the tomb of Anne of Cleves in
front of the Royal Box, while the former is reserved for the
High Altar itself. The effect is magnificent.

NOTE

The various pieces of plate described above did not form
the sum total of the treasures of metal-work once belonging to
the Abbey.

Records exist of 'a cup set in silver, given by Dean Goodman'
and a 'Cann set in silver' given by Peter Birch, who was Prebendary from 1689 to 1710. The dates at which these pieces
of plate were respectively bestowed upon the Abbey plainly
indicate that they possessed considerable value.

The Precentor's Book records that both pieces were delivered
to the new Precentor, the Rev. George Carleton, by the
Magister Choristarum on January 30, 1729.

Sixty-seven years come and go. Carleton passes away and
likewise his two successors the Rev. Edward Lloyd and the
Rev. Dr. Anselm Baily, Sub-Dean of the Chapel Royal. A new
Precentor takes up the duties of his office, the Rev. Weldon
Champneys, a man of some note in his day, who was Minor
Canon of the Abbey for nearly half a century.

The gifts of both Dean and Prebendary have disappeared
and no explanation is forthcoming. Evidently much perturbed,
Champneys has recorded the fact in the Precentor's Book and
the entry is attested by one of his colleagues, the Rev. W. W.
Dakins, who followed him in the office of Precentor, and
George Catling, a Verger, to the effect that when the key of

the Precentor's Vestry was handed to him the two pieces of plate were not to be found!

It forms a lurid illustration of the culpable carelessness which characterized the administration of many churches in the eighteenth century.

2. THE VERGES AND MACES

The Abbey possesses today three verges, two silver and the third plated; but it is not easy to assign an exact date to all three. Probably there have been losses due to theft or accident.

The first record is dated October 24th, 1660. The restored Chapter were anxious to repair past misfortunes with the minimum of delay and commissioned one, John Smith, to supply a 'verge rod' weighing 7 oz. 2 dwts. He charged the Dean and Chapter £2. 12s. 0d. for the rod and another 16s. 6d. for fashioning it.[1] Again, the Treasurer's Accounts for the following year contain the entry of a payment of £3 for a silver verge to Thomas Merrill, one of the principal Vergers at that time. Five years later, Thomas Kettlewell received £3. 6s. 0d. for a similar article, while in 1681 a bill for £9. 10s. 0d. occurs divided into two portions as follows: 'Mr. Plucknett in part of a Verge £4. 2. 6: Mr. Cox for Verge £5. 7. 6.'[2] In the Treasurer's Accounts for 1713, £16 was expended upon 'two silver rods for the Vergers by order of the Chapter'.[3] Another still more expensive purchase—£16. 18s. 6d., took place in 1726. The sum of £2. 11s. 6d. was expended in 1748 on the repairing and mending of the Abbey verges. Two years later an order was given to the Treasurer to pay £4. 3s. 0d. being half the cost of a new verge, while judging by another bill, dated 1756, some further expenditure was deemed necessary for upkeep.

Twenty-eight years later a burglary is recorded as having taken place necessitating the purchase of a sub-

[1] W.A.M. 44009.   [2] W.A.M. 33745.   [3] W.A.M. 33758.

stitute for the victim of this sacrilege. According to one of
the Abbey muniments, John Legrix was paid the sum of
three guineas for a French plated verge, while John Catling,
a Verger, received 11s. 6d. for 'advertising the former
verge which was stolen out of the Church'.[1] The last record
is dated 1830, in which year Hugh Beaver provided a
verge of silver for the sum of twelve guineas.

Of the three existing verges that which is plated must
almost certainly be the one provided by John Legrix in
1788, while one of its two companions must be that which
was added to the Abbey treasures in 1830. All three are
precisely similar as regards design, viz. a thin hollow rod
expanding at one end into a shield on which are engraved
the arms of the Collegiate Church. Unfortunately there
are no marks by which their respective dates can be verified.

According to these accounts eight verges were purchased between 1660 and 1830. Two are definitely identi-
fiable today but of the remaining six all save one have
disappeared!

Two pieces of eighteenth-century origin still remain
to be described among this group of instruments of worship.

The oldest is usually entitled the Porter's Staff—a long
rod of ebony surmounted by a round head of silver engraved with the Abbey Arms. The Treasurer's Accounts
for 1714 record its arrival: 'Mr. Stocker for a Porter's
Staff with a silver Top Engraved £5. 7. 6.'[2] It is supposed
to have been the gift of Dean Atterbury, who provided a
similar ornament for Rochester Cathedral.

The Mace, borne by the Beadle, is similar to the Porter's
Staff, though of a much more massive description. In this
case bamboo has been substituted for ebony, terminating
in the customary round top. The date of its addition to the
Abbey ornamenta has not as yet been discovered. The
Treasurer's Accounts for the year 1750, however, prove

[1] W.A.M. 33819.   [2] W.A.M. 33746.

that it must already have been in use for some time: 'The Silversmith's Bill for repairing the head of the Beadle's Staff and ingraving the same, and for mending the poculum and verges £1. 15. 0.'[1]

It should be borne in mind that the Vergers with their gowns and maces have a long and honourable history. They are a direct survival from Pre-Reformation times. No break has ever occurred to mar the continuity of this feature of Anglican worship. At the very beginning of the Elizabethan period, as soon as Dean Goodman was installed, it was ordered that the verger having conducted the preacher to the pulpit was to 'bring him agayne to his place in the quyer when sermon is don and to go before the prest to the communyon'.

A few years before, too, at the Installation of John of Feckenham the Abbot with thirteen monks 'went in processions after the old fashion . . . with two vergers carrying two silver rods in their hands . . . and after his prayer made was brought into the choir with his vergers, and so into his place'.[2]

NOTE

In 1944 a magnificent mace of ebony and silver gilt was presented to the Dean and Chapter by Councillor Walter Stanley Edgson, D.L., Mayor of Westminster from 1942 to 1943. The head is surmounted by a figure of St. Edward the Confessor with eight richly enamelled shields in the base. It was almost the last of the many highly competent designs of the late Mr. George Kruger Gray.

3. THE ANCIENT FABRICS

I. FRONTALS

The traditions of medieval magnificence never wholly faded at Westminster Abbey during the generations which followed the Reformation. Praiseworthy attempts were made to repair the awful pillage of the sixteenth century.

[1] W.A.M. 33781.   [2] Machyn's Diary, Nov. 22nd, 1555.

An occasional entry in the Chapter Book or the Treasurer's Accounts shows that down to the middle of the eighteenth century, save for the sad interval between 1641 and 1660, the capitular body sincerely desired to clothe the official worship of the Abbey with becoming dignity. The famous Restoration copes were carefully preserved and now and again costly hangings were provided for the Altar which, if they still existed, would arouse immense interest.

At the end of the nineteenth century, however, the High Altar was in a condition almost as woe-begone as that which met the eyes of the restored Chapter in the year 1660. Its hangings consisted of a cheap purple cloth for use in Lent, and another of inferior black serge. A distinguished antiquarian remarked to the writer in the year 1902 that, apart from the splendid plate, he had never in all his experience come across any great church, the equipment of which was so utterly miserable and unworthy! Time, however, has not stood still and a quite considerable collection of ancient fabrics are today the property of the Dean and Chapter.

The Chapel of St. Faith possesses a fine frontal of crimson velvet divided into panels by stripes of gold lace, with an elaborate centre-piece consisting of the Sacred Trigram surrounded with rays of gold and silver; and a frontlet of crimson velvet embroidered in silver and gold with crosses and heads of cherubs, together with the inscription *Qui Propter Nos Homines*. Frontal and frontlet are both adorned with a heavy gold fringe.

This frontal is one of the most interesting of our relatively ancient fabrics. That it dates from the early eighteenth century is clear; material and decoration speak for themselves. It may have been intended for use at the High Altar. Had it not suffered mutilation the dimensions would have agreed. It is more probable, however, that this crimson velvet was used to decorate the east end of Henry VII's Chapel when an Installation of Knights of the Bath took place therein. A print exists representing one of these ceremonies in which a dorsal behind the Altar bears considerable resemblance to this fabric.

The crimson velvet is of great beauty, while the heavy embroideries of gold and silver lace eminently characteristic of the end of the seventeenth and the beginning of the eighteenth centuries, add immensely to its general interest.

It lay in a mutilated condition for unknown years, packed away in a chest and almost forgotten. In 1920 the happy suggestion was made that it should be applied to some useful purpose. Everything pointed to the Chapel of St. Faith and it proved an easy matter to convert it into a frontal. Very little adaptation was necessary, for the dimensions of frontal and altar were identical. A frontlet of crimson velvet harmonizing with the older work was designed by the late Mr. W. D. Caroe, F.S.A., and the general effect suits the severity of St. Faith's Chapel admirably.[1]

The Altar in the Chapel of My Lady Margaret is covered at festal seasons with a superb frontal of white satin embroidered with coloured silks and silver and gold thread. It is a fine specimen of Italian work of the last half of the seventeenth century. The design consists of an elaborate display of flowers and fruit enclosing a number of medallions containing scenes in the life of an abbess, probably St. Scholastica, sister of St. Benedict, and Foundress of a small Community of women near Monte Cassino. On one occasion when her brother came to visit St. Scholastica, she endeavoured to prolong his stay, having a secret premonition of her approaching death. In answer to her prayers, a violent storm of thunder and rain broke forth, compelling St. Benedict to remain, though anxious to return to his own monastery. His sister died two days later. This scene has been depicted with remarkable effect

[1] See illustration facing p. 31.

SEVENTEENTH-CENTURY FRONTAL OF CLOTH OF GOLD AND CLOTH
OF SILVER

SEVENTEENTH-CENTURY FRONTAL OF CRIMSON VELVET

THE FUNERAL ARRAY OF THE HIGH ALTAR

in the top right-hand medallion of the frontal. In one of the lower medallions Our Lord appears in the act of addressing the Woman of Samaria at the well of Sychar.

In 1934 the present magnificent altar and baldacchino in the Chapel of King Henry VII were set up in close conformity with the sixteenth-century work of Pietro Torrigiano. Since then a generous gift has provided a number of fine fabrics of Renaissance character and the Altar is now vested in a dignified and comely manner. They include a white and a red frontal of rich Italian seventeenth-century embroidery, a third consisting of cloth of gold and cloth of silver, and a Russian fabric of cloth of silver adorned with floral sprays.[1]

One of the rubrics in the *Order of Service for the Coronation* lays down the nature of the official gifts to be made by the Sovereign and his Consort at the time of the Offertory. It has been repeated on each occasion with practically no variation in its wording. The Coronation Order of William III and Mary II will suffice for illustration:

'This, being done, the King and Queen each of them supported by two Bishops, attended (as allwaies) by the Dean of Westminster and the Lords that carry the Regalia, going before them, go down to ye Altar, and kneeling down upon the Steps there, make each of them their first Oblation: which is, each of them a Pall (or Altar Cloth or Cloth of gold) delivered by the Master of the Great Wardrobe to the Lord Great Chamberlain, and by him to their Majesties; and each of them an Ingot or wedge of gold . . . to be received by the Archbishop standing, (in which posture he is also to receive all other Oblations) the Palls to be reverently laid upon the Altar, and the gold to be received into the Basin, and with like reverence put upon the Altar.'[2]

Dean Neile with characteristic vigour converted one of the palls offered at the Coronation of James I into a splendid altar frontal.[3] Twelve Coronations succeeded that

[1] See vol. ii: illustration facing p. 208; also illustrations opposite.
[2] J. Wickham Legg, *Three Coronation Orders*, pp. 16 and 17.
[3] *Cornhill Magazine*, 1884, p. 208.

of James I, but all of these royal gifts, which might well have been similarly utilized, disappeared. Not until the twentieth century, with the Coronation of Edward VII, was any attempt made to follow the example of Dean Neile.

In the days of pluralities and perquisites, it was customary to divide up the Coronation furniture (all of which was left in the Abbey) into fourteen portions, one for each of the twelve Prebendaries with a double portion for the Dean. They were free to dispose of their respective shares as they chose.

Thus, after the Coronation of George II in 1727, the 'rich Coronation furniture' was parcelled into fourteen shares so as to produce £28 per share. The Bible on which the Oath was taken was valued at £4; the Altar Cloth at £11; the Pulpit Cloth at £6; a Brocaded Vestment at £25. 5s. 0d.; and a Parcel of Gold Tissue at £25. 5s. 0d.[1]

Again, in the division of the spoil after the Coronation of George III in 1761, the Bible, which on this occasion happened to be in two volumes, was valued at £8. 8s. 0d.; a Communion Table Cloth at £24; and the 'Gold Stuff and Tissue at the Altar' at £15.[1]

Sixty years later a welcome change for the better took place. The ingot of gold and five sovereigns were applied to the Choristers' Fund. Fifty yards of blue Persian carpet were reserved for the Presbytery on which Bernasconi and Wyatt were about to lay their 'restoring' hands, while some crimson velvet with trimmings of gold lace and gold fringe was set apart for the pulpit. On the other hand, a certain portion of the furniture was divided up as before in accordance with past precedent, for instance, 'the gold pall, lined with yellow silk, the blue silk embroidered altar cloth, and a gold altar table cloth lined with crimson silk'.

A portion of one of the precious cloth of gold fabrics,

[1] Chapter Book.

used at a nineteenth-century Coronation, may be seen today at the Cathedral Church of Christ at Fredericton in New Brunswick where it is used as a festal frontal for the High Altar. The late Bishop of Fredericton (the Right Rev. John Richardson) informed the writer that attached to the frontal is a small silk label stating that the material was given to the first Bishop of Fredericton (the Right Rev. John Medley) by 'Mr. Edwards'. The latter must have been the Rev. Howel Holland Edwards who became Prebendary of Westminster in 1803, and occupied his stall for forty-three years. In 1806 he became Curate-in-Charge of St. John's Church, Westminster, with its huge, undivided parish, and at once procured a licence for non-residence! The parish remained without an active head for twenty-one years!

The connexion between the zealous missionary bishop and this venerable Georgian survival from the days of pluralities and non-residence, and the reasons which impelled the latter to bestow the cloth of gold upon so eminently worthy a recipient as Dr. Medley, are likely to remain unknown. The Bishop, a man of great artistic taste, was devoted heart and soul to the building of Fredericton Cathedral, designed by Butterfield, and the gift must have given him unbounded delight.

After the Coronation of Queen Victoria, the Sub-Dean (the Rev. Lord John Thynne) gave his share or a portion of his share to the Church of St. Mary Hawnes, in which parish was situated his Bedfordshire estate. It consists of the altar carpet, a fine piece of cloth of gold, and forms today an effective frontal.

The Cathedral of Quebec is also the fortunate possessor of another of these Coronation treasures, viz. a fine frontal of crimson velvet and cloth of gold, the gift of George III after his Coronation. This fabric and certain other ornamenta were given by the King to this 'Royal foundation' in which he took a great personal interest.

These three fabrics are the sole pieces of Coronation furniture which it has been possible to trace.

II. COPES

The Restoration Chapter found their great church stripped bare. The most elementary essentials for the offering of Divine worship were lacking; but nothing was allowed to discourage them. They determined to make good forthwith some at any rate of the lengthy list of deficiencies, and the provision of new copes was almost the first task they assayed. These 'ornaments of the ministers' were, in the judgement of Dean Earles and his twelve Prebendaries, only less essential for the worship of the Abbey than the new sacramental plate.

The evidence is fully conclusive. An interesting document entitled 'Particulars of money expended by the Dean and Chapter in 1660 and 1661' states that the lordly sum of £1,031. 7s. 2d. had been expended upon 'copes and vestments'.[1] Again the Inventories of 1661[2] specify most distinctly the existence of '12 copes in Mr. Shene's Custody'.[3]

No doubt the great solemnity of the Coronation then drawing near, and invested with a very special significance, weighed considerably in their minds when they sanctioned this large expenditure[4] upon 'copes and vestments'. It would have been difficult, however, to justify their lavish action, if the said 'copes and vestments' were restricted to use at a Coronation. The evidence indicates that the Restoration Chapter fully intended to follow in the footsteps of their early Stuart predecessors. In other words, they determined that Canon XXIV of 1603 should be meticulously observed. 'The Principal Minister, using

[1] W.A.M. 44024; see Appendix VI.
[2] W.A.M. 44026; see Appendix III.
[3] The Sacrist of that date, a layman.
[4] The Coronation of Charles II did not take place until Apr. 23rd, 1661, nearly a year after the Restoration of the Monarchy.

a decent Cope and being assisted with the Gospeller and Epistoler vested agreeably.' They felt themselves wholly debarred from allowing this plain direction to remain a dead letter, anyway in the Church of Westminster.

The Dean and Chapter provided then twelve new copes in four sets of three each at a cost of £1,031. 7s. 2d. By this means it enabled the three ministers at a Celebration in accordance with the Canon to be 'vested agreeably'. At the same time a sufficiency of copes was secured which should enable practically the entire capitular body, then consisting of thirteen members, to be arrayed uniformly at Coronations and other functions of a specially solemn character.

A certain number of copes were manufactured at that period in England, but very few have survived. Hence these Westminster examples possess a special value.

Cloth of gold woven in a delicate floral pattern of great beauty was used for the first of the four sets. In the opinion of experts this material must be assigned to a period anterior to the Restoration, possibly even the commencement of the seventeenth century. Copes, hoods, and morses are all alike, and are devoid of embroidery. Their effect is derived entirely from the material of which they are composed. One of the three is still in fairly good condition, but the two others have suffered badly with the passage of years.

The second set consists of three splendid specimens in crimson velvet of the most sumptuous description. Hoods and orphreys are heavily embroidered with appliqué decorations in gold and silver, consisting of five petalled flowers with curved stems, trefoils, and stars. Their entire surface is powdered with these devices in immense profusion, but by far the richest treatment has been reserved for the border, which forms a kind of orphrey in front, continued thence in a running pattern all round the lower edge.

Similar decoration has been employed on the third set. The material in this case consists of velvet of a dark purple hue, almost black in fact. In the embroidery of gold and silver thread great prominence is given to the pomegranate.

The fourth set closely resembles the first, but gold has played a much less important part in the weaving of the material, producing a brownish effect which is not altogether pleasing. This set is unfortunately incomplete, one of the three having disappeared, though it seems to have been used at the Coronation of George IV.

In every one of these copes the hood occupies the ancient position coming right up to the neck. Not only is this arrangement more in accordance with tradition, but it is infinitely more effective than the clumsy practice of today by which the hood is suspended below the orphrey.

The twelfth cope consists of a foundation of blue damask silk into which has been introduced a charming rococo scroll-work pattern, together with a quantity of foliage and floral details. It is lined with crimson silk. It has been pronounced by experts to be the work of French craftsmen, and assigned to the early eighteenth century. Differing *in toto* from its eleven companions, alike in material and general character, its existence seems to be something of an anomaly. The explanation can almost certainly be found in the personality of Dean Sprat.

The long connexion, covering nearly half a century, of that famous ecclesiastic with the Abbey, first of all as Prebendary, then as Dean, terminated with his death on May 20th, 1713. During the following year, his widow, Mrs. Helen Sprat, presented a 'rich gold flowered cope lined with crimson silk' to the Dean and Chapter.[1] Her offer was duly accepted and a record of their cordial thanks was inserted in the minutes of their meeting on November 14th, 1714. Sprat was a typical high churchman of the Restoration period. His personal sympathies would have

[1] Chapter Book.

been all in favour of the regular use of a cope. It is conceivable, too, that he found it convenient to possess a personal cope of his own, which he could wear not only in the Abbey, but also when officiating in the Cathedral and Diocese of Rochester, which he served as chief pastor throughout the whole of his Westminster decanate.

Certain expressions in Sprat's Will and the fact that his successor, Francis Atterbury, made no claim upon his estate for dilapidations, suggest that the widow was left somewhat scantily provided with this world's goods, and hardly able to maintain a house of her own.[1] In her limited quarters the cope, possessing no more than a sentimental value in her eyes, would probably be in the way. It was therefore a happy inspiration on her part, when leaving the Deanery, her home of many years, to place this fine work of art in the hands of her husband's old colleagues.

An unwritten tradition appears to have reserved this beautiful blue cope for the use of the Dean. At the Coronation of George IV Dean Ireland is recorded to have worn 'a purple and gold flowered cope', a description which exactly fits this vesture. On the other hand, in Sir George Nayler's monumental history of that event, Ireland is twice represented arrayed in a cope of wholly different character, save for its colour, as compared with that of Dean Sprat. Faced with these conflicting statements, it seems more reasonable to accept the evidence of the Chapter record than that of the picture.[2] On the other hand, the Dean might have provided himself with a special cope for the occasion, since disappeared.

At the Coronation of Queen Victoria, Dean Ireland was precluded from officiating owing to the burden of years and other infirmities. His place was accordingly taken by the Sub-Dean, Lord John Thynne, who is depicted in more than one picture of that Coronation

[1] Crull, *Antiquities of St. Peter's Westminster*, vol. ii, appendix viii, p. 28.
[2] W.A.M., C., 51350.

arrayed in this particular cope. The Sub-Dean would not have acted thus without good reason. Probably he simply desired to conform to tradition.

This remarkable collection of copes appeared at successive Coronations from Charles II down to Queen Victoria without a break. There is good reason, too, for thinking that they also continued in regular use at the Celebrations of the Holy Communion for a great number of years as was undoubtedly the case at Durham and possibly at Norwich also.

Five interesting specimens still survive, preserved in melancholy dignity in the Cathedral Library at Durham as so many archaeological curiosities. Their disappearance from public worship was due to the childishness and ill-temper of William Warburton, Bishop of Gloucester, who held one of the wealthy Durham prebends in connexion with his bishopric. Irritated by the fact that 'the stiff high collar used to ruffle his great full bottomed wig', that un-attractive prelate threw his cope aside. The Durham Chapter then stultified themselves by gradually following the example of their hot-tempered colleague, though it would seem that the use of the cope did not wholly disappear till about 1784. Thus, the tradition inherited from none other than John Cosin was abandoned without the slightest justification.[1]

As regards Westminster Abbey, the strict observance of the Canon was maintained for several generations. It has been conjectured, not without reason, that the use of the cope, on occasions other than Coronations, continued here to an even later date than at Durham. No supporting documentary evidence has so far come to light, but a tradition to this effect was undoubtedly in existence at the time of the Accession of Queen Victoria.[2]

---

[1] *Hierurgia Anglicana*, vol. i, pp. 202 and 203.
[2] Jebb, *The Choral Service of the United Church of England and Ireland*, pp. 216 and 217.

The Abbey muniments contain several pieces of miscellaneous information the general tendency of which undoubtedly tells in this direction.

Thus, in 1683, the Sacrist 'Mr. Shene' was accorded by the Dean and Chapter an honorarium of £10 as a recognition of the work he had carried out during the previous twenty years in 'keeping and brushing of the copes'.

In the same year, the sum of twenty-one shillings was expended[1] in providing 'a trunk for the copes'.[2]

In the following year and again in 1687 the Treasurer's Accounts record the payment of the sum of one shilling for 'the portage of the copes'. It would be interesting to know the occasion to which this entry refers.[3]

We come then to the significant year, 1689. The Treasurer's Accounts contain a bill dated April 10th for 'the mending ye 12 Copes against ye Coronation'. The reparation required could not have been very extensive for the Treasurer of the Abbey, Dr. Pelling, only spent three shillings![4]

In 1714 authority was given for the 'mending and cleaning of the copes'. Obviously the Dean and Chapter were making preparations for the Coronation of George I. The bill of three shillings in 1689 had swollen in a quarter of a century to three pounds five shillings.[5]

Again, the Accounts for 1721 contain the strange entry that one Elizabeth Coldwell was paid the sum of 8s. 6d. for 'cleaning and making a bag for the copes'.[6]

Lastly there comes in 1738 a bill of £1. 5s. 6d. paid to Edward Bell 'for mending the copes and repairing the Vergers' and Sacrists' gowns'.[7] The date is not without

---

[1] W.A.M. 33781.
[2] In all probability the trunk in question was an interesting seventeenth-century chest covered with leather and inscribed with the two words 'West Col' in nail heads. Down to 1903 several of the copes were stowed away within its recesses.
[3] W.A.M. 33719 and 33721.   [4] W.A.M. 44337.
[5] W.A.M. 33746.   [6] W.A.M. 33753.   [7] W.A.M. 33770.

significance, for no outstanding public event is associated with that year. Two of these entries are obviously connected with the Coronation but this is by no means the case with the remainder. There would appear therefore to be only one possible inference, namely, that the copes were being regularly used, and that their upkeep demanded a certain amount of expenditure, which was met by the Dean and Chapter as a piece of routine.

The use of the cope on certain important public occasions, other than Coronations, is now and again specifically recorded. The Funeral of the Duke of Buckinghamshire on March 11th, 1720–1, is a case in point.

'The corpse of the late Duke of Buckinghamshire was interr'd here with great solemnity, being received by the Dean and Chapter in their copes, the whole choir in their surplices singing before the corpse which was carried up to a vault in King Henry VII's Chapel.'[1]

Such entries, however, become fewer as time goes on. All mention of the copes disappears from the Treasurer's Accounts after 1738. They were used at the funeral of George II in 1760, but from this time forward they ceased to be mentioned save in connexion with the Coronation. Evidently the Dean and Chapter of Westminster, like their brethren at Durham, deliberately abandoned the regular use of the cope at some unknown date, reserving it as an additional compliment to royalty at the commencement of a new reign.

Four times only during the whole of the nineteenth century were these magnificent old fabrics brought into publicity: viz. the Coronations of George IV, William IV, and Queen Victoria, and the great Service of Thanksgiving for the Golden Jubilee of the latter Sovereign in 1887.

The first of these occasions has been recorded in the fullest detail by Sir George Nayler, Garter King at Arms,

---

[1] Crull, *Antiquities of St. Peter's Westminster*, vol. ii, p. 48.

THE PROCESSION OF THE REGALIA AT THE CORONATION OF GEORGE IV

CHOIR OF WESTMINSTER ABBEY AT THE CORONATION OF JAMES II

in two sumptuous volumes. The vast expense involved in their production landed the erudite but unfortunate compiler in the Bankruptcy Court. This work contains a beautifully coloured full-page drawing depicting the Dean and Chapter of Westminster delivering over the Regalia to George IV in Westminster Hall shortly before the start of the outdoor Procession, since abandoned.

A Memorandum relating to this Coronation mentions six 'plain gold copes' worn by the six senior Prebendaries, viz. the Rev. Dr. Fynes-Clinton, the Rev. H. H. Edwards, the Rev. Dr. Allen, the Rev. F. W. Blomberg, the Rev. Lord Henry Fitzroy, and the Rev. Dr. Causton. They apparently preferred the simple cloth of gold copes to their heavily embroidered companions of velvet.

In the illustration six of the twelve Prebendaries are represented, each of whom is carrying one of the pieces of the Regalia. All are vested in 'plain gold copes' which are, without a doubt, those existing today.[1]

The choirs of the Abbey and the Chapel Royal regularly took part in this great outdoor Procession. The illustration from Sandford's *History of the Coronation of James II* shows the former arrayed in cassocks, long surplices, and ruffs. The reintroduction of the ruff at the Abbey in 1923 was no innovation but the welcome revival of an ancient custom which ought never to have been dropped.

When the great Golden Jubilee Service on June 28th, 1887, drew near, it was found that the condition of several copes had seriously deteriorated since the Coronation of Queen Victoria. Two of the velvet copes in particular were almost unusable. Unfortunately, the Dean and Chapter did not content themselves with pronouncing a veto upon their use. They even allowed two of them to be stripped of a goodly portion of their ornamentation with the object of enhancing the splendour of their companions, a deplorable piece of Victorian vandalism. Fortunately,

[1] W.A.M., C., 51350.

wiser counsels have prevailed in more recent years, for these ill-used copes have been renovated with such consummate art as to remove almost every trace of former deterioration or mutilation.

During the long interval between 1838 and 1887 the Church of England had been passing through much tribulation. Five clergy had been successively imprisoned under the Public Worship Regulation Act for what were supposed to be infractions of ecclesiastical law. The Rev. James Bell Cox, Vicar of St. Margaret's Church, Liverpool, had been released from one of Her Majesty's gaols only a few weeks before the celebration of the Golden Jubilee. Hence, the appearance of these forgotten copes, as the merest matter of course in Westminster Abbey on this great national occasion startled many people who were totally ignorant of their existence. The Press seized upon this welcome 'copy' with avidity. Pictures were on sale all over the country in which not only the Dean and Chapter of Westminster, but also Archbishop Benson and Archbishop Thomson, unexpectedly appeared arrayed in the gorgeous robes associated in the public mind solely with churches of an 'advanced' character. A curious situation thus came into existence, and one not devoid of humour, for this unusual experience appeared by no means unwelcome to these pillars of the Church.

One or more photographs were taken, the College Garden with the Dormitory as a background providing not unsuitable surroundings. They are full of interest in that they display more than one figure which may fairly be termed historical and afford valuable evidence upon the appearance of these ancient copes after half a century of disuse.[1]

No doubt it was an act of graceful courtesy on the part of the Chapter to rescue the two Archbishops from their distressing plight, by lending them two copes, but it could claim no precedent. It was twice repeated, however, during

[1] See illustration facing p. 167.

the ten years that followed, under circumstances still more open to criticism, for certain copes were even removed out of the Abbey. A crimson cope adorned the person of Bishop Creighton at the Coronation of the late Czar in 1894, while at the Diamond Jubilee service of 1897 on the steps of St. Paul's Cathedral, Archbishops Temple and Maclagan were vested in two purple velvet copes. The fact deserves to be recorded that one of these venerable fabrics has figured alike at the Coronation of our second Charles in Westminster Abbey and that of the unfortunate Nicholas II at Moscow. It is to be regretted that no record was made at the time which of our three crimson velvet copes received this honour.

III. THE TAPESTRIES

It has generally been assumed that no document exists recording the history of the older pieces among the superb tapestries of Westminster Abbey. Evidently an entry in the Inventory of 1661 must have been overlooked: 'Item: ffour large pieces of tapistree hangings for the Altar imagery work given by His Majesty at ye Coronation.'[1] The two great volumes by John Ogilby and Francis Sandford, which describe the Coronations of Charles II and James II in considerable detail, contain pictures showing the three sides of the presbytery heavily hung with tapestry. It is possible, too, to identify one of the fabrics depicted therein with tapestries suspended today in the Jerusalem Chamber and in the Chapel of St. Faith. The connexion with Charles II is clear enough.

The purpose served by these tapestries at occasions other than those of special solemnity is by no means clear. Although they are not indicated in the oil painting of the choir[2] they were probably in regular use, for the Treasurer was ordered on December 17th, 1731, to see that the 'two large pieces of tapestry be taken down, scoured, mended

[1] W.A.M. 44026, A and B.   [2] See vol. i: illustration facing p. 64.

and put up again' as well as to carry out other reparations at the east end.[1]

At some date unknown it was decided to distribute the tapestries in different parts of the building, mostly in the Jerusalem Chamber. It was a difficult and complicated task, but the Dean and Chapter found a rough and ready solution, and carried it out with drastic thoroughness. The tapestries were actually cut to fit the walls of their new home and mutilations inflicted which can never be made good. These priceless treasures were treated as if they were so many pieces of cheap wall-paper. The most splendid piece of all was even divided up into two separate sections.

Two of the Westminster tapestries have been identified as forming part of the famous Abraham series designed by the painter Bernard Van Orley of Brussels about the year 1530. Complete sets of this series still exist at Madrid and Vienna. Each of them comprises ten separate pieces. Our own country can also claim the possession of one complete set, though they are not all housed beneath the same roof. Eight adorn the Great Hall at Hampton Court, while the two remaining pieces are at St. James's Palace. All are plentifully enriched with gold and silver thread and surrounded with magnificent borders containing allegorical figures. They bear the signature of a famous sixteenth-century weaver, William Pannemaker.

The pieces preserved at Hampton Court were purchased by Cardinal Wolsey for the adornment of his great palace shortly before his disgrace. They were evidently appropriated by Henry VIII, for they are duly recorded in an inventory of that monarch's possessions under the date 1548.

Two of the Westminster tapestries clearly belong to another set of the Abraham series but the home of their companion pieces, supposing them to be still in existence, is unknown. They differ from the sets at Madrid, Vienna,

[1] Chapter Book.

and Hampton Court in that the borders are not enriched like the others with metal thread.

A magnificent panel of remarkably vivid colouring hangs in the north-west corner of the Jerusalem Chamber, partly covering a door. Experts have identified it as forming the major portion of the piece representing the Circumcision of Isaac. The smaller picture, viz. the Birth of Isaac which flanks it on the left, still remains *in situ*, but the piece which should complete the panel, viz. the Expulsion of Hagar and Ishmael, was for lack of space shamelessly severed therefrom. It has been effectively hung in the Chapel of St. Faith where it adds greatly to the comeliness of the building.

The Jerusalem Chamber also contains four smaller mutilated pieces which originally formed part of another panel of the Abraham series depicting the return of Sarah to Abraham from the Egyptians. The two principal figures have so far eluded discovery, together with a considerable portion of the border. Of the maltreated pieces which survive, the first contains about one-half of the main subject: the second and third display a camel and several men laden with treasures, while the fourth consists of a portion of the border on which are depicted figures of Luxus, Caristia, &c. The latter piece has been ingeniously utilized to form a narrow strip on the wall between two of the windows.

The remainder of the wall of the Jerusalem Chamber is graced by two other tapestried panels, of seventeenth-century date. Although extremely beautiful they display a decidedly lower standard of workmanship. One of them was executed by some Flemish weaver, possibly Pieter Wanders, who had a workshop in London during the seventeenth century. It belongs to a series entitled the Acts of the Apostles, other portions of which are preserved at Boughton and Haddon Hall. It is a simplified version of one of the Raphael Cartoons, viz. St. Peter and St. John at the Beautiful Gate of the Temple.

The last panel hangs on the left-hand side of the fire-place. It is attributed to certain Flemish artists of the late seventeenth century and depicts Rebecca in the act of giving water to the servant of Abraham at the well.

The two latter fabrics were presented to the Abbey by the Sub-Dean, Lord John Thynne, who brought them from his country seat, Hawnes Park, in Bedfordshire.

According to the Inventory of 1661, there remain '3 lesser pieces of tapestree hangings, lyned with canvice formerly given by Sir Paul Pindar'. These panels, alike in their general character, were suspended in various parts of the Abbey. One has long occupied a prominent place on the south side of the Presbytery,[1] a second panel hangs on the south wall of the Chapel of St. Faith, while the third formerly adorned the great staircase of the Deanery. All three specimens are rectangular panels of the 'vase and arcade' type, together with enriched composite columns, and a frieze consisting of amorini, fruit, &c. They are Brussels work of the late sixteenth century. It is probable that these are the three identical panels which found their way to the Abbey thanks to this generous citizen of London Town, a most strenuous supporter of the Royal cause. One of them unfortunately perished during the blitz days of 1941.

Similar tapestries form part of the two greatest collections in Europe, viz. those which formerly belonged to the King of Spain and to the late Imperial Dynasty of Austria. Another set is in existence, stamped with the arms of Cardinal Richelieu, while an almost perfect duplicate of the largest of the three pieces possessed by the Abbey is contained in a private collection in Sweden.

Mention must also be made of a fine specimen of Flemish Tapestry, on which is represented the Descent from the Cross, given to the Abbey in 1929. It hangs in the Chapel of My Lady Margaret, where it serves as a dorsal.

---

[1] See vol. i: illustration facing p. 98.

PART XI

WORSHIP AND ORDER
1560–1950

1. THE ELIZABETHAN CHAPTER AND THE WORK OF RECONSTRUCTION

WHEN Queen Elizabeth ascended the throne on November 17th, 1558, she found the monastic life re-established and the Church of Westminster in the hands of a small body of Benedictine monks, their Abbot being John of Feckenham, an excellent man who inspired respect wherever he went. The foundation could, however, claim but little stability. It had been set up barely two years before. Queen Mary had spared no pains to foster it; but its strength was slender and it had already experienced its share of difficulties.

The chief mark left upon the Abbey by the Feckenham régime has been the restoration of St. Edward's Shrine, a righteous act indeed; but the makeshift methods employed by the Abbot proclaim his shortage of money and the unsettled conditions of the times.[1]

For the moment things were left undisturbed. The Coronation of the new Queen took place on January 15th, 1559. Save that the Litany was recited in English and the Epistle and Gospel in both Latin and English, the old rite was followed throughout, Feckenham, as a matter of course, taking the same prominent part in the ceremonial as his abbatial predecessors. Ten days later Elizabeth attended High Mass, prior to the opening of her first Parliament, and from that time things moved quickly.

The Abbot was undoubtedly *persona grata* to the new Queen. It is more than possible that his intercession had

[1] Machyn's Diary, Mar. 21st, and Apr. 21st, 1556, 1557.

saved her from the fate of Lady Jane Grey. A tradition exists that she even offered him the Archbishopric of Canterbury; but, despite his conciliatory disposition, Feckenham was a zealot for the old ways and the offer (if ever made) was unhesitatingly refused.[1]

On May 5th, 1559, Parliament passed a bill decreeing the dissolution of all monasteries, for Westminster was not the only one refounded by the late Queen. Greenwich, Shene, and Syon had all been staffed by monks or nuns. There is some reason for thinking that the Abbey would have been excepted if Feckenham could have been brought to terms. Provided that the services were rendered in accordance with the Third Revision of the Book of Common Prayer, then on the eve of publication, and that they took the Oath of Supremacy, the monastic brethren might conceivably have remained in security within their precinct. The Feast of the Nativity of St. John Baptist was fixed as the last day for the taking of the Oath under pain of forfeiture; but as Feckenham remained silent, the Queen and her advisers had no alternative. The blow fell on the twelfth day of July. The Abbey was dissolved and two days later the black-robed Benedictines disappeared from the Isle of Thorns for ever.[2]

For nearly a year the Abbey remained in a state of suspended animation, devoid of staff and governing body. A public funeral took place, it is true, during this interim period, that of Frances Duchess of Suffolk, the mother of Lady Jane Grey, but the records are provokingly silent as to the performance, if any, of the customary services.

Ultimately the Queen decided to re-establish, with some minor variations, the Collegiate Church founded in 1540 by her father. The Charter of Foundation was dated May 12th, 1560. Three Commissioners, Matthew Parker, Archbishop of Canterbury, Gilbert Berkeley, Bishop of

[1] Fuller, *Church History*, pp. 6, 38.
[2] Richard Widmore, *History of the Church of St. Peter Westminster*, p. 138.

Bath and Wells, and William May, Dean of St. Paul's, were appointed to give possession on June 21st to the new Dean, William Bill, Master of Trinity College, Cambridge, and Provost of Eton. Nine days later the twelve Prebendaries provided in the Collegiate foundation were duly installed and the great church was 'sped upon its way', to play its part in the shaping and moulding of the new England that was to be.[1]

The first Chapter displayed a strange theological mixture. It included on the one side, John Hardiman, whose iconoclasm speedily brought about his deprivation, and Alexander Nowell who, ejected from the Abbey by Queen Mary and compelled to take refuge at Frankfort, had now returned strongly confirmed in his Protestantism. On the other side were Richard Cheney, a future Bishop of Gloucester, most loyal of churchmen, and Humphrey Perkins, upon whom had been bestowed the name of Charity. He had entered Westminster Abbey as a novice in 1517, said his first Mass in 1524, and was appointed by Henry VIII to a prebendal stall after the Dissolution. Ousted in 1556, shortly before the return of the monks, he was re-appointed to a stall in 1560 and continued to hold it till death in 1577 ended his remarkable career. A fifth member of the Chapter was that unsatisfactory ecclesiastic William Barlow, now become Bishop of Chichester, who not long before had taken the principal part in the consecration of the new Primate. Two others, Edmund Scambler and William Downham, became in due course Bishops of Peterborough and Chester. All without exception must have found it difficult to accommodate themselves to one another and to the complex conditions of the new Elizabethan régime.

The Dean at once embarked upon the task of drawing up Statutes and the countless details of reorganization, but he quickly succumbed, as well he might, beneath the

---

[1] Ibid., p. 139.

heavy burden of the simultaneous headship of three great foundations!

A surprising appointment followed. The junior of the twelve Prebendaries of Westminster, Gabriel Goodman, a Welshman, was installed in his place and the longest decanal reign in the annals of the Abbey commenced. This preferment was probably due to William Cecil, already all-powerful in the counsels of the Queen. The two men were close friends and at one time near neighbours, for Cecil was for many years a resident in Dean's Yard.

Goodman was in many ways a remarkable man. He laboured earnestly for the well-being of the Abbey, together with that of the town of Ruthin, his birthplace. To the former he gave two bells still in use, indeed both places had good cause to bless his generosity. It will always remain something of a mystery that, although more than once nominated, he never reached the episcopal bench.

The Church of Westminster has from time immemorial been renowned for its fabrics. During Pre-Reformation times, when the great churches of England were inspired with an ardent desire to render the worship of God's House in a manner exceeding magnifical, it occupied a position in the front rank. The vast record of treasures set forth in the Inventory drawn up in the year 1388 almost takes away one's breath. In the single item of copes, the Abbey could claim the possession of several hundred.[1] This enormous number is fully intelligible when the circumstances of the age and place are remembered. A prominent feature of the Westminster Customary was the great Sunday Pro-

---

[1] A sidelight is thrown upon the fate of some of our medieval treasures by a manuscript belonging to the Earl of Ancaster at Grimthorpe in which is recorded the deposition of Mr. John Copley concerning John Cotton (June 28th, 1612): 'And further he knoweth that he had divers copes of great worth, which, as he hath heard, did sometimes belong to the Westm Church and these he would never lend unto the secular priests, but unto the Jesuits, and that Father Garnett had two of them when he was taken . . . and two others he thinketh of these copes are now at St. Omer's being entreated thither by the Jesuits'. (*Historical Manuscripts Commission*, Report of the Manuscripts of the Earl of Ancaster, p. 367.)

THE STONYHURST COPE

cession when the whole monastic body passed round the building, visiting and censing each of the numerous altars in turn. Presumably the brethren would all be vested in copes, which fact goes far to explain the provision of this vast collection of costly fabrics. Grievous to relate, all of them disappeared before the end of the reign of Edward VI. The King's Commissioners, like so many birds of prey, swooped down upon the Abbey and stripped it of everything which had escaped at the Dissolution, save the barest necessities of worship, 'a silver pot, two gilt cups with covers, two hearse cloths, twelve cushions, one carpet, eight stall cloths for the choir, three pulpit cloths, a little carpet for the Dean's stall and two table-cloths'. In the temperate words of Richard Widmore, the most reliable of all the Abbey historians, 'to leave so fine a place so very bare, when there was no other public necessity but what greedy courtiers had made could hardly be excused'.[1]

Thus, it must have been a sadly impoverished church over which Bill and Goodman were called to preside. It is clear, however, that something had been done during the brief Marian period to make good the losses of the past, for on July 13th, 1559, Abbot Feckenham and John Moulton, gentlemen, the day after the deprivation of the Abbot entered into a bond with Sir Thomas Curtys, Alderman of London, pledging with him certain pieces of plate, including nine chalices of silver and a pax for the sum of £40. These ornamenta were to remain at the Abbey for the time being. If authorized by the Queen's Injunctions or by the bench of Bishops for Divine Service prior to the ensuing Easter, they were to continue in use without any payment being made, otherwise they were to become the property of Feckenham. Whether these ornamenta ever actually passed into the hands of the Dean and Chapter is, however, extremely doubtful.[2]

[1] Richard Widmore, *History of the Church of St. Peter Westminster*, p. 134.
[2] W.A.M. 9490.

In April 1563 a surprising windfall fell into the hands
of the Dean and Chapter; for Feckenham then conveyed
to Goodman, for the use of the Chapter, all such goods as
had been in his custody and not given by him to one Sir
Thomas Parry, now deceased. The various items are set
forth one by one in a schedule and included seven red
copes, fifteen blue, one green, one black, six complete sets
for the three Sacred Ministers, two canopies of blue and
red cloth respectively, some cushions and other cloths,
among the latter being 'two foore fruntes for the Communion Table'.[1]

The Dean and Chapter did not, however, display much
appreciation of the treasures which now came into their
hands. They converted a number of these valuable fabrics
into cushions and on March 11th, 1570, they even decided
to cut up 'the best copes remaining in the vestry' for the
manufacture of a canopy to be suspended over the head of
the Queen when she was received by them at the Abbey on
the first day of the next Parliament![2] The Treasurer's
Accounts, too, for the following year contain this sinister
entry: 'Thome Holmes upholster for thalering of certain
coapes into Quisshions &c. and for the workemanship and
stuffe thereunto as appereth by a bill xjii viish vid.'[3]

This remarkable collection of fabrics, though small when
compared with the well-nigh fabulous splendour of the
past, was amply sufficient to render the Abbey almost, if
not quite, unique among the great churches of England
during those dreary times. Hence, it is tragic to think that
the Dean and Chapter should have held the treasures,
which they had done but little to deserve, in such cheap
estimation.

The early years of Dean Goodman's long decanate must
have been a time of considerable financial stringency. A

[1] W.A.M. 9490.
[2] W.A.M. 9491A and 9491B—quoted by H. F. Westlake, *Westminster Abbey*, vol. i, pp. 234-5.   [3] Chapter Book.

few months after this holocaust of copes the Dean and Chapter actually embarked upon a lottery having for its object the raising of funds for the purchase of the necessary communion plate![1] The method employed is hardly one to be commended; but the Abbey had been so terribly depleted that there can be no question of its dire need.

Little evidence has so far been revealed regarding the High Altar and east end during Elizabethan times. Information drawn from divers sources is a good deal fuller where the ordering of the Services and the general customs of the establishment are concerned.

An entry in the Chapter Book dated October 12th, 1561, states that orders were given for a monthly celebration of the Holy Communion at which all the priests were to communicate. Failure to carry out this injunction was to be punished by the imposition of a fine curiously graduated in its amount, viz. in the case of the Dean 3*s*. 4*d*., a prebendary 2*s*. 0*d*., and other priests 1*s*. 4*d*. The Lay-vicars and Almsmen were to be present in sequence, four at a time.

The Dean was bound to preach four times a year, viz. on Christmas Day, Easter Day, Whitsunday, and All Saints' Day; but was permitted to appoint a Prebendary as his deputy.

Omission to perform his official residence involved a defaulting Prebendary in a fine of forty shillings.

Further regulations regarding sermons were made in 1571. It was decided that a Prebendary might invite any 'bishop deane or other worthie mane being a preacher' to occupy the pulpit of the Abbey Church; but he must give the Dean several days' notice that he might 'allow of him'.

In 1573 this regulation was somewhat strengthened:

'It is decreed that so oft as any Prebendary dothe not preache his sermon in his course, that he shall vj days at the least before give knowledge to Mr. Dean, whom he deputeth to preach for

[1] W.A.M. 33631. f. 5 quoted by H. F. Westlake, *Westminster Abbey*, ii. 247.

him, and if Mr. Dean shall not like of the preacher, then shall
Mr. Dean in that case, and also when no knowledge is given
by the prebendary being absent, of any preacher wtin the said
vj days, appoynte a fitt man to preache, and then the prebendary
shall paye to the preacher six shillings eight pence!'[1]

The Dean's veto on the appointment of preachers continues at the Abbey to this day and has been exercised
during the present century.

This information regarding the services and other matters already quoted from the Chapter Book was amplified
in an important letter addressed by the Dean to Lord
Treasurer Burleigh about sixteen years later.

The former was evidently much concerned about the
lax behaviour of some of the Prebendaries as regarded
both residence and preaching. Accordingly he appealed
to the Lord Treasurer for the confirmation of the statutes
of the Collegiate Church, 'in order to a reformation of
some things in the College'.

In response to Burleigh's request Goodman then forwarded a lengthy document which contains a deeply interesting description of the internal life and organization of
the Collegiate Church during the Elizabethan régime.
Little in the way of change had taken place since 1561,
while the various analogies between the sixteenth and the
twentieth centuries are both numerous and remarkable.[2]

Prayers were said daily in Henry VII's chapel at 6.0
a.m., a lecture being added on Wednesdays and Fridays.
'Daily Service Song' took place 'in the chancel of the great
church according to the order of Her Majesty's Chapel'.
The services must have been of the most protracted character for, according to Goodman, they lasted from 8 till 11
on Sundays: and on weekdays from 9 to 11 and 4 to 5.
A solemn Communion was celebrated on the Great Festivals and on the first Sunday of each month: on which occasions it was directed that the Dean, Prebendaries, and other

[1] Appendix IV.   [2] See Appendix V.

clergy present were all to communicate, likewise four of
the clerks and four of the Almsmen. A sermon was
preached either by the Dean or one of the Prebendaries
or some one acting for them.[1]

In 1592, during the decanate of Dean Goodman, and
again in 1610, two of the Dukes of Wurtemberg made
what they termed a 'Bathing expedition' to England.
Fortunately for posterity the extremely interesting journal
in which they recorded their adventures was preserved
and translated. Westminster Abbey was one of the places
visited by the Dukes and the choral service seems to have
impressed them: 'In this beautiful church the English
Ministers, who are dressed in white surplices such as the
Papists wear, sang alternately and the organs played.'[2]

2. PROGRESS AND DEVELOPMENT UNDER THE EARLY STUARTS

It fell to the lot of Dean Goodman to install no less than
forty Prebendaries during his lengthy decanate. The
majority left no mark either on the Abbey or anywhere
else. When they were not nonentities their records do not
bear too close investigation.

Towards the close of the Elizabethan period, however,
a change set in and appointments took place of men of
high character and outstanding ability.

Richard Bancroft came to Westminster in 1587 and we
can well imagine that the Abbey derived no small benefit
from the organizing capacity of this brilliant man, before
he departed ten years later for the See of London en route
for Lambeth.

Lancelot Andrewes, 'the angell in the pulpit', already
famous both as preacher and divine, became a Prebendary
in 1597. Four years later he received preferment no less

[1] Strype, *Annals of the Reformation*, vol. ii, part ii, App. X.
[2] W. B. Rye, *England as seen by Foreigners in the Days of Elizabeth and
James the First*, pp. 9–10.

striking than that of Goodman, for while still the junior member of the Chapter he was elevated to the Deanery.

For several years, then, Westminster enjoyed the direct influence of this splendid son of the English Church and many people had abundant cause for gratitude. A permanent memorial of his rule survives in the beautiful heraldic glass which he placed in the window of the Jericho Parlour.[1]

In his Funeral Sermon Buckeridge, Bishop of Rochester, paid a glowing tribute to Andrewes, for he stated that all the places where he held preferment were the better for him! Although his tenure of the Deanery lasted a bare four years, sufficient information is available to show that his administration was characterized by both wisdom and vigour; and fully merits Buckeridge's eulogy.

In addition to the manifold gifts familiar to all students of English Church history, the Dean displayed all the qualities of a first-rate man of business. He instituted a fabric fund, and 'left a place truly exemplarily collegiate in all respects, both within and without, free from debts and arrearages, from encroachment and evil customs'.[2]

Andrewes took the warmest interest in the well-being of the School which was already producing men of high distinction. One of the King's Scholars, a future Bishop of Lichfield, has left a delightful picture of the patriarchal relations between the Dean and the boys and the personal influence he brought to bear upon them. Possibly it was here that Bishop Hacket learnt the maxim which so abundantly characterized his own career and which he never ceased to reiterate, 'serve God and be cheerful'.[3]

Four stalls fell vacant during Andrewes' decanate. They were filled by excellent appointments in which it is impossible not to see the hand of the Dean. The installation of

[1] J. Armitage Robinson, *The Abbot's House at Westminster*, p. 60.
[2] Richard Widmore, *History of the Church of St. Peter Westminster*, p. 144.
[3] John Hacket, *Scrinia Restaurata*, p. 45.

such men as William Barlowe, an able preacher and the historian of the Hampton Court Conference; the erudite Old Westminster Richard Hakluyt; Adrian de Saravia, a strenuous upholder of episcopacy; and Christopher Sutton, whose sermons and devotional writings attained a wide popularity both in his own and in Tractarian times. Such men could not fail to strengthen the spiritual influence of the Abbey enormously.

We know little of Andrewes' policy at Westminster as regards the ordering of the services; but it is inconceivable that a man of such churchmanship could have tolerated anything unworthy in the great church of which he was the chief custodian. He has left on record a detailed description of his own private chapel with its instrumenta of worship, during his subsequent career. So beautiful and attractive was the ordering of the services that 'some that had been there desired to end their days in the Bishop of Elye's Chapel'. He left Westminster in 1605 for Chichester after a brief rule of four years; but he has made it abundantly clear that the 'Monastery of the West', τό ἐπιζεφύριον, for ever after occupied no small place in his affection and prayers.[1]

Richard Neile was utterly different from Andrewes in character and temperament though his theological outlook was similar. In spite of the unattractive features in his personality, we cannot withhold our respect from the son of the Westminster tallow-chandler who ended his career as Archbishop of York. The oft-quoted tale of his sycophancy in the presence of royalty has predisposed many to form an estimate of him which does less than justice to his many good qualities. He was one of Westminster's outstanding Deans, though his tenure of that office lasted barely five years, held moreover, for part of the time, *in commendam* with the Bishopric of Rochester. His industry

---

[1] Library of Anglo-Catholic Theology: Andrewes, *Works: Preces Privatae*, p. 13.

was extraordinary; for, when he was translated to the Bishopric of Lichfield and Coventry in 1610, he could point to an astonishing record of work accomplished by him at the Abbey, where despite extensive outgoings he greatly improved the unsatisfactory revenues of the Chapter.

A remarkable document[1] dated 1608 has set forth in full detail the achievements of Neile during his decanate. Evidently he was determined that the High Altar should display both dignity and splendour. Allusion has already been made to the magnificent frontal provided out of the palls or altar-cloths offered in accordance with the rubric by James I and Anne of Denmark at their Coronation,[2] together with another of simpler character for daily use costing £22. A dorsal, too, was required, in the Dean's opinion, in order to impart adequate dignity to the east end. At a cost of £55, no small amount in those days, he provided, therefore, 'a large backe Fronte of Cloathe of gold and blue velvett'.

Unfortunately, Feckenham's twenty-four copes had by Neile's time been reduced to eleven, while the sets of vestments for the three Sacred Ministers had apparently disappeared altogether. Neile's inventory drawn up in 1608 suggests, however, that the survivors were fabrics of remarkable beauty and interest.

'Imprimis one olde Cope of Blew Cloth of Golde with ye Salutacion in ye Cape.

Item. One Other Cope of Blew Cloth of Golde with the Resurrection in ye Cape.

Item. One other Cope of Blew Cloth of Golde with God the father and the Crucifix in ye Cape.

Item. One other Cope of Blew Cloth of Golde with St. Paul in ye Cape.

Item. One other Cope of Cloth of Golde with Blew velvet with a border of beaten golde and a Cape to the same.

Six Copes receaved of Mr. Standen viz. fower of them

---

[1] W.A.M. 6612. See Appendix II.   [2] See p. 71.

with borders of flower de luces and are thus distinguished viz.

The first with a Salutacion in ye Cape.

Item. The second with God the Father and Christe dead in his arms.

Item. The third the Salutacion in ye Cape being of cloth of beaten golde.

Item. The fowrth, with the death of our Lady in ye Cape.

Item. The other two of red cloth of golde, viz. the one with the Epiphanie in ye Cape, th' other with the Nativite in ye Cape.'

Whatever may have been the practice at the Abbey during the long forty years' rule of Dean Goodman, the cope was undoubtedly in regular use during the reign of James I and this practice continued down to the revolutionary days of the Long Parliament.

It would seem, too, that on certain occasions, not only the officiating clergy, but a portion of the choir also were vested in copes, according to the description by Bishop Hacket, himself an Old Westminster, of an extremely interesting event, which took place on December 15th, 1624.

The occasion was an entertainment which included a sacred concert given by the Dean, John Williams, to the French Ambassador in honour of the engagement of Charles Prince of Wales and Princess Henrietta Maria. The historian states that 'the quiremen vested in their rich copes with their choristers sang three several anthems with most excellent voices before them'.[1]

Montaigne followed in the steps of his predecessors. The conservative spirit which had always prevailed at the Abbey was consistently upheld by him. Customs and practices lingered here which had long been discarded elsewhere. A statement made by Bishop Cosin suggests that some of these practices had been maintained without a break all through the Reformation period. 'Though

---

[1] John Hacket, *Scrinia Restaurata*, part i, p. 210.

there was no necessity, yet there was a liberty still reserved of using wafer bread which has continued to divers churches of the Kingdom, and Westminster for one, till the 17th of King Charles.'[1]

In such embittered times as the first half of the seventeenth century it was impossible, however, for the conservative Abbey to escape criticism. It was 'the feare of the copes and wafercakes' in use there which produced the historic protest of the House of Commons in 1614, followed by their migration to the Parish Church of St. Margaret, as more suitable for their corporate worship. A serious breach with the past took place and no small amount of bile was stirred up at the time; but the loss was accompanied by gain, for this intolerant attitude of the popular representatives brought about the establishment of a permanent link between that beautiful Church and the Lower House, still jealously preserved.

The pompous funeral in the Abbey of a certain favourite of the Duke of Buckingham, Sir John Grimes by name, in 1616, not only raised a storm of criticism, but was also the occasion of the loss of two of the copes together with some altar hangings. The thieves apparently were never brought to justice.[2]

Before long, William Laud, then aged forty-eight, became a member of the Chapter. Neile had bequeathed his mantle to this rising ecclesiastic. In the year that he himself ceased to be Dean, he managed to secure the stall then occupied by Dr. Bulkeley for his protégé, though Laud was condemned to wait a good ten years for the vacancy. He was not installed until January 1620.

It is, of course, possible that the High Altar of the Abbey, like that of many other churches during the reign of Queen Elizabeth, had been removed into the body of

---

[1] Cosin, *Works*, vol. v, p. 481. John Jebb, *Choral Service of the United Church of England and Ireland*, p. 523.
[2] *State Papers, Domestic, James I*, vol. lxxxvi, No. 132.

the church and there placed tablewise. Dean Stanley has stated this as a definite fact,[1] and claims as his authority a passage in Wiffin's *History of the House of Russell*, describing the baptism of a scion of that distinguished family.[2] His interpretation is, however, extremely far-fetched and can hardly be accepted. Whatever may or may not have been the case during Elizabethan times it is certain that the High Altar was occupying its ancient position long before Laud embarked upon his great campaign. The changes instituted by Dean Neile between 1605 and 1610 establish this fact beyond all possibility of doubt.

A further improvement took place during Laud's six years' service as Prebendary; for a set of rails was interposed between the presbytery and the main body of the church. That the future Archbishop had no small share in this development may be taken for granted.[3]

A curious Chapter Order of this period indicates an attempt on the part of the Abbey authorities to control the members of their congregation, for it lays down that admission to the Church is to be refused to ladies attired in yellow ruffs![4]

In the year of Laud's installation Puritanism invaded the Deanery in the person of John Williams. He represented, fortunately, the Puritanism of Milton rather than that of Cromwell, indeed the records of his rule do not suggest that he inaugurated any radical changes. On the contrary, he spent his money with a lavish hand and he took the warmest interest in the music, which for a time was under the direction of our 'English Palestrina', Orlando Gibbons, whom he appointed *Magister Choristarum*.[5] He has even received the credit, though quite erroneously, for effecting the change from 'tablewise' to

[1] Stanley, *Historical Memorials of Westminster Abbey*, p. 494.
[2] Wiffin, *House of Russell*, p. 503.
[3] W.A.M. 41620.
[4] Chapter Book.
[5] Barnard, *Life of Heylin*, pp. 162 and 194.

'altarwise',[1] despite his own Puritanical leanings.[2] He apparently acquiesced in the state of things which he found already in existence at the Abbey, indeed he was wont to say that his great exemplars were Abbot Islip and Dean Andrewes.

Before long Williams fell into dire disgrace. James I had a sincere regard for this clever Welshman; but Charles I could not abide him. For a long while his decanal duties were in abeyance. He rarely, if ever, came near Westminster during those years, some of them spent in the Tower. For all practical purposes he was under suspension. Consequently, the influence of Laud and his disciple, Peter Heylin, a leading personality among the twelve Prebendaries and a representative of the High Anglican School, remained in the ascendant.

This state of things continued to prevail in the Church of Westminster until the great tempest arose in 1640, no less calamitous than that of a century before. Abbey and Chapter alike sank into what seemed to be irretrievable ruin.

3. PURITANISM RAMPANT

With the assembling of the Long Parliament on November 3rd, 1640, the position of the Abbey soon became critical. Williams was promptly released from the Tower and restored to royal favour. A year later he was rewarded with the Archbishopric of York to be held *in commendam* with the Deanery of Westminster for the ensuing three years.

The Puritan Dean returned to his old haunts from which he had been unjustly expelled and found himself a popular hero. Such, however, was the embittered state of the public mind that, although his Puritan views were known to all

---

[1] Hacket, *Scrinia Restaurata*, p. 63.
[2] E. W. Benson, *Lincoln Judgment*, p. 112.

and applauded by many, he was powerless to avert disaster from the church of which he was the chief officer.

The day after Christmas Day 1641, a furious attack was made upon the Abbey by a number of London apprentices under the leadership of one Sir Richard Wiseman, shouting 'no Bishop, no King'. A portion of the north door was battered in; but so spirited a defence was put up by the staff of the Abbey and the King's Scholars that the assailants were repelled. Unfortunately, the leader of the assault was slain by a tile hurled from the battlements by an unknown hand and the mob became infuriated to madness. Williams himself was in some danger, while his hot Welsh blood was roused to boiling-point partly by reason of the insults hurled upon the episcopal order, partly because he feared for the safety of the Regalia, of which in those days the Dean and Chapter enjoyed the custody.

Furious at the treatment received by the Abbey and the personal violence which he had himself suffered in making his way from the House of Lords to the Deanery, Williams assembled a dozen Bishops in the Jerusalem Chamber the next day and headed a protest against their exclusion from the Upper House. It was of no avail. The whole twelve were arrested, and Williams, in return for his pains, for the second time in his life found himself an inmate of the Tower. He was released a few months later and his signature appears for the last time in the Chapter Book at a meeting held on May 18th, 1642. He followed the King to the north and never returned to Westminster again.

During this year of increasing difficulty and unrest, the Chapter continued to function though Peter Heylin, and probably others among the Prebendaries were driven from their posts and compelled to seek places of refuge. The Treasurer's Accounts[1] for the year ending Michaelmas 1642 indicate that all the members of the Chapter were

[1] W.A.M. 33690.

receiving their customary stipends up to that date. The services of the Abbey were evidently being maintained. The choir is recorded as being at full strength. The Precentor and Minor Canons were still at their posts. The year 1642 must have passed away in comparative though cheerless peace.

With the opening of the dark year 1643, the storm burst with renewed fury and a frontal attack was made. Blow after blow fell upon the place, and before long the entire capitular establishment collapsed.

On April 24th, 1643, a Parliamentary Committee was appointed under the chairmanship of Sir Robert Harley, an iconoclast of the first order. His delight must have known no bounds when the terms of reference were made known. The Puritan majority could hardly have invented a task better calculated to give pleasure to the chairman and his colleagues than the demolition of the 'monuments of superstition and idolatry in the Abbey Church and the windows thereof'.

Torrigiano's altar and reredos and the glorious windows in Henry VII's Chapel speedily fell victims to their sacrilegious zeal, while the doom of the copes was sealed. No power on earth at that time could have saved them. Orders were given for them to be burnt and their gold and silver ornamentation sold for the benefit of the poor of Ireland. The proceeds of the sale, whether great or small, have never transpired. Every trace of Pre-Reformation magnificence disappeared for ever. Two tragic relics alone remained to tell the melancholy tale. In the Chapel of St. Faith there survived 'a set of cranes of wood, swinging as if in a rack on which formerly the copes and vestments in common use were hung'. They lingered here in this useless manner for at least eighty years after the pillage, and probably a good deal longer,[1] only to disappear in their turn. An interesting fifteenth-century cope chest of quad-

---

[1] Dart, *Westmonasterium*, i, p. 64.

rant shape with chamfered framing and strap hinges had better fortune, for it has survived to this day.

An investigation of the Abbey and its Precincts, under the suspicion of a Royalist plot, speedily followed and on June 2nd an attempt was made to seize the Regalia housed in the Chapel of the Pyx. For the moment this abominable outrage was foiled. A motion that the Chapter be requested to deliver up the keys was lost by 58 to 37 votes; but a second debate followed the next day as a result of which the doors of the Chapel were forced open, on the suspicion that Williams, an out-and-out man of action, might have carried away its precious contents on his flight to the north. So great was the sanctity attached to the Regalia in the public mind, however, that even at that time of upheaval, the resolution authorizing this outrage only passed the House of Commons by one vote.

A few weeks later a foul desecration of the east end took place. The Parliamentary soldiers destroyed the organ, burnt the altar rails, played hare and hounds inside the church, dressed up in surplices and sat round the Communion Table eating, drinking, smoking, and singing. Still worse outrages took place, upon which one can only draw a veil, for the hideous story is utterly unfit for publication.[1] The veracity of the Very Rev. Dr. Bruno Ryves, Dean of Chichester and subsequently Dean of Windsor, who is said to have written this account under the pseudonym of Mercurius Rusticus, has been questioned: but it is difficult to see on what grounds. In the eyes of the chief actors desecration and profanation stood for nothing.

Simultaneously with the destruction of the furniture and instrumenta of worship, a savage attack was made upon the whole Catholic position. On August 21st the Sub-Dean, Thomas Wilson, and his colleagues were ordered to throw over their Statutes and Customs and place the pulpit

---

[1] Crull, *The Antiquities of St. Peter's Westminster,* ii, App. ii, p. 14.

on Sunday afternoons at the disposal of such Lecturers as the House of Commons should think fit to appoint.

Meanwhile, the famous Westminster Assembly of Divines had started its meetings. They had been entrusted with the duty of revising the liturgy and government of the Church of England. To quote the words of Dean Stanley:

'For five years six months and twenty two days through one thousand one hundred and sixty-three sessions the Chapel of Henry VII and the Jerusalem Chamber witnessed their weary labours. Out of these walls came the Directory, the Longer and Shorter Cathechisms and that famous Confession of Faith, which alone within these islands was imposed upon the whole Kingdom, and which alone of all Protestant confessions, still, in spite of its sternness and narrowness, retains a hold on the minds of its adherents.'[1]

Among the early proceedings of the Assembly was the enactment of the Solemn League and Covenant. The document was brought 'with tears of pity and joy' into Henry VII's Chapel on August 16th. Eight days later it was solemnly signed in St. Margaret's Church by the members of the Assembly in company with those of the House of Commons.

It is hardly surprising that the Treasurer's Accounts for the year ending Michaelmas 1643[2] tell a very different tale as compared with those of its predecessors. The numerous omissions are highly significant. There is no trace of payment to any of the Chapter. On the other hand, the Choristers and Lay-vicars are still at work, likewise the Precentor, Dr. Pierce, and four Minor Canons, William Hutton, Edmund Nelham, Robert White, and James Taylor. The fact, however, that the Precentor only received three-quarters, and James Taylor one-half, of their respective stipends during the year just ended suggests that before its close they, too, had become obnoxious to

[1] Stanley, *Historical Memorials of Westminster Abbey*, p. 467.
[2] W.A.M. 33692.

the dominant party, and had been unable to continue at their posts.

One member of the Chapter was still on the spot, and in high favour, Lambert Osboldstone, the ex-Headmaster. In former years he had been foolish enough to style Laud the 'Little Vermin' and 'Hocus-pocus'. He narrowly escaped the pillory and was compelled to go into hiding. With the triumph of Puritanism, he had returned to his old haunts and his prebendal stall. For a time he was surrounded by a halo of veneration.

During 1644 disasters continued to crowd thick and fast upon the place. It is possible that Osboldstone still strove to maintain his position, though his name ceased to occupy a place in the Treasurer's Accounts. But, extreme Puritan though he was, and apparently in favour with members of Parliament, he could do nothing to avert the ruin which now descended upon the unfortunate Abbey.

On January 13th, sixteen members of the Lower House, to whom four others were added later on, were appointed a Committee to inquire into the state of the Church of Westminster. They soon got to work. The daily service which had still been maintained somehow or other during these last terrible months was now officially suspended, and on February 28th a new order of things came into being. For Matins and Evensong there was substituted a daily 'morning exercise' lasting half an hour and ending at eight o'clock, conducted by certain Presbyterian divines, among them Stephen Marshall and Philip Nye, a sorry substitute for the exquisite music and the lofty devotion of the Book of Common Prayer.[1] The official residences of the Chapter were seized, and doubtless proved very acceptable to those intruding divines.

The year which started in this ill-omened manner was even more tragic than its predecessor, for the breaking-point was reached. It was laid down by order of Parliament

---

[1] *Journals of the House of Commons*, vol. iii, p. 410.

that all persons connected with the Chapter and College of Westminster must signify their acceptance of the Covenant on April 22nd. Osboldstone alone out of the capitular body assented though even his extreme Puritanism was soon found all too mild for the Parliamentary vandals. We are told, however, that two Prebendaries were 'skulking about' and that Mr. Busby, the distinguished Headmaster of the School, was 'sickly'. Surely this must have been a diplomatic illness! It would seem that two of the Minor Canons followed the example of Osboldstone, for the names of Hutton and White appear once more in the Treasurer's Accounts. They could scarcely have held on so long without pronouncing the Puritan Shibboleths.

All through this year things grew steadily worse, if such were possible. The sum of £1. 8s. was paid to Thomas Stevens and others 'for taking down the angels in the Abbey and cleansing out pictures'. Professor Lethaby has suggested that this may refer to the cherubim on the rood-beam above the High Altar; but it is impossible to speak positively. An order was also given on April 24th for the sale of the brass and iron in Henry VII's Chapel. Fortunately for posterity, this outrage was not carried out. A payment is recorded in this same year for 'taking down part of the organ loft', while one John Stevens was recompensed for 'cutting out a crucifix at the north end of the Abbey'.

Far away back in the thirteenth century even before Henry III had started to rebuild the church, Richard de Berkyng, one of our outstanding Abbots, enriched the two sides of the choir with magnificent tapestries of cloth of Arras. They were divided into forty-eight different scenes, on the south side events in the life of Our Lord, and on the north the story of St. Edward the Confessor.[1] Although four centuries had come and gone the tapestries

[1] Flete, *History of Westminster Abbey* (edited by J. Armitage Robinson), pp. 24–31, 105.

were still occupying their accustomed place. But their doom was now sealed. Dugdale in his *History of the Civil War* has told the story. The Long Parliament, in order to 'glorify their doings the more', and for the further adornment of their own building, removed 'the whole suit of Hangings which were placed in the Quire of the Collegiate Church at Westminster and some other taken out of the King's Wardrobe'. They have never been seen again.

The High Altar must have disappeared together with the costly furnishings provided by Dean Neile. Whether it was actually destroyed or not it is impossible to say, but a table was undoubtedly substituted and placed in the centre of the Church for the Communion of the Commons.[1] The Presbytery was filled up with a great mass of pews. The plan for their allocation still exists among the Abbey muniments. The clergy had been driven forth to seek refuge as best they could. The Abbey had become a mere preaching-house.

There is a curious minute among the proceedings of the Parliamentary Committee on March 28th of this year. It runs as follows: 'Plate of ye College carried into one of ye vaults of ye Church and there buried.'[2]

The suggestion that a quantity of Pre-Restoration plate is at this moment lying intact in some unknown place beneath the floor of the Abbey is full of fascination; but it is not easy to harmonize this theory with the statements of Widmore, by far the most trustworthy of all the Abbey historians. According to him, an order was given by the House of Commons on May 8th, 1644, that 'the plate lately found that belongs unto the College of Westminster now in the possession of Sir Robert Harley, was to be melted and the produce applied by the Committee for the use of the Church and for the payment of the servants and

---

[1] There is a tradition to the effect that this table is identical with one which long stood at the west end of the Confessor's Shrine, and today occupies the centre of the Jericho Parlour. That it is of seventeenth-century origin is unquestionable.

[2] W.A.M. 42198.

workmen'. Again, on October 9th two of the members were ordered to inform the House what superstitious plate was in the place where the registers were kept, that it might be melted and sold and the produce employed to buy horses.[1] As regards any burial of the plate Widmore says nothing. His silence is significant.

On November 18th, 1645, another Committee consisting of eleven Lords and twenty-two Members of the House of Commons was established by an Ordinance of the two Houses of Parliament for the better ordering, directing, and disposing of the rents, issues, and profits belonging to the College and Collegiate Church of Westminster. It was laid down that all those members of the Collegiate body who had departed, or who were 'delinquents' or had omitted to take the Covenant were suspended, with the exception of Osboldstone; and the Committee was empowered to take their place.[2]

The reasons for the establishment of the Committee are set forth in the preamble to the Ordinance as follows:

'For asmuch as the present Dean and Prebends (except only Mr. Lambert Osbolston) have deserted their charge or are become delinquents to the Parliament, whereby the said College and Collegiate Church is destitute of government, and the said School, Almsmen, servants and officers deprived of all means of subsistence, by reason no person is appointed to take care for the same.'[3]

In September 1649, by another Act of Parliament, the management of the Church and College of Westminster was put in the hands of fifty-six Governors.

Save for the beautiful building itself, nought remained to suggest the ancient worship for the constant offering of which it had been erected by its Royal founders. The Puritan majority in Parliament had carried out their wild

[1] Richard Widmore, *History of the Church of St. Peter Westminster*, p. 156.
[2] *Harleian Miscellanies*, ix, 545.
[3] Richard Widmore, *History of the Church of St. Peter Westminster*, p. 214.

work only too well. The wreck of everything represented by the word 'churchmanship' was complete. So far as the Puritans were concerned there was nothing further to be done. Let one of them speak for himself:

'And about 26 of this instant March my intelligence put me in minde here to make mention of God's admirably and most wise ordering and disposing of things to the glory of his name, joy of his children and vexation of his base *Brats of Rome* and malignant enemies of Reformation, in the most rare and strange alteration of things in the *Cathedral Church of Westminster*. Namely, that whereas there was wont to be heard nothing almost but *Roaring*—Boyes, tooting and squeaking *Organ Pipes*, and the *Cathedral catches of Morley*, and I know not what trash; now the Popish Altar is quite taken away, the *bellowing Organs* are demolisht and pull'd down, the *treble* or rather *trouble* and base singers, Chanters or Inchanters driven out; and instead thereof, there is now a most blessed Orthodox Preaching Ministry, even every morning throughout the weeke, and every weeke throughout the whole yeare a Sermon Preached, by most learned grave and godly Ministers, of purpose appointed thereunto, and for the gaudy, gilded Crucifixes and rotten rabble of dumb Idols, Popish Saints and Pictures, set up and placed, and painted thereabout, where that sinfull Singing was used; now a most sweet assembly and thicke throng of God's pious people, and well affected, living teachable Saints is there constantly, and most comfortably, every morning to be seen at the Sermon. O our God! what a rich and rare alteration! What a strange change is this indeed!'[1]

In the years 1649 and 1650 it was customary for a corporal and nine soldiers to be present at the Abbey on Sunday from early morning until the conclusion of the afternoon service to suppress interrupters. When vitriolic utterances were being poured forth from the pulpit, we can well believe that these guardians of public order found their office no sinecure.

One bright spot alone appears in this gloomy picture. The indomitable Headmaster, Dr. Richard Busby, despite

[1] John Vicars, *God's Ark overtopping the World's Waves*, p. 184.

his sound churchmanship and royalist opinions, remained unshaken at his post all through these depressing years, gallantly riding upon the storm. Neither did the great Doctor make any attempt to hide his light under a bushel. Day by day was prayer offered up in the Royal School for the well-being of the Sovereign, even on the day of his martyrdom at Whitehall. The boys were compelled, it is true, to attend the ministrations of the Puritan preachers in the Abbey, but to quote the words of one of Busby's most distinguished pupils, Robert South, afterwards the great preacher of Restoration days—'Though we had some of those fellows for our governors yet, thanks be to God they were never our teachers . . . though our ears still encountered with such doctrines in the Church, it was our happiness to be taught other doctrines in the School.'[1] Well might John Owen, the Puritan Dean of Christ Church, Oxford, exclaim that 'it will never be well with the nation till Westminster School is suppressed'.[2] Dr. Busby was all the while building even better than he knew.

4. THE REBUILDING OF THE WASTE PLACES

Eleven dreary years came and went after the hideous tragedy of 1649. The Church was driven to take refuge in the caves and holes of the earth and the Abbey endured the full blast of the tempest. Williams' successor, Richard Steward, could not be installed and passed away in a foreign land. Four only out of the full complement of twelve Prebendaries had survived. The redoutable Peter Heylin still retained his energy though he had lost his sight. Three

[1] Robert South, *Sermon on The Virtuous Education of Youth*. This Sermon was 'planned and proposed to have been preached at Westminster Abbey at a solemn meeting of such as had been bred at Westminster School. But the death of King Charles II happening in the meantime the design of this solemnity fell to the ground with him.' The Sermon was subsequently published at the command of 'A very great person (Lord Jeffries) whose word was law as well as his profession'.
[2] Stanley, *Historical Memorials of Westminster Abbey*, p. 440.

colleagues, William Heywood, William Laney (destined to occupy the See of Ely), and Matthew Nicholas returned with him, after cruel sufferings, to their homes in the Precincts. The houses and stalls of which they had been so wickedly dispossessed were once more occupied by their lawful owners.

A cleric named William Hooper is found officiating as Minor Canon during these early months. It is probable that he was one and the same as a Lay-vicar bearing that name, who appears in the last set of the Treasurer's Accounts before the final débacle.

The names of three elderly men, Thomas Heywood, John Harding, and Christopher Chapman reappear as Lay-vicars in the Treasurer's Accounts for 1660–6, the sole representatives of the famous choir. Richard Portman, the Organist, a pupil of Orlando Gibbons, had died the previous year. Of Choristers or Choir School there was not a trace. In the midst of their joy for the overthrow of the sour Puritanism which had brought the Abbey to the verge of ruin, this little band of veterans must have experienced many a bitter heartache as they recalled the glories of the past.

The King lost no time in filling the vacant Deanery. Barely a fortnight after the Restoration his choice fell on John Earles, a man of the most delightful and attractive character, 'being universally beloved for his sweet and gentle disposition, an excellent scholar and a rare preacher'. He had served Charles as Tutor and Chaplain during the days of exile in Paris.[1]

One of the first duties of the new Dean was the installation of eight new Prebendaries to fill the places which had become vacant during the long interregnum. Save in the case of Francis Walsall, who did not arrive until September, this task was completed before the end of July. At least two of the new Prebendaries were men of outstanding

---

[1] *Diary of John Evelyn*, p. 225.

ability, viz. Busby, who now received this richly merited reward, and John Sudbury, destined to serve as Dean of Durham in the days of Cosin. Before long, powerful reinforcements arrived with the great Caroline theologian, Herbert Thorndike, and Robert South, the Old Westminster, now become a distinguished preacher. The Westminster Chapter was soon functioning as of old.

At the same time the Dean and Chapter felt obliged to go slow. They allowed the intruding Independent clergy to continue their ministrations until Michaelmas. Accordingly, Pepys, most inveterate of sermon tasters, attended service at the Abbey on Sunday, September 23rd, eager to enjoy a valedictory sermon. He was not disappointed for he sat under the well-known Independent, John Rowe. His sense of humour was, however, severely tickled by the extemporaneous effusion of one of the divines present who besought the Almighty 'that he would imprint his word on the thumbs of our right hands, and on the right great toes of our right feet'.[1]

The Treasurer's Accounts show that Seth Wood, who acted as Assistant Minister to the Independent congregation in the Abbey, was paid his stipend up to Michaelmas Day, on which date the Chapter Book states in colourless, businesslike fashion, his appointment came to an end.

From Michaelmas Day onwards the Church was in full possession once more, but reorganization could not be achieved in a day. At a second visit, on October 2nd, Pepys found 'but a thin congregation' at Vespers,[2] while on the following Sunday afternoon (October 7th) he came away grievously disappointed. 'After dinner to the Abbey where I heard them read the Church Service, but very ridiculously. A poor cold sermon of Dr. Lamb, one of the Prebendaries came afterwards, and so all ended.'[3] It is only

[1] *Diary and Correspondence of Samuel Pepys,* vol. i, p. 191.
[2] Ibid., p. 196.
[3] Ibid., p. 234.

fair to say that Dr. James Lamb, whom Pepys castigates so severely, was an Oriental scholar of great learning. Presumably his oratorical gifts had failed to keep pace with his erudition.

Pepys's churlish remarks were most unreasonable, considering the difficulties of the times, but he had to eat his words three weeks later when to his surprise and delight he found an organ in use. 'The first time that ever I heard the organs in a Cathedral.'[1] The fame of the Abbey organ spread rapidly through the metropolis, for on the last Sunday of the year this indefatigable gossip again made his way from the City and noted the immense crowds. 'Lord's Day. I to the Abbey and walked there, seeing the great confusion of people that came to hear the organs.'[2] It speaks volumes for the energy of the Dean and Chapter that in less than six months an organ should have been in use once more. Whether it was an entirely new instrument or the old one repaired after the damage inflicted by the Puritans is not very clear.[3] The cost was £120.[4]

The choral portion of the establishment was another matter altogether. During the winter a capable man, by name Philip Tynchare, was secured for the post of Precentor together with two new Minor Canons, William Tucker, not unknown as a composer of chants, and Jonas Caldecote.

By degrees a number of adult singers were secured. At first they were only 'allowed to do service in the church'. Presumably they were found reasonably efficient, for they were officially installed on February 16th, 1661, when the Lay-vicars on the foundation were once more brought up to the full complement of twelve.

For some considerable time the daily services were rendered by adult voices only. The Court was plunged into mourning at Christmas with the death of the Princess

[1] Ibid., p. 275.   [2] Ibid., p. 315.
[3] W.A.M. 44024.   [4] See vol. i: illustration facing p. 64; also Appendix VI.

Royal, the King's eldest sister, mother of the future William III. A State Funeral followed, but no Choristers were available. Not until after the appointment of an older Henry Purcell as *Magister Choristarum* did the choir attain its full strength, and not until the funeral of a child of James Duke of York in the following May did the Choristers attend on any State occasion save, no doubt, the Coronation on April 23rd.

The difficulties which confronted the Dean and Chapter were enormous. Old traditions had sunk into oblivion, and in rebuilding it was necessary to start from zero. The voice of thanksgiving and melody had well-nigh disappeared out of our land during the dreary years which had just terminated. The awful persecution to which the Church had been subjected had inflicted a wound upon her musical art which has never been completely healed. A generation was growing up devoid of any musical knowledge whatsoever. Matthew Locke, in his book entitled *Present Practice of Music Vindicated*, has stated that

'For above a year after the opening of His Majesty's Chappels the orderers of the Musick there were necessitated to supply the superior parts of their Musick with cornets and men's feigned voices there being not one lad to be had for all that time capable of singing his part readily.'

The Abbey as well as the Chapel Royal had to endure this anomaly. Only by thus supplementing the organ with the tones of the cornet[1] was it found possible to render the daily offices with any approach to decency or dignity, for lack of efficient boys. The sum of £4 was still being paid to John Hill, the cornet player, four years later.[2]

The post of Organist was the last to be filled, with the appointment of Christopher Gibbons, son of a greater

---

[1] This is not the same instrument as that with which we ourselves are familiar. It has been described as a 'delicate, pleasant musick if well played'. 'Nothing comes so near or rather imitates so much as an excellent cornet pipe.' Grove, *Dictionary of Music and Musicians*, i, p. 728.

[2] Treasurer's Accounts.

father. Appointed to Winchester Cathedral in 1638, he left his post a few years later and joined the Royalist Army. He survived the great Civil War and the troublous times of the Commonwealth and with the Restoration he once more resumed his musical art. He did not, however, immediately make his appearance at Westminster, for his name does not appear in any official document until February 27th, 1661, when he received a fee from the Treasurer, Dr. Busby.[1]

The refurnishing of the rifled Abbey involved the Dean and Chapter in a heavy burden. The Puritans had done their evil work thoroughly. The great church had been stripped bare. The tombs had been left for the most part untouched, the thirteenth-century stalls were still *in situ* and, for some unexplained reason, a quantity of metalwork, though specially marked out for destruction, had been spared, but that was all. Of the various *instrumenta* of public worship not a solitary vestige remained.

Evidently the restored Dean and Chapter believed, rightly or wrongly, that some at any rate of the treasures seized by Sir Robert Harley had not gone far away and might perhaps be recovered. Accordingly, on October 20th, 1660, they published a Chapter Order to the effect that 'if any person shall give notice to the Dean and Chapter by word or writing of any money, goods or utensils detayned or embezzled from the said Church, shall for their paynes and faithfulness in discovering the same, receive one fourth part of the full value of all such money, goods or utensils which shall be discovered by their industry and intelligence'.[2] This laudable effort does not appear to have met with any success.

Down to the time of the great catastrophe, when the Dean and Chapter were expelled by the Long Parliament from church and home and scattered to the four winds, the twelve Prebendaries had invariably been admitted to

[1] J. E. West, *Cathedral Organists*, p. 144.   [2] Chapter Book.

particular stalls. These they retained throughout the entire period of their service, long or short, as the case might be. The seat into which each had been officially installed by the Dean or his representative never varied and presumably he never occupied any other unless he happened to become Sub-Dean.[1]

The Restoration found the Chapter sadly depleted in numbers, no installation having taken place since 1642. During the dreary years which had just terminated, the influence of tradition had inevitably weakened. Many customs and practices must have passed into oblivion. The excellent Dean, John Earles, was a new-comer. He had had no previous experience of life at the Abbey and with all the goodwill in the world he must have been completely ignorant of traditions which had been in abeyance for at least seventeen years. All four of his colleagues were elderly and one was totally blind. That a breach with the past should have taken place at the time of the hurried installation of eight new Prebendaries in July 1660 was scarcely wonderful, though most regrettable.

Thus, the ancient custom by which each Prebendary on his installation was placed in the first, second, or third stall, as the case might be, ceased from the Restoration onwards. Henceforth, a new Prebendary took his place in the junior stall on either the Decani or Cantoris side and moved upon a vacancy occurring. Today the twelve Prebendaries of the Elizabethan foundation are meagrely represented by five Canons, a sad falling off for which early-Victorian legislation can hardly be sufficiently blamed. Thus, the junior stall at the present time stands next but one to that of the Sub-Dean on the north side and installations take place in that stall alone. This slovenly practice can claim the precedent of many years; but it compares unfavourably with other churches in which the

[1] Richard Widmore, *History of the Church of St. Peter Westminster*, Appendix, p. 114.

'laudable customs' of the past have been more jealously guarded by former generations.

An important piece of pictorial evidence as to the condition of the east end at this time has come down to us in a picture by Wenceslaus Hollar of the Coronation of Charles II which appeared in the volume by John Ogilby describing that ceremony.[1]

This highly popular event did not take place until St. George's Day (April 23rd), 1661, some nine months after the vacant stalls had been filled. Thus, a breathing space had been accorded to the Dean and Chapter enabling them to restore some semblance of decency to the worship of the sorely tried Abbey. During the first year twelve copes and a quantity of plate (q.v.) were purchased.

Hollar's picture indicates the High Altar in its ancient position. It is covered with a frontal, while on the mensa is grouped a quantity of plate in accordance with the ancient English use. The customary pair of candlesticks are in their usual position. There is no sign of an Altar Cross and the altar is far shorter than in Pre-Reformation times. The Altar screen and the Presbytery are hung with tapestry which suggests an endeavour to follow the ancient tradition which had prevailed down to the time of the great upheaval.

The Coronation of James II followed twenty-four years later. The fine prints contained in Sandford's exhaustive history portray admirably the scheme of decoration and the arrangements of the east end generally.[2] It would seem that in the arrangement of the church, the authorities closely adhered to the precedent of Charles II's Coronation.

It must be remembered, however, that these interesting pictures record the special arrangements set up for the great Solemnity of the Coronation, hence they can hardly

[1] See vol. i: illustration facing p. 60.
[2] See vol. i: illustrations facing pp. 60, 62.

be regarded as affording conclusive evidence for the normal condition of the High Altar and Presbytery in Restoration times. For this we are dependent upon various documents in the Muniment Room, entries in the Chapter Book, and above all the oil painting acquired by the Dean and Chapter in 1930 to which allusion has already been made.[1] In one way and another considerable light is thrown upon the appearance of the Choir and Presbytery and also the customary method of rendering the services.

The interesting Inventory dated January 30th, 1661 (see Appendix III),[2] records the existence of '4 brasse candlesticks for ye Altar and 3 branches for ye Altar and Quire'. In 1661 one of the vergers, Anthony Tingle by name, was paid the sum of thirty shillings for scouring three pairs of hangings and cleaning and repairing four candlesticks and four branches.[3]

Again, there is a Chapter Order dated May 27th in the following year commanding that 'the new hangings belonging to the Greater Altar in the Church be taken down and cleaned'.

In 1673 John Tynchar, the Precentor, was paid twenty shillings

'for mending the carpet in Henry VII's Chapel, and for washing and cleaning the Altar and Vestry and for taking down the hangings at the Altar and putting them upp and the branches and for washing the Altar linen and for brooms and for scouring the cloaths of the Bishop's seats and Sub-Dean's curtains'.[4]

These entries in the capitular records confirm the evidence afforded by the two prints of the Coronation as regards the existence of tapestried hangings at the east end, though the earlier fabrics alluded to by Weever and others disappeared for good during the Great Rebellion.

The 'branches' have been omitted by the artists who

---

[1] Vol. i: illustration facing p. 64.   [2] W.A.M. 44026, A and B.
[3] W.A.M. 33695.   [4] W.A.M. 33706.

drew the Coronation pictures: but they are indicated in the oil painting and they still survive, though in a somewhat different position. Each of these 'branches' or chandeliers contains six candles. They date from the seventeenth century and are said to be of Dutch manufacture. Possibly they formed part of the new furniture provided by the Dean and Chapter at the Restoration. Of the five chandeliers in use today the three nearest to the High Altar are ancient work, the other two being twentieth-century copies. They are excellent specimens of their kind; but the need of a centre-piece similar in character to the existing 'branches', though larger and more elaborate in design, is only too apparent. A noble piece of metal-work, such as the great chandelier given to Southwark Cathedral in 1680 by Dorothy Applebee, would add immense dignity to the east end of the Abbey when combined with the chandeliers already *in situ*. Nothing, however, can possibly make up for the loss of Henry III's corona or basin of silver, a disaster of unknown date.

All through this Restoration era there are indications of a real desire on the part of the Chapter to restore their impoverished Presbytery to something more nearly approximating to its former comeliness. Apart from such things as plate, copes, and tapestries, they evidently determined, like Dean Neile, that the High Altar should be equipped in a fully adequate and dignified manner.

Thus, in the Inventory of 1661 mention is made (in addition to fair linen) of a 'large purple clothe . . . trymed with a deepe Silk fringe; 2 large cushions . . . lined with crimson damaske; one fronte behind ye Altar; a fronte before ye altar panned with clothe and damaske trymed with fringe suitable to ye Altar cloth and cushions'; also '14 yards of black bayse for ye altar and 12 yards of course black bayse for ye foote place before ye Altar . . . to be used ye 30 of January.'[1]

[1] W.A.M. 44026 A.

In 1687 the sum of £6. 8s. 2d. was paid 'for an altar and pulpit cloth above ye remainder of Mr. Cary's money',[1] while in the Chapter Book for the same year there is an entry dated February 14th which refers to 'three pieces of Crimson Velvet embroydered and two cushions of the same being the gift of Madam Katherine Dolben,[2] and laid up in the custody of my Lord Bishop of Rochester, Dean of Westminster'. The bill for these hangings is still in existence,[3] viz.

> 'Velvet for the Altar and Pulpit Cloths £ 9. 0
> and fringe for them   7.19. 0
> and making them,   3. 6. 3'

The year 1690 is marked by the appearance of a still more notable ornament, viz. 'a large Altar Cloth of Purpell Velvet and Sattin and flowered with gould, lined throw and fringed with gould and silk fringes:' also of '7 yards and a half of Purpell Caleco to line ye Altar Cloth at 18d per yard.'[4]

Seven years later still further additions were made, viz.:[5]

> 'Caldicot the mercer for serge to line the vestments of ye Altar, Pulpit, etc.   £3. 15. 0
> Crane ye upholsterer for making do.   23. 14. 0
> Heygate the silkman for strings, etc.   38. 15. 0
> for Altar Cloath, Pulpit and Cushions.'

Allowing for the change in the value of money the sum of £66. 14s. represents a generous expenditure.

Again, in 1707, allusion is made to 'The Upholsterer's 2 bills for making up the Pulpit and Altar Cloath of Purple Cloath and for putting up the hangings £12. 8. 3d and Mr. Billingham for the Purple Cloath £9. 15. 0.'[6] This last-mentioned item refers, no doubt, to a Chapter Order passed on May 5th of the same year to the effect that 'an Altar Cloth with a glory in it be provided for the Abbey'.

---

[1] W.A.M. 33921.   [2] The wife of the Dean.   [3] W.A.M. 33724.
[4] W.A.M. 44221.   [5] W.A.M. 33730.   [6] W.A.M. 33739.

Then a long interval follows till in 1744, during the rule of Dean Wilcocks, a 'Pulpit Cloth and a Covering for the Communion' were ordered costing £19. 1s. This Chapter Order is evidently alluded to in a bill dated the same year, for 'a Communion Cloth, a Pulpit Cloth and Cushion Fringe, Tassels and making'. The cost, however, worked out at rather less than the original estimate, being only £18.17s. 9d.[1]

Not until the nineteenth century had long entered upon its course did the Abbey authorities concern themselves again with matters of this description.

These odds and ends of information do not constitute a very impressive record. They are at the best but the faint echo of a glory which had passed. It is, however, worth remarking that some sort of modified Colour Sequence was still being maintained even in the middle of the eighteenth century. It is clear that the Dean and Chapter possessed certain hangings set apart for best occasions; also a 'common altar cloth' and 'black furniture for the altar'.[2]

According to Henry Keepe, whose *Monumenta West-monasteriensia* was published in 1682, the Presbytery was entirely surrounded by hangings. When describing the 'five noble monuments' therein he states that they were not 'visible but by drawing the hangings which are hung before them for the better adorning of this place'.[3] What then was the nature of these hangings? The oil-painting portrays very distinctly six or more curtains of rich blue material each surrounded by a wide border of gold wholly unlike the tapestries used at the Coronations. This discrepancy suggests that the tapestries suspended in the Presbytery in 1661 and in 1685 were placed there for the Coronations only, in which case a Chapter Order issued on July 13th, 1706, for 'taking down ye tapestry and putting y^m forwarde' would seem to imply that the word

---

[1] W.A.M. 33775.　　[2] W.A.M. 6613. See Appendix III.
[3] Keepe, *Monumenta Westmonasteriensia*, p. 34.

'tapestry' was held to include hangings of any kind of material. Possibly the discrepancy may be explained in this way, but the matter is by no means clear.

The oil-painting shows a good-sized altar decidedly longer than those used at the Coronations of Charles and his brother.[1] It is vested with a frontal consisting of seven alternate panels of crimson velvet and some other material. The dorsal is similar and like the frontal fully harmonizes with the description given in the Inventory of 1661, viz. 'a fronte before ye altar panned with clothe and damaske'[2] or again, with the 'purple velvet and sattin' of 1690. With the aid of a magnifying-glass it is even possible to make out the detail of the ornaments on the altar. The large alms-dish provided in 1685 is distinctly recognizable and likewise the two fine silver gilt candlesticks, the result of Sarah Hughes's bequest. Altar books are standing on either side of the alms-dish, a custom which still prevails in at least one English cathedral. Only in recent times did it cease at the Abbey, and then quite accidentally.

The Presbytery is separated from the Choir by a dwarf screen placed at the head of a flight of steps (shorter than today) which gives access from the floor of the choir. Whether or not it was the barrier erected while Laud was a member of the Chapter, it is difficult to say. The baluster shafts and their bulbous swellings or 'melons' do not look very attractive. The colour suggests that it was composed of stone or marble.

It would be a deeply interesting experience could we be present in the stalls of Westminster Abbey some Sunday morning in (let us say) the reign of William and Mary. We should find ourselves confronted with a strange combination of the familiar and the unfamiliar.

The High Altar would certainly be vested in a frontal which would do duty for most of the Church's year. The

---

[1] See vol. i, p. 64.   [2] W.A.M. 45245 A.

ancient Colour Sequence of the Abbey had disappeared. Probably it had passed altogether out of men's minds. Of Lenten white hangings of any kind our Restoration records do not give a hint.

An Altar Cross was in those days unknown. On the other hand, the two massive candlesticks would undoubtedly be lighted at Evensong during the winter months and whenever the condition of the atmosphere made it necessary to employ artificial light. An interesting entry in the wax chandler's bill for 1690, viz. 'eight yelow tapers for the use of the Altar every day',[1] is conclusive on this point. Possibly (though this is more doubtful) they would also have been lit at Celebrations of the Holy Communion during this Post-Restoration period.[2] This latter service which took place once a month and on the three great Festivals, if not with greater frequency, would be marked, as today, by a magnificent array of gold plate on the High Altar. The Celebrant, Gospeller, and Epistoler would be vested in copes.

On the other hand, a Choral Celebration of the Holy Communion would be unknown. The Sanctus and the Nicene Creed would be chanted to a musical setting, the former by a strange piece of liturgical perversity being employed as an Introit. After the Nicene Creed the voice of melody would be heard no more.

In the north choir aisle stood the tiny organ over which Purcell, Blow, and Croft presided. Devoid of pedals and possessed of but few speaking stops, it would sound incredibly thin to our ears, attuned as they are to modern conditions, even when one of those mighty men of music was seated at the keyboard. The general standard of the singing would in all probability not be particularly high,

[1] See Appendix VI.
[2] The late Mr. Beresford Hope has stated that in his possession was an old print representing the east end of the Abbey at the beginning of the eighteenth century and that the candles were distinctly represented as lighted. Beresford Hope, *Worship in the Church of England*, p. 227.

least of all in the rendering of the Psalms. The troubles of
the Civil War and the Commonwealth had inflicted deep
wounds on the music of the Church. A great gap stood
between the period of the Restoration and those spacious
days when ability to take part in the singing of a complicated madrigal was accounted a mark of good breeding
and education.

There would be no formal entry of singers and clergy.
The Choristers probably walked as one unit; but the other
members of the Collegiate body would enter, one or two
at a time, for the most part through a door in the parclose
screen which separated the choir from the south transept.[1]
Having reached their places they would remain seated
until the striking of a clock announced that the hour of
Divine Service had arrived. This arrangement, until recent
years, was universal in all English Cathedral and Collegiate
Churches. It hardly survives anywhere in England today
save at Magdalen College, Oxford.

Many years prior to his Installation in 1660 Dean
Earles had inflicted his lash upon the 'common singing
man in Cathedral churches'. His *Microcosmography* first
appeared in 1628 before its author had been ordained, and
the future Dean has given us therein seventy-seven
cleverly delineated character sketches, among them one
on Lay-vicars. He states that they

'are a bad Society and yet a Company of good Fellowes that
roar deep in the Quire, deeper in the Taverne. Their pastime
or recreation is prayers, their exercise drinking, yet herein so
religiously addicted that they serve God oftest when they are
drunk. . . . Upon worky dayes they behave themselves at
Prayers as at their pots, for they swallowed them down in an
instant. . . . Long liv'd for the most part, they are not,
especially the base. They overflow their banks so oft as to
drown the organs. Briefly, if they escape arresting they dye
constantly in God's Service; and to take their death with more
patience they have Wine and Cakes at their Funerall; and now

[1] See vol. i: illustration facing p. 166.

they keepe the Church a great deal better, and help to fill it with their bones as before with their noyse.'[1]

It is to be hoped that Earles, starting with a clean sheet as he did in 1660 (when he had to appoint nine new Lay-vicars all at once), may have managed to secure a higher standard of life and manners in the choral portion of the Abbey establishment than that which appears to have prevailed in some of our Cathedrals during early Stuart times. He, if anyone, was the man to do it.

There is some reason for thinking, however, that the standard of discipline at the Abbey still left something to be desired in Restoration times. The 'best scholar in England', as Charles II once described Isaac Barrow when appointing him to the Mastership of Trinity College, Cambridge, had abundant cause for complaint after the following trying experience:

'Another time Dr. Barrow preached at the Abbey on a holiday. Here I must inform the reader that it is a custom for the servants of the church upon all Holidays Sunday excepted, betwixt the Sermon and Evening Prayers, to show the Tombs and Effigies of the Kings and Queens in Wax, to the meaner sort of people, who then flock thither from all the corners of the town and pay their twopence to see the Play of the dead Volks, as I have heard a Devonshire Clown most improperly call it. These perceiving Dr. Barrow in the pulpit after the hour was past and fearing to lose that time in hearing which they thought they could more profitably employ in viewing—these, I say, became impatient, and caused the organ to be struck up against him, and would not give over playing till they had blow'd him down.'[2]

It is, however, only fair to remark that the vast length of Barrow's discourses was a trial even to an age which revelled in pulpit oratory!

Criticism was not unknown though it was an age less careful of ceremonial than our own. The historian John

---

[1] J. Earles, *Microcosmography*, pp. 83–4.
[2] Pope, *Life of Seth Ward*, pp. 147, 148.

Dart, whose words were penned rather later, during the decanate of Dean Atterbury, roundly condemned certain slovenly customs still in vogue. A plan contained in this historian's *Westmonasterium* shows the south-west corner of the south transept (formerly the Chapel of St. Blaise) screened off by a wainscot partition so as to form a vestry for the Choristers and Lay-vicars.

'It is a great pity', Dart complains, 'this enclosure was never taken away, it being a scandalous blot on the beauty of this part of the church, and a place for the same use may with more convenience be made in some square of the cloisters, where there may be a regular procession of the Choir with the Prebendaries. Whereas now the south cross is made a news-walk by the singing men, till the Sub-Dean or any of the Prebendaries come, and then in a hurried, confused manner, run different ways to get into their seats in time. This I have heard many complain of, and was told that the Dean, my Lord of Rochester, intended some alteration upon that account, which I hope his Lordship, than whom there was never a stricter observer of church decency and discipline, will in due time proceed in.'[1]

More than a century passed before Dart's aspirations were fulfilled. The unsightly partition disappeared in 1735, the space being subsequently utilized for the erection of the great Argyll monument. The Chapter Order giving effect to this alteration has already been quoted.[2] But the adjoining Chapel of St. Faith continued to be used as a vestry for many more years; while, save on the Great Festivals, when all the members of the Collegiate body used to meet before service in the Jerusalem Chamber, proceeding thence to their stalls to the strains of a voluntary, the old method of entry continued unchanged.

The Vergers are seen at work once more before the year 1660 had reached its close. The cost of providing them with silver verges appears among the earliest items of ex-

[1] Dart, *Westmonasterium*, vol. i, p. 41.
[2] J. Armitage Robinson, *The Abbot's House at Westminster*, p. 78.

penditure incurred by the restored Chapter. Gowns, too, are bestowed upon the Almsmen 'according to the Statutes of the College', while orders are given for their renewal every two years, as was anciently accustomed.

Evidence is not lacking to show that the Restoration Chapter were not content with the provision of comely ornamenta, but were also doing their best to raise the general standard of worship in their great Church. Shortly after the Restoration the following curious Chapter Order was drawn up. It is dated November 11th, 1660.

'That the back door of the organ be shut, and that the organist come into the quire at the beginning of prayers in his surplice and betake himself to his stall till towards the end of the Psalms except on festival days when the answers are to be performed with the organ; then to go up the stairs leading from the choir and perform his duty. And it is further ordered that neither the organist nor any other permit any person to be in the organ loft during the time of Divine Service; and that the organist and the blower keep themselves private and not expose themselves to the view of the people during their stay in the organ loft.'

This Chapter Order throws considerable light upon the method of rendering Divine Service in early Restoration days. Evidently the choir could not be relied upon to chant the Psalms effectively, neither did the authorities perceive any likelihood of their being able to do so in the near future. On the other hand, they specially desired that the Great Festivals be marked by the addition of an organ accompaniment to the Preces and Suffrages; hence, the Organist was directed to be in readiness at his post.

Later on the Choristers are directed to attend Church in their 'Gowns and Surpluses'. The former word almost certainly means a cassock which we know from other sources was in regular use. Sandford's pictures of the Coronation of James II portray the Choir, Lay-vicars, and Choristers alike, clad in cassocks, long surplices, and broad white bands. Five years later the sum of £8 was expended on 'making 8 Quiristers Gowns', twenty-six yards of 'fine black cloth being provided at a cost of £9. 17. 0.'[1]

During the early years of Dean Sprat's rule, the Dean and Chapter again manifested their determination to secure reverence of demeanour on the part of the staff at the time of Divine Service, for they issued another most interesting Chapter Order on January 12th, 1685. In addition to that of the Dean it bears the signature of seven Prebendaries: including such famous names as those of Richard Busby, Robert South, and Simon Patrick.

'That when any of the Prebendaries shall come into the Quire, the Scholars and the Singing Boys there shall stand upp to show their respect to them according to the old custom and practice: And also that they pay all due respect to them in all other places.

'Ordered that the Quiremen as they pass in the Quire to do their office shall according to the old Customs come into the Middle of the Quire, and there make due Reverence toward the Dean and Prebendaries' Stalls after they have first done it towards the Altar.'[2]

The custom of making a reverence to the Altar formed then part of the official Westminster ceremonial (as was also the case at Durham and Christ Church, Oxford). It fell into desuetude at some date unknown until its revival under Dean Ryle, but the bow towards the stalls of the capitular body has continued without interruption. To this day the Choristers and Lay-vicars at the conclusion of the Office turn towards the senior dignitary present and bow to him before leaving their seats.

During this period it was customary at the Abbey, as in other great churches, to chant the Litany at a special desk.[3] The reason for the abandonment by the Dean and Chapter

[1] W.A.M. 44245 B.
[2] There is a marked similarity between the ceremonial thus laid down and that which may be seen on any Sunday in the Cathedral of Rheims and other great French Churches.
[3] See pp. 43, 44: also John Jebb, *The Choral Service of the United Church of England and Ireland*, p. 194.

at some date unknown of this time-honoured Anglican custom forms an insoluble problem.

It was the custom to mark the Christmas Festival by decking the choir with greenery. Thus, in 1676, Ivy Walters was paid £3. 6s. for supplying 'Laurel, Holly and Ivy for dressing the Church at Christmas'.[1] Year after year does an item appear in the Treasurer's Accounts, with almost monotonous regularity for the cost of the rosemary and bay used in decorating the church. No reason has ever been given for the disappearance of this pleasing custom in the middle of the nineteenth century. A certain revival has, however, taken place during recent years, for every Christmas big bunches of holly and other evergreens are suspended over the stalls with excellent effect.

The Restoration Chapter, it is clear, had no intention of confining their efforts to the maintenance of an orderly ceremonial. They earnestly desired to secure a high spiritual standard on the part of all engaged in the worship of the Abbey. We may perhaps regret the dictatorial tone of a certain Chapter Order promulgated in 1686, but the excellence of the intentions of those who framed it is beyond dispute.

'It is ordered that the Quiremen and the Officers of this Church and College do receive the Holy Communion in this Church three times in the year at least (according to the Rubric) viz., at Easter, Whitsuntide and Christmas, and particularly this next Easter Day after the date of this Order. And that a copy of this Order be delivered to the Chanter who is to give notice thereof.'

By the time the eighteenth century had arrived the hours of service had undergone some variation as compared with those customary during Elizabethan times. According to an interesting little guide-book to the London Churches, published in the reign of Queen Anne, the

[1] W.A.M. 33710.

week-day services were three in number as before; but
the hours of Matins and Evensong had been altered to
ten and three. The early prayers in Henry VII's Chapel
were read at six in summer and seven in winter 'for the
convenience of the Scholars and the devout people there
inhabiting'.[1] The two Sunday services were at nine and
half-past three. Lectures were delivered on the Wednesdays and Fridays in Lent at the morning service, while on
the thirtieth day of January, the twenty-ninth day of May,
and other solemn occasions, a sermon was preached before
the House of Lords by some eminent divine.[2]

The history of the Abbey indicates plainly enough the
value attached to the oratory of the pulpit, more especially
during the sixty years which followed the Restoration.

So far back as the reign of Queen Elizabeth the Dean
and Chapter received a bequest from that munificent personage, the Lady Frances Sidney, Foundress of the College which bears her name at Cambridge. According to
the inscription on her monument in the Chapel of St. Paul
it was to be expended in providing for the delivery of a
lecture in Divinity.

In 1672 there died the Rev. John Doughty, one of the
Prebendaries, appointed in 1660. The staunchest of
Royalists, he had at one time enjoyed considerable renown
as a preacher; but according to Anthony à Wood 'he lived
to be twice a child'. His widow, Katharine Doughty, together with William Dolben, Esq. (probably a younger
brother of the Dean and subsequently a well-known
Judge) gave to the Dean and Chapter a fee farm rent on
certain houses in Tothill Fields, the income derived from
which was to be partly bestowed upon the preacher at the
morning service on Good Friday and partly upon a gift
to certain deserving Westminster poor, any surplus to be
applied to the purchase of books for the Chapter Library.

[1] Keepe, *Monumenta Westmonasteriensia*, p. 170.
[2] Paterson, *Pietas Londinensis*, pp. 244–55.

Katharine Doughty subsequently married Sir Thomas Heath of Stoke in Surrey, dying in 1694.

Another bequest surrounded by somewhat curious circumstances was received by the Dean and Chapter at the end of the seventeenth century.

On October 11th, 1697, there died Dame Grace, the young wife of Sir Richard Gethin of Ireland, daughter of Sir George Morton of Abbots Leigh in the County of Somerset and Frances his wife. The lady must have been an extremely attractive character and it was tragic that 'all this excellence was bound within a compass of twenty years'.

So greatly impressed were her relatives by her gifts of intellect that a few years after her death they brought out a volume, now very scarce, entitled *Reliquiae Gethinianae* in order to preserve her memory. It included (1) a number of loose papers, found among Dame Grace Gethin's effects, written in her spare hours. They were calculated to astound readers with the maturity of their thought, 'a miraculous rather than a human production'; (2) a set of verses from the pen of William Congreve, who had been inspired to flights of song by the perusal of the young lady's literary 'remains'; (3) a sermon delivered at the Abbey by Peter Birch, one of the Prebendaries on March 28th, 1700. The *Reliquiae Gethinianae* were prefaced by the words from the thirty-first Chapter of the Book of Proverbs: 'Let her own works praise her in the gate.'

Alas! the unwelcome fact was revealed to a subsequent generation that these remarkable tokens of the genius of this precocious young lady which had so wrought upon the minds of Congreve and others were simply extracts which she had herself copied from the works of Francis Bacon![1]

The bereaved parents were allowed to erect a monument

[1] Ballard, *Memorials of British Ladies*, p. 263; Isaac Disraeli, *Curiosities of Literature*, vol. ii, pp. 272–3.

as 'a lasting memorial of her godly and blessed end' in the south choir aisle of the Abbey; and one of similar character in the Church of All Saints, Hollingbourne, in Kent. Further they made a donation to the funds of the Dean and Chapter, the interest derived from which was to be applied partly in providing a fee for the preacher of the Ash Wednesday sermon who was directed to make a Commemoration of Dame Grace Gethin 'for perpetuating her memory for ever', and partly in providing a gift of bread for certain Westminster poor.

More important still was the bequest of Dame Joan Upton, the wife of a City merchant, who died in 1713. The income was to be paid to 'five learned and orthodox Divines of the Church of England for five sermons to be preached in the Collegiate Church of St. Peter, Westminster, on the second, third, fourth, fifth, and sixth Fridays in every Lent for ever' together with fees 'to two Vergers for attending the sermons'. The lectures still continue, Lent by Lent. If Joan Upton could have lived to see the vast crowds drawn by the lectures of Charles Gore, Armitage Robinson, and others, she would have felt that her bequest had borne fruit a thousandfold.

Unfortunately no definite information is extant as regards the frequency of the Celebrations of the Holy Communion, for which a monthly arrangement only had been prescribed by Dean Goodman. It has been assumed by Dean Stanley on the strength of a statement made by Simon Patrick in his interesting *Autobiography*, that a weekly Celebration was established at the Abbey during the time when he was occupying one of the prebendal stalls (1672–89).

'This year also [1683] the Archbishop required that according to the rubric we should have a communion every Sunday in Cathedral churches; which I began about Whitsuntide, and preached several sermons concerning it, persuading to frequent communion. Which, blessed be God, had such good effect that we had for several Sundays larger communions that I expected.'[1]

It is clear, however, from the context that Patrick is here referring to his action at Peterborough, which Deanery he held *in commendam* with his stall at the Abbey. The three intensely earnest sermons which he delivered in Peterborough Cathedral on this subject were subsequently published, together with a dedication to Archbishop Sancroft, in which he expressed his deep thankfulness for the Primate's action. On the other hand, the Rev. Alexander Taylor, Fellow of The Queen's College, Oxford, Patrick's editor, states that the vigorous search which he himself instituted for further information on this subject proved fruitless. No record whatever of Sancroft's meritorious action could anywhere be found in the Library of Lambeth Palace.[2] Hence, although there can be no doubt as to Patrick's policy at Peterborough, we are left uncertain as to whether the Primate did in the end make the strong effort he had certainly intended to raise the general standard of our Cathedral and Collegiate churches. It would be gratifying to think that the Church of Westminster had kept in line with that of Peterborough: but no written evidence to that effect has so far come to light.

The extremely prosaic information afforded by the expenditure upon tent or sacramental wine suggests that people made their Communion in very large numbers on 'Sacrament Sunday'. Among the Muniments is a document entitled 'Mr. Tinker's[3] bill', which was presented by the Sacrist to the Rev. Dr. Birch, the Treasurer of the Abbey, for tent. It covers the period of one half-year, viz. from Michaelmas 1691 to Lady Day 1692. The same item appears with undeviating regularity month by month, an

---

[1] Patrick, *Works*, vol. ii, pp. 3, 91, 269.
[2] Ibid., p. 54 note.
[3] John Tinker or Tynchare, Minor Canon from 1663 to 1694, also Sacrist.

extra amount of wine evidently being provided for the Christmas festival. The details of the bill are as follows:[1]

Oct.	3.	2 gall. of tent				18.	0
,,	31	,,	,,	,,	,,	18.	0
Dec.	5	,,	,,	,,	,,	18.	0
,,	25	3	,,	,,	,,	1. 7.	0
Jan.	2	2	,,	,,	,,	18.	0
Feb.	6	,,	,,	,,	,,	18.	0
Mar.	5	2	,,	,,	,,	18.	0
						6.15.	0

The picture which results from the piecing together of these fragmentary details will doubtless appear tame and perhaps even trivial compared with the more grandiose ideas which have grown up among ourselves during the last two or three generations. It testifies, however, to the earnestness and zeal of a body of churchmen who, finding themselves placed in charge of a great institution which had been cruelly maltreated and stripped bare, laboured in the face of manifold difficulties to restore beauty and comeliness once more to their desecrated sanctuary. Twenty years of Puritan ascendancy had left their mark. It could not be otherwise. The changes and improvements which took place at the Abbey during the last forty years of the seventeenth century would arouse little comment today, but it was different in the time of the later Stuarts. The cessation of all Anglican worship during a period covering many years was bound to have an effect upon the public mind. A falling away even on the part of church people from the standard which had prevailed immediately before the Great Rebellion was both inevitable and regrettable.

The considerable alterations made in the great Classical Altar-Piece when it was re-erected in the Abbey in 1708 illustrate some of the difficulties which beset those who

[1] W.A.M. 44407.

were patiently endeavouring to bring back the spirit of beauty to our churches at that time.[1] Although Dean Sprat and many of the twelve Prebendaries were possessed of High Anglican sympathies, they felt constrained to remove certain harmless figures including even one representing Our Lord, for fear of raising a storm![2]

It is interesting to learn that Herbert Thorndike, the great Caroline theologian, left instructions in his will that an inscription commending his soul to God was to be engraved upon his tombstone. Evidently his capitular brethren feared to bring a hornet's nest about their ears. The grave in the east cloister has remained incomplete to this day!

To some people it will appear strange that there is not the slightest indication of an Altar Cross. Splendid plate was being provided all over England at this time, candlesticks, patens, chalices, flagons, and the like with which to 'garnish' the altar; but of an Altar Cross, there is not a sign. In a later generation, a cry of Romanism was raised against Bishop Butler for having placed a cross of white marble on a black shelf on the eastern wall of his private chapel at Bristol and Archbishop Secker even expressed a mild disapproval of his Suffragan's action.[3] It would have created a veritable hurricane if the Dean and Chapter of Westminster had ventured to take such a step during the closing decades of the seventeenth century.

The Abbey was fortunate in its Deans at this period, all of whom threw themselves energetically into the work of reconstruction. Earles soon departed to the Bishopric of Worcester, but the influence of Sheldon, the future Primate, his uncle by marriage, brought about the appointment of John Dolben, an Old Westminster, wounded years before at Marston Moor. The latter together with

[1] Richard Widmore, *History of the Church of St. Peter Westminster*, pp. 165, 166, and Appendix XIV.
[2] Ralph Thoresby, *Diary*, vol. ii, p. 38.
[3] Halifax's Preface to Butler's *Works*, vol. i, p. xxxiii.

his friends, Fell and Allestree, secretly maintained in subsequent years the worship of the proscribed and persecuted
English Church in a house in Merton Street, Oxford.
Dolben now found himself in the strange position of
presiding over a Chapter which included the formidable
personality of his old headmaster, Richard Busby, at whose
hands he had probably endured bodily suffering in his
younger days! He at once instituted a much needed Fabric
Fund and in a variety of ways showed himself an excellent
Dean.[1] When some twenty years later he received a well-
deserved translation to the Archbishopric of York he left
behind him at Westminster the highest reputation.[2]

Sprat, his successor, was a man of lesser account, but he
closely followed in Dolben's steps in his care for the Abbey
and its services, which remark applies with equal force to
the next Dean, Francis Atterbury.

The latter, another Old Westminster, was a first-rate
scholar, a brilliant speaker and preacher and a devoted son
of the Church of England. His rule at Westminster was
marred, however, by certain faults of temperament and
was destined to end in tragedy. His sympathies with the
King over the water brought about his downfall. A lengthy
imprisonment in the Tower culminated in the deprivation
of all his preferments and perpetual banishment from the
realm. None the less his zeal for the service of God's house,
his labours in the Muniment Room, and his strenuous
efforts in the face of tremendous opposition to provide the
King's Scholars with a new Dormitory will always ensure
him a place among our greatest Deans.

Lastly, a word must be said regarding the munificence
displayed by certain members of the Chapter. Sudbury's
splendid addition of plate for the High Altar has already
been mentioned. His colleague, Dr. Busby, was respon-

[1] Paul Dolben, *Life of John Dolben*, pp. 7, 8, 9, 12.
[2] Richard Widmore, *History of the Church of St. Peter Westminster*, pp. 162
and 164.

sible for the complete repaving of the choir, a scarcely less generous gift. We may deplore the inappropriateness of these lozenges of black and white marble in their gothic surroundings without withholding our admiration for the donor.[1] Two inscriptions again record the fact that another Prebendary, Henry Killigrew, who served the Abbey for the long period of forty years, made a similar addition to Henry VII's Chapel.[2]

From the Restoration down to the early years of the nineteenth century the Deanery was held *in commendam* with the Bishopric of Rochester. It was an indefensible arrangement, and the frequent absences of the chief officer of the Church of Westminster which it entailed must have severely handicapped the labours of these excellent men. When later on the Deanery fell into less capable hands, the Abbey was bound to suffer and disaster supervened.

5. THE END OF THE GOOD DAYS

The good days lasted for the best part of a century and the momentum created by the four Deans appointed after the Restoration, strong churchmen and members of the school of Laud, did not cease until the death in 1756 of Joseph Wilcocks, the penultimate successor of Atterbury, a most high-minded man. Few ecclesiastics at the time when the Church was suffering from the rampant jobbery associated with the names of Walpole and Newcastle would have had the self-restraint to decline the attractive offer of the Archbishopric of York. A born administrator, Wilcocks has left a permanent mark upon the fabric. The completion of the great restoration, inaugurated by Wren, and the building of the two western towers form an achievement of which any man might be proud.

But Wilcocks did not confine himself to the material fabric. He strove hard to raise the general level of devotion

[1] Vol. i, p. 129. [2] Vol. ii, p. 185.

and the efficiency of the Abbey services. He made a gallant effort, which fell short unfortunately of complete success, to enforce a stricter observance of the duties and responsibilities of residence upon the twelve Prebendaries. He increased the number of Minor Canons. He was partly, if not wholly, responsible for the provision of a large organ and its erection on the choir screen.

Everything indicates that, down to the time of this good man's death, there had been little if any falling away from the Restoration standard, indeed, in some respects there was a distinct improvement.

Down to 1731 the Lessons had, by a curious arrangement, been read by the Lay-vicars. In some regulations issued on November 29th of that year this duty was entrusted for the future to the Minor Canons.[1] Careful instructions were given at the same time as regards the choice and the frequent rendering of anthems. Indirect evidence suggests that the wearing of the cope was still being maintained, while both the Litany stool and the Church Pall, the disappearance of which has never been explained, were in regular use. Save that Evensong had been altered to four o'clock on week-days and a quarter past three on Sundays, the services display no variation from the customs of the early seventeenth century. A document found among the papers of the Rev. William Battell, who died in 1728 after serving the Abbey as Precentor and Minor Canon for nearly forty years, states that sermons were delivered twice on Sundays, and on every Red-Letter Day without exception. The Festivals assigned to the Dean were the same as today.

Another custom prevailing during the first half of the eighteenth century, but long since dropped, was the annual giving of a dinner to the choir, as each St. Peter's Day came round.

In one respect only, so far as we can gather, did Wil-

---

[1] Precentor's Book.

cocks fall short on the disciplinary side, for he formally authorized such members of the Abbey choir as were on the staff of the Chapel Royal to disappear after the Nicene Creed on Sunday mornings and before the Sermon on Sunday afternoons 'when required to be at St. James' Palace'. This indefensible practice persisted for another century and a half![1]

No doubt there were weak spots and the standard achieved fell short of that which we should expect today; but the sincere and consistent attempt initiated at the Restoration and carried on by several Deans to render the worship of the Abbey in a manner which should be at least seemly and perhaps even magnificent, was deserving of the highest praise. When Wilcocks, full of years and honour, passed away in 1756, the words 'senex sanctissimus' were applied to him in an oration delivered over his coffin by the Captain of the School. It was a well-merited tribute to one who took as his motto, 'Let me do all the good I can'.

So soon as this grand old veteran was laid in his grave beneath the south-west Tower, in the building of which he had been so largely instrumental, the loss was felt severely. A downward movement set in destined to leave deep wounds, both spiritual and material, upon the great church he had served so faithfully and loved so well.

6. DRABNESS AND DULLNESS

The bad times started during the early part of the reign of George III and continued until approximately the Accession of Queen Victoria.

The neglect suffered by the fabric was unbelievable. The exterior of Henry VII's Chapel was allowed to become almost ruinous before any attempt was made to grapple with the situation. The condition of the monuments was filthy in the extreme. The Westminster boys

[1] See vol. i, pp. 184, 185.

were even allowed to jump from tomb to tomb.[1] The south transept remained as of old, a mere appendage. Doubtless, the members of the choir still continued to treat it as their promenade or 'news-walk', in spite of Dart's protest in the distant days of Dean Atterbury.[2] No one troubled to emphasize its sacred character. A late Georgian print exists which shows that it was even being used for the weekly distribution of bread and meat to forty Westminster widows every Saturday morning—a venerable charity entitled the Dean's Gift, probably due to the bounty of Lady Margaret Beaufort. Save at the hours of services admission could not be obtained to any part of the Abbey without the payment of a fee!

John Carter, on the architectural and archaeological side, dealt faithfully with the Dean and Chapter at the beginning of the nineteenth century. They must have regarded their brilliant but uncomfortable neighbour in Great College Street with anything but friendly feelings. Most of his protests seem, however, to have fallen upon deaf ears, for little or no improvement manifested itself, rather the reverse. The close of this period witnessed the loss of numbers of precious things, among them the Renaissance organ case, the Classical Altar-Piece, the grates round the tombs of Queen Elizabeth and Lady Margaret Beaufort and a vast quantity of metal-work, sold at so much a pound!

The erection of the new stalls and the other changes effected by Henry Keene in 1775 produced no marked effect upon the worship. The choir had from the first been walled in and segregated from the rest of the building by Henry III, and this arrangement, respected at the time of the Reformation, survived without a break until early Victorian days. The Post-Reformation Chapter took the place of the Benedictine brethren and the forms of worship

---

[1] J. P. Malcolm, *Londinium Redivivum*, p. 163.
[2] See Dart, *Westmonasterium*, vol. i, p. 41.

set forth in the Book of Common Prayer were rendered under conditions and in surroundings differing little from those associated with the Pre-Reformation rite. Hence, the seating space available in the choir for the celebration of Divine Worship was scanty in the extreme. Not more than a few hundred people at the very most could have been accommodated therein. At the same time all the evidence goes to show that during the eighteenth century even this limited space amply met the demand.

Daniel Defoe, when visiting the Abbey on September 24th, 1725, commented upon the decrease in the number of 'the gazers, the readers of epitaphs and the country Ladies'. He went on to say that 'the appearance of the Choir was diminished for, setting aside the families of the clergy resident and a very few more, the place was forsaken'.[1]

Possibly it was this state of things which led the Dean and Chapter in 1769 to revert to three o'clock for the hour of Evensong. Two years later they distributed twenty guineas among the eight Vergers 'as a compensation for the last two years' deficiency in their respective perquisites from wax candles occasioned by the alteration in the hour of Evening Prayers'.

The congregations continued however to be lamentably small and the early years of the nineteenth century showed no improvement, judging by an incident which occurred during the decanate of Dean Vincent. Among the various offices of the Collegiate Church was the Lectureship endowed by Joan Upton, who died in 1711, usually held by a different Prebendary each year. Possibly it had been the hope of the Foundress that a series of solid contributions to Anglican Theology would result. John Heylin the 'Mystic Doctor'—an unusual description of an eighteenth-century divine—who was Prebendary from 1742 to 1759 and preached the Sermon at the Consecration of Bishop

[1] Daniel Defoe, *Works*, vol. iii, p. 427.

Butler, published in 1749 a volume entitled *Theological Lectures in Westminster Abbey with an Interpretation of the Four Gospels*. Another volume appeared thirty-six years later from the pen of Dr. John Blair, another Prebendary, on 'the Canon of the Scriptures'. But with these exceptions none of the lectures thus delivered found their way into print—a striking contrast to the happenings of more recent days.

Dean Vincent, on being appointed to the Deanery in 1802, turned to Dr. Ireland who, coming from the Vicarage of Croydon, had succeeded him in the prebendal stall he had vacated and was destined to follow him a dozen years later as Dean. Vincent urged the new Prebendary to deliver a course of lectures, intended more especially for the boys of Westminster School, pointing out at the same time that it was difficult to discover any other source from which a congregation could be drawn! Ireland consented and his Lectures were in due course published under the title of *Paganism and Christianity Compared*. We can scarcely withhold some measure of sympathy for the congregation!

From the Restoration onwards emphasis had been laid upon the three official services prescribed for January 30th, May 29th, and November 5th. On these occasions a departure from the normal Abbey custom took place, for an ecclesiastic not on the foundation, usually a Bishop, was invited to deliver the sermon.

The Abbey has been recognized from time immemorial as the official Church of the House of Lords, and during Stuart and Hanoverian times the members of the Upper House were wont to attend these special Services in state. It is to be feared, however, that these 'Visits of the Lords to the Abbey' ultimately dwindled into a sadly perfunctory affair. The Precentor, the Rev. Dr. Dakins, has recorded that on January 30th, 1808, the attendance was sparse in the extreme, consisting of the Lord Chancellor

(Eldon), the Archbishop of Canterbury (Manners Sutton), eight Bishops, and two Temporal Peers. Neither were things much better at a General Fast Day ordered for February 17th of the same year, when the Lord Chancellor was supported by only eleven Spiritual and Six Temporal Peers.

A characteristic of the régime of Dean Vincent was an antipathy to the appearance of any stranger in the Abbey pulpit save on special occasions. In certain regulations drawn up by him on January 5th, 1807, he explicitly laid down that no one other than a Minor Canon was to preach if for any reason a member of the Chapter was not available. It would seem that in those days the preacher was habited in cassock, gown, scarf, and hood.[1]

The music was in all probability of a relatively high order. An organ, immense for those days, was erected at the beginning of George II's reign. It was the first in our country to be equipped with a pedal board. Benjamin Cooke and Samuel Arnold both enjoyed considerable repute in their day as composers and organists, while Greatorex was a Fellow of the Royal Society. In the Abbey choir there were educated under their guidance a remarkable number of boys who subsequently made their mark in the world. Apart from musicians, they included a Headmaster of Harrow and a President of the Royal Academy. More than one of the Minor Canons, too, acquired some fame as a composer. It would seem that this department alone displayed anything at all approaching to activity.

The Funerals of the great ones of the land, at which the members of the College of Arms played an important part, must have been events of appalling magnitude, especially when a stupendous catafalque was erected copiously embellished with an array of heraldic achievements and other decorations.

Interments, rare events today, were of relatively frequent

[1] Precentor's Book.

occurrence. During the seventeenth and eighteenth centuries they sometimes reached a total of twenty or more
in any given year. They varied from great state functions
carried out on an elaborate scale to the burial of some
obscure individual, who found a last resting-place in the
Dark Cloister or on the large space north of the church.
Interments which took place outside the Church were
conducted with a strange lack of ceremony, and even
decency. The body was never carried into the building at
all, and a portion only of the Office for the Burial of the
Dead was recited. A note appended to the record of the
Burial in the west cloister of one, George Lane Blount, of
84 Baker Street, on March 26th, 1847, speaks for itself:
'This was the first Cloister Funeral that the Corpse was
taken into the Abbey and the whole of the Funeral Service
read over its interment.'[1]

With the eighteenth century the practice of interring
distinguished personages by night became an established
practice. More than one writer has borne testimony to the
mysterious unearthly beauty of the Abbey lit solely by
candles and torches. At the Funeral of Joseph Addison,
for instance, when Atterbury, 'one of these Tories who had
loved and honoured the most accomplished of the Whigs',[2]
officiated, a youthful King's Scholar who was present
holding a lighted taper carried away with him a lifelong
impression of this midnight ceremony, not least the beauty
and solemnity of Atterbury's voice.[3]

A very different fate awaited Atterbury himself. When
at length death ended his sad exile, the remains of the Dean
were brought from Paris, to be interred beside those of his
wife and daughters in the vault constructed years before
under his direction 'as far as possible from Kings and
Caesars'. Dean Wilcocks at once decided that full honour

[1] J. L. Chester, *The Marriage, Baptismal and Burial Registers of the Collegiate Church of Westminster*, p. 512.
[2] Macaulay, *Critical & Historical Essays*, p. 774.
[3] *Autobiography of Bishop Newton*, p. 15.

should be done to his great predecessor by performing the ceremony himself and ordering the attendance of the whole Collegiate body. The report that a solemn funeral would, however, be regarded with scant favour at Court led Wilcocks, who had barely been installed in the Deanery, to cancel this order. The ceremony was therefore handed over to the junior Minor Canon and Atterbury was interred at dead of night. No member of the Chapter was present. His son-in-law and two former Chaplains were the sole congregation. It is regrettable that so excellent a Dean as Wilcocks did not adopt a more courageous attitude.[1]

Horace Walpole has bequeathed to us in picturesque prose a matchless description of the torch-lit Abbey at the midnight Funeral of George II.[2] Unfortunately this first impression was sadly marred by the miserably inadequate rendering of the ceremonial to which both the Chapter Book and the Precentor's Book testify. Evidently, careful preliminary staff work was not a strong point with Dean Zachary Pearce and his collaborators:

'When we came to the Chapel all solemnity and decorum ceased—no order was observed, people stood where they could or would, the Yeomen of the Guard were crying out for help, oppressed by the immense weight of the coffin, the Bishop read sadly and blundered in the prayers; the fine chapter "Man that is born of a woman" was chanted not read, and the anthem besides being immeasurably tedious would have served as well for a nuptial.'

On the other hand the Abbey traditions were most carefully observed, in that the Prayer of Committal and other prayers were read by the Dean, who thus assumed precedence over both Secker, Archbishop of Canterbury, and Gilbert, Archbishop of York.

Towards the close of the eighteenth century, the very real dangers associated with midnight funerals in the

---

[1] H. C. Beeching, *Life of Atterbury*, pp. 341, 342.
[2] See vol. i, p. 86.

Abbey came to be more fully realized. The free fight
which developed out of the confusion at the Funeral of
Pulteney, Earl of Bath, in 1764 inflicted permanent injury
upon the tomb of Edward I and must have scandalized
many people. Bad though this was, it was far surpassed by
the terrible disaster at the Funeral of Elizabeth, Duchess of
Northumberland, in 1776.[1]

The Funerals of the great were sometimes imbedded in
Evensong, a custom which long continued. Even so late
as July 23rd, 1881, we find Gladstone, then Premier, com-
menting that 'the strange arrangement of Dean Stanley's
funeral which is to begin at 4 and last until 6 entirely shuts
me out from the power of attending'.[2]

The Precentor must have been a man to be envied seeing
that he received a fee of £2. 8s. at every Funeral, for 'Wax
Lights and Torches'; and another £5 for 'Mourning at
Every Person of Quality's Funeral'. The Dean naturally
enjoyed a still greater rate of remuneration for he received
£10 for mourning, and his four servants £8. In 1761 ten
yards of the black velvet used at the Funeral of the Princess
Caroline in 1758 were given for the adornment of the
altar in the Widows' College at Bromley, an institution in
which the Deans of Westminster owing to their frequent
residence at Bromley Palace as Bishops of Rochester took
considerable interest.

Westminster was still a comparatively small area cut off
from London, alike in an ecclesiastical, civic, and geo-
graphical sense. Ecclesiastically the old City formed a
Peculiar under the Dean who occasionally held a Visitation, while on the civil side its administration was in the
hands of the High Steward, the High Bailiff, the High
Constable, and the Court of Burgesses, all of whom derived
their authority from the same potentate. The increase of
population did not commence till the nineteenth century
was well upon its way. For many years the inhabitants con-

[1] See pp. 20, 21.   [2] *Gladstone to his Wife*, p. 235.

tinued to live what elderly citizens were wont, till recently, to designate their local 'village' life.

Their spiritual well-being was on the whole adequately served by the two large churches of St. Margaret and St. John of which members of the Chapter acted as Curates-in-charge. There was also the Broadway Chapel (a delightful seventeenth-century Gothic structure of brick, mercilessly destroyed in Victorian times) holding one thousand people, and two smaller chapels in Queen Anne's Gate and Delahay Street. The daily offering of prayer and praise in the Abbey continued to be the Office of the Chapter, and that alone. The desirability, much less the necessity, of extending its scope so as to include people other than members of the foundation and their families (with of course the School), or the establishment of the place as a strong centre of devotion, probably never entered anyone's head for a single moment. Everything indicates that the spiritual life of the Abbey had become a very slender thing indeed. This quiet, easy-going place, suggestive of one of our country cathedrals, reflected in short the conditions generally prevailing in the Church of England at the time.

It is hardly surprising that at the close of this dreary epoch a scathing indictment against Westminster Abbey and all its works was delivered by the learned John Jebb, Canon Residentiary of Hereford.

'The Church of Westminster, though most richly endowed, and so situated as to command every advantage required by so magnificent a foundation, though connected in a peculiar manner with the chief Estates of the Kingdom, as the place of Royal Coronations, the Chapel of the House of Lords, and the frequent scene of the Councils of the Church, though made famous by the gravest religious and historical associations, has long claimed the pre-eminence of setting the most perfect example that perhaps any Collegiate Church in the Realm affords, of coldness, meagreness, and irreverence in the performance of the divine offices. Of the richly endowed Prebendaries,

instead of the simultaneous residence of at least four, as required by the ancient regulations, but one at a time usually
attended, except during the height of the London season: the
Prebends being of course considered as mere sources of revenue
to individuals, or as appendages to Parochial incomes. The residences were in many instances alienated to laymen. The Choir,
till of late years, wretchedly few in number, were permitted to
perform their duties by deputy; and these were discharged in
a manner which at best was barely tolerable, without life or
energy. The Lessons were commonly read with the same
degree of solemnity as the most ordinary document by a clerk
in a Court of Law. The service was opened in a manner the
most careless: no decent procession was made; and the striking
of a wretched clock was the signal for beginning to race through
the office: there was a squalid neglect in all the accessaries of
divine worship; the books were torn and soiled, and the custom
of the place apparently enjoined on the Choir boys the use of
surplices more black than white. The whole aspect of the
Church plainly indicated the mechanical performance of a
burthensome duty. . . . To these abuses I need hardly add the
disgraceful traffic carried on at the doors, which required
payment for looking at the Nave or the Aisles; the blocking up
the whole Church except the Choir, and a small portion of the
side Aisle. . . .'[1]

NOTE

Two remarkable Funerals were witnessed in the Abbey
during the early years of the nineteenth century which have
been left almost unrecorded.

On May 18th, 1807, Anthony Duc de Montpensier, younger
brother of Louis Philippe, died, an exile in England; eight
days later, after a solemn Requiem in the French Chapel in
King Street (close to Portman Square), the body was brought
to the Abbey and interred in one of the vaults of Henry VII's
Chapel. The site is marked by an uninteresting tomb, designed
by the sculptor Westmacott. Dean Vincent was officially
thanked for his 'very safe and human care'.

Three and a half years later a ceremony even more remark-

---

[1] Jebb, *The Choral Service of the United Church of England and Ireland*,
pp. 130 ff. It is only fair to point out that the 'disgraceful traffic' which Jebb
rightly condemned had been abolished by Dean Ireland years before the publication of this book.

able took place when the body of Marie Josephine Louise de Savoie and de Lille, Queen Consort of Louis XVIII, was similarly interred, the office in our Book of Common Prayer being used.

Everything possible was done to invest the occasion with dignity. The whole Collegiate establishment attended, including the King's Scholars and the Almsmen, while the aisles of the Abbey were lined by the St. Margaret and St. John Volunteers.

Louis XVIII was not present himself; but Monsieur, his brother, the future Charles X, acted as chief mourner supported by his two sons, the Duc d'Angoulême and the Duc de Berri, by representatives of the Spanish, Portuguese, and Sardinian Embassies, of the ancient French Military and Chivalric Orders, and by prominent members of the exiled French Court.[1]

Save that the Procession, after entering the Abbey, passed straight to the grave, which involved the omission of the Psalm and the Lesson, the Anglican rite and ceremonial were followed throughout, Dean Vincent officiating. The Funeral Sentences were chanted, presumably to Croft's music, and an anthem followed the Prayer of Committal.

Evidently a special pall was used on this occasion, for two Chapter Orders early in the following year directed that a Black Velvet Pulpit Cloth and Curtain were to be made 'out of the Pall accruing to the Church from the Funeral of the Queen of France', at a cost of £10. 8s.[2] They have long since disappeared.

It is strange that these two remarkable Services, in which we see the Churches of England and Rome joining hands, should have passed into complete oblivion. Save for a very brief reference by Dean Stanley, they have been completely ignored by every Abbey historian.[3]

7. THE STIRRINGS OF NEW LIFE

Jebb's indictment was severe in the extreme and it must be frankly admitted that he touched a number of undoubtedly weak spots, but the picture he has drawn is far from just. He has written in a highly censorious spirit and above all he was a full generation out of date. Had the book

[1] Precentor's Book.   [2] Chapter Book.   [3] Precentor's Book.

appeared during the time of the Regency its accuracy could hardly have been impugned. It was not published, however, till 1843, by which time a considerable stirring of the waters had already manifested itself. The long easy-going decanate of Dean Ireland had just ended, a period in Westminster annals usually regarded as the reverse of glorious. It must, however, always be remembered to this Dean's credit that he had taken a warm practical interest in the rebuilding of the organ and the development of the music. Jebb himself admits that some of the twelve Prebendaries were 'labouring for reformation, as far as their influence and the obstinacy of long rooted abuse would permit' and again that 'the present Chapter is laudably rectifying abuses'.

Lord John Thynne, a first-rate man of business and of progressive mind, had arrived from Lincoln some years before and was already making his influence felt on the Chapter. Another like-minded colleague was Henry Hart Milman, destined to make a real mark as Canon and Rector of St. Margaret's Church before he left Westminster to become one of St. Paul's greatest Deans. Later on, there came a great accession of strength in Christopher Wordsworth, a ripe Cambridge scholar, who gave nearly a quarter of a century of his life to the Abbey before his preferment to the Bishopric of Lincoln.

It is clear, too, that the general public had commenced to attend the services in increasing numbers, thereby producing a serious problem. The Dean and Chapter had been forced to adopt the desperate expedient of filling the space between the two sides of the choir with benches facing eastwards,[1] in order to secure additional accommodation. It sadly marred the beauty of the Church, but the additional seating was without doubt badly needed.

The first impressions of Milman when he entered upon his duties in 1835 have already been recorded[2] and Mr.

[1] See vol. i, pp. 155, 156 and illustration facing p. 155. [2] See vol. i, p. 155.

Gladstone has related that one December afternoon in 1841 he attended Evensong expecting to find but a sparse body of worshippers: 'but it was crammed'.[1]

People were to be found, too, whose opinion was as fully deserving of respect as that of Jebb, to whom the Abbey services (far below the standard of today though they may have been) were a joy and delight.

During the reign of George IV there was often seen in the organ loft a brilliant boy

'listening with profound attention and evident delight to the solemn and impressive effects of the choir, when chanting the glorious works of Tallis, Blow, Orlando Gibbons, Purcell, Croft and other great writers of the real English School, and gradually forming his taste upon the noble simplicity, grand harmonies, the solid and masterly counterpoint, and the magnificence and sublimity of style to be found in the admirable productions of our old Cathedral composers.'

The gifted boy thus described by Vincent Novello was none other than Thomas Attwood Walmisley, who frequently used to slip into the Abbey from his father's house in Cowley Street, hard by.

Sir George Grove, subsequently the first Principal of the Royal College of Music, has recorded, in tender and beautiful language, his own recollections of the Abbey Services about the time of Queen Victoria's Accession.

'Many an entrancing hour have I spent in the Abbey at the afternoon service in the winter months with the dim candles below and the impenetrable gloom above, when I thought my heart must have come out of me with emotion and longing.'[2]

Once more, a grand old churchman, who devoted the whole of his life to the cause of Church music, the Rev. W. E. Dickson, for thirty-seven years Precentor of Ely Cathedral, has recorded with delight a series of visits to the Abbey in 1842 'where the style of music exclusively

---

[1] *Gladstone to his Wife*, p. 39.
[2] Graves, *Life of Sir George Grove*, p. 17.

in use was that of the strict ecclesiastical School. The Services of Aldrich, Gibbons, and Rogers were often heard at Matins and Evensong on Sundays most effectively rendered by the choir of ten lay-clerks, and as many boys.[1] The anthem was usually by Boyce, Croft, Greene, or the mighty Purcell.'[2]

The early Prayers at 7.15 a.m. in summer and 8 a.m. in winter met a real need. They were regularly attended by the Students of the National Society's Training College then in Westminster, and a certain number of other residents in the neighbourhood. Dr. Hook, for instance, when in town, invariably made a point of being present.

Celebrations of the Holy Communion were deplorably infrequent, being restricted to the first Sunday of the month and the three Great Festivals. There is no trace of a Celebration on Ascension Day or Red Letter Days. At the same time there is good reason for thinking that the number of persons who made their Communion on 'Sacrament Sundays' was extremely large.

It must be remembered too that the singing of Matins and Evensong was most punctiliously observed. The rendering of the Daily Office without choir and organ, an abuse which since the First World War has become deplorably widespread in many 'quires and places where they sing', was unknown at the Abbey even during the slack Hanoverian times. It was something to have maintained the principle, however faulty the details of its observance, and we cannot withhold a well-merited tribute to our forefathers for their loyalty to Anglican tradition and the example they have set to the Deans and Chapters of today.

[1] Not many years before, in 1821, the Choristers numbered only eight. A proper balance of parts must under such conditions have been unobtainable. Maria Hackett, *A Brief Account of Cathedral and Collegiate Schools*, p. 54.
[2] W. E. Dickson, *Fifty Years of Church Music*, p. 16.

8. A BRIGHTER DAY

The lengthy decanate of Ireland terminated with his death in 1842. He was followed by Thomas Turton, Regius Professor of Divinity at Cambridge, a vigorous controversialist and a musician of some ability. Two of his hymn tunes are frequently heard today. His colourless administration of less than three years ended in 1845 with his preferment to the See of Ely.

To Turton succeeded Samuel Wilberforce, who might well have become one of our greatest Deans. Unfortunately for Westminster his decanate lasted less than six months. Before the close of the year 1845 he was enthroned as Bishop of Oxford. To those who love the Abbey it will always remain a gratifying reflection that the 'Remodeller of the Episcopate'[1] once occupied the chief stall in our Collegiate Church, if only for a brief space. Even those few months gave promise of an epoch-making decanate.

The vacant stall was filled by William Buckland, Canon of Christ Church, Oxford. He owed his appointment to Sir Robert Peel, who often congratulated himself on the wisdom of his choice. The new Dean was a highly distinguished man of science whose geological researches had secured for him a European reputation, but he was in no sense a great divine, much less a preacher. Only two of his sermons ever found their way into print. On the other hand, he was a man of untiring energy and, although already elderly, he threw himself into the life of the Abbey with an almost boyish enthusiasm. The rebuilding of the organ and the erection of the present stalls were only two out of the many developments in which he led the way. The School in particular will always have good reason to bless his memory. In his short decanate clouded at its close by a complete failure of health, during which time Lord

[1] J. W. Burgon, *Lives of Twelve Good Men*, vol. ii, p. 1.

John Thynne took over the helm, he left a deep mark upon the whole life of the Abbey.

Just over a century has passed since Buckland was installed, years crowded with activity and manifold developments. His decanate will always be recognized as the starting-point of the forward movement. It is difficult to tell the story of these changeful years. Development has often been uneven and lop-sided. Movement has never ceased, but the pace has constantly changed. At the same time a single glance will suffice to show the greatness of the gap which intervenes between the decanate of (let us say) Dean Zachary Pearce and that of Dean de Labillière. The many blessings with which the past century has been crowded must be regarded as the sign and the promise of those which will, we trust, mark that century's successor.

Buckland had been at work less than two years when two events occurred, both of them in the June of 1847; one of them quiet and unobtrusive, hardly attracting any notice at all, the other creating almost a national sensation and surrounded by the widest publicity.

The Abbey has been the scene of numerous episcopal Consecrations. During the half century which followed the Restoration they took place in Henry VII's Chapel in considerable numbers, but this custom ceased after the consecration of Sir William Dawes to the See of Chester in 1708.

Rather less than a century later Consecrations in England of Bishops for the Anglican Communion Overseas commenced with that of Charles Inglis to the See of Nova Scotia. The ceremony was performed in the privacy of Lambeth Palace Chapel, a practice which continued for a great number of years and was accepted as the merest matter of course. The Consecration of Dr. Middleton to the newly founded See of Calcutta on May 8th, 1814, was regarded by many people with such downright aversion and even alarm that it was thought prudent to abstain from everything calculated to attract public attention. Hardly anyone was present save the necessary officials; and permission to print the admirable sermon of Dr. Rennell was actually withheld. A few years later the wife of Middleton's successor, Reginald Heber, was only allowed as a great favour to bring two friends to the Consecration of her husband! Small wonder was it that after the Consecration of George Augustus Selwyn to the See of New Zealand in 1843, likewise hidden away in Lambeth Palace Chapel, his friend the Rev. Edward Coleridge was provoked into writing the following indignant comments:

'I could not help feeling that we ought to have been thousands rather than ten, gathered together to witness the sending out by the Church of the first Bishop of the appointment and not, as we were, a few persons in an upper chamber— as if we were afraid and ashamed of that great deed which we came to sanction by our presence and our prayers. It is an actual fact that my own cousin, the present Bishop of Barbadoes, was admitted to that sacred office in the presence of only two persons besides the necessary attendants. Such cannot last much longer. The feeling of the Church will become so strong and the cry of indignation so loud that it will pierce even the walls of Addington and rouse its Archbishop from his slumbers.'[1]

Not long after this outburst, a change for the better took place. Caution and hesitation were thrown over and on St. Peter's Day 1847 Robert Gray was consecrated in Westminster Abbey to the Bishopric of Cape Town, together with three colleagues destined for Australia,[2] in the presence of a vast congregation. The barriers separating the transepts from the choir were removed. Seven hundred and sixty persons communicated, the alms collected

[1] It is only fair, however, to say that five Bishops had been publicly consecrated in the Abbey the year before on St. Bartholomew's Day. See vol. i, p. 100.
[2] Rev. F. Tyrell, Newcastle, N.S.W., Rev. C. Perry, Melbourne, Rev. A. Short, Adelaide.

amounting to £550.[1] Public opinion throughout the country was deeply stirred by this remarkable event, for such it was regarded at the time. The Church of England was at long last awake once more to a sense of her mission to the world. The age of Willibrord and Boniface had returned.

The Consecration of the four Bishops, so full of profound significance to the Church, was not strictly speaking an Abbey event, though the authorities threw themselves into it heart and soul. Less than three weeks before, however, an innocent-looking Chapter Order, purely domestic in character, had been issued. To ourselves it looks almost common-place, but it was hardly less significant than the great ceremony on St. Peter's Day. It was a sincere attempt, the first of many, to restore the second Sacrament of the Gospel to its rightful position. A movement having for its object the development and enrichment of the official worship of the Church of Westminster then started upon its way. The Dean and Chapter of that day were building better than they knew.

This Chapter Order of June 9th, 1847, laid down that an early Celebration of the Holy Communion should in future take place on those Sundays in the month on which people were not accorded the opportunity of participating in that Sacred Feast. Harmless though it was, this privilege was not provided unconditionally. Its future existence depended on the average number of communicants reaching a minimum figure of seven in any one year. The alms were to be divided among such objects as the Dean and Chapter might think fit to direct.

In pursuance then of this Chapter Order, the first Early Celebration of the Holy Communion took place on Sunday, June 13th, 1847. The Celebrant was the Canon in Residence, the Right Rev. James Henry Monk, who

---

[1] Rev. J. McLeod Campbell, *Christian History in the Making*, pp. 88, 113, 114.

was also Bishop of Gloucester and Bristol. He was a pluralist of the old school, though by no means unsympathetic to Tractarian influences, and it must be recorded to his credit that he accomplished a remarkable work of church extension in his western diocese. Fifteen communicants gathered together before the Abbey altar on this historic occasion. The alms collected amounted to £1. 5s. 6d.[1] Such, then, was the unobtrusive beginning of the Early Celebration of the Holy Communion at Westminster Abbey, which henceforth took its place as a normal feature of the worship conducted therein.

The Dean and Chapter hardly received the encouragement they deserved. The Abbey must have been the first, or at any rate one of the first of the great Churches of England to inaugurate this important development and one could wish that our records showed evidence of a greater appreciation than appears to have been the case. Growth was slow and the communicants remained pitifully few. Only on a few occasions for many years did they reach such a relatively small total as thirty. None the less the early Celebration survived. Despite the small numbers who availed themselves of this privilege there never seems to have been any question of its discontinuance. Hence, for upwards of a score of years on the first Sunday of the month, 'Sacrament Sunday', and on the three great Festivals, the Holy Communion continued to be celebrated after ten o'clock Matins, while on the remaining Sundays it took place at 8 a.m. In the year 1871, however, a change, not wholly satisfactory, was inaugurated. The late Celebrations were increased to twice a month, but at the expense of their companion, which now underwent a corresponding reduction in frequency. Apparently, it was the prevailing idea among the Abbey authorities of that time that two Celebrations of the Holy Communion on the same day could not by any possibility be contemplated!

[1] Sacristy Records.

On Easter Day 1848 the present choir was opened, the Dean being the preacher. The scheme had been long under consideration and Buckland must be given full credit for bringing it to fruition. Grievous mistakes were made in carrying out this great piece of work, but on the whole the gain outweighed the loss. The disappearance of Keene's atrocious eighteenth-century stalls, the division of the organ into two portions thus revealing the glorious full-length view which we enjoy today, and a great increase in the seating accommodation were solid achievements for which the Dean and Chapter merited high commendation.

The opening of the new choir signalized an important improvement in the ceremonial. Up to that time it had been customary for clergy and choir to drop into their places independently of each other, but on certain festivals they met in the Jerusalem Chamber and entered the choir in procession. This practice was now extended to all choral services.[1]

The organ was completely rebuilt and much enlarged at the same time, another great achievement; but it is to be feared that for many years to come the rendering of the music was sadly inadequate while various slovenly practices occupied a long time in dying![2]

Dean Trench, in a letter written in 1860, made an unwilling admission as to the low standard of the Abbey music. After attending Evensong one Sunday at St. Paul's, Brighton, a church which, thanks to the ministrations of the Rev. Arthur Wagner, had become widely renowned, he wrote: 'In the evening I was at St. Paul's (very high) where the music is certainly wonderful and puts the best of our Abbey services in this line in the shade.'[3]

During the greater part of the nineteenth century the huge length of the Sunday services continued unabated.

[1] John Jebb, *The Choral Service of the United Church of England and Ireland*, p. 229; also vol. i, pp. xx and 183.

[2] See vol. i, pp. 183–6.

[3] *Letters and Memorials of Richard Chenevix-Trench*, p. 324.

People living today would regard them as intolerable. In the course of the evidence given in 1841 by the Rev. Henry Hart Milman (at that time Treasurer of the Abbey) before the Select Committee on National Monuments and Works of Art[1] he stated that the Sunday morning service normally occupied a full two hours, while on Sacrament Sundays it lasted from ten till one o'clock. Evensong, commencing at the hour of three, was sometimes not over until five. Such was the result of the eloquence, mainly canonical, which streamed from the Pulpit.

Milman was then describing the state of things prevailing during the forties of last century, but sermons of colossal length continued to occur ten, twenty, and even thirty years later. To quote a distinguished Old Westminster:

'We dreaded Canon Wordsworth. He would preach for an hour or sometimes even an hour and a half. Our hearts sank into our boots when we saw the verger bow to him. The Abbey was fearfully cold. The pulpit placed near the altar rails, was far off, and without close attention the sermon was difficult to follow. We tried to keep ourselves warm with rugs round our knees and the Collegers could put on what wraps they liked under their surplices.'[2]

People must have possessed Spartan constitutions indeed. In no other way, surely, could they possibly have survived religious exercises of such gigantic proportions, conducted in the icy atmosphere for which the Abbey enjoyed an evil renown. Not until the eighteen-sixties was a heating apparatus installed.

One of the most famous and popular of the spiritual developments witnessed by Westminster Abbey during the nineteenth century was, without doubt, the Sunday

---

[1] *Report of the Select Committee on National Monuments and Works of Art*, p. 44. This must have included the time when the chiming of the bells began, half an hour before service.

[2] Markham, *Recollections of a Town Boy at Westminster*, p. 65.

evening service. It attracted an immense amount of public attention when first started and for many years afterwards. A Sunday evening service in any Cathedral or
Collegiate Church was in early Victorian days an unheard-
of event. To Westminster Abbey must be assigned the
honour of having made the first move, with the institution
of a series of such services for the benefit of the multitudes
drawn to London by the Great Exhibition during the
summer of 1851.

Some years passed away before there was any repetition
of these services and the honoured name of Dean Trench
must never be forgotten in this connexion. The first took
place on the evening of Sunday, January 2nd, 1858. It
must surely be regarded as another historic occasion.

An extract from an undated letter by this Dean indicates
some of the difficulties which confronted the Abbey
authorities in those experimental times.

'Many of our arrangements last Sunday were a manifest
improvement on those of the preceding: the pulpit far better
placed, against a pillar; the amount of draught and cold air
much diminished by the addition of curtains; more chairs, more
matting, and perfect order and quietness in the admission of
the people. This I know as an eye witness, and on the same
authority I can say that the number of poor, meanly, shabbily
dressed people was very large, much larger than on the first
occasion, while the gentle folks were in much diminished
numbers. We were quite as full as on the first occasion.'[1]

During the Exhibition of 1862 the sermon at one of
the Sunday evening services was delivered in French.
The preacher was the Rev. Francis Jeune, a Jerseyman by
birth, at that time Master of Pembroke College, Oxford,
and subsequently Bishop of Peterborough.

Under Dean Stanley the Abbey Sunday evening services became one of the most prominent features in the
spiritual life of the metropolis. The 'great little Dean'

---

[1] *Letters and Memorials of Richard Chenevix-Trench*, vol. i, p. 321.

threw himself heart and soul into the task of securing the best and most representative preachers of all shades of religious opinions which the land could provide. The pains he took must have been enormous, and he never slackened in his good work, despite the rebuffs he received from time to time. Pusey and Keble resolutely declined to allow their names to be associated with some of Stanley's Broad Church nominees, while Liddon only consented after declining a long series of invitations. The lists of preachers which have survived from those now distant days form a deeply interesting study.[1]

A voluntary choir, too, was organized, while the 'good Duke of Westminster' and various well-known inhabitants of the West End together with Old Westminsters and others rendered valuable service as Stewards.

The Sunday evening services did not, however, become a regular weekly custom for a very long time. Until the closing years of the nineteenth century they were restricted to the seasons of Advent and Lent, together with the months of June and July. During the summer they formerly took place in the Nave.

A resident in the Cloisters during those early years when these nave services had scarcely emerged from the experimental stage, has recorded the existence of a strangely grotesque practice. The congregation, almost invariably a large one, 'sang the hymns from large posters placed on the columns of the great church'.[2] He goes on to say 'we had many noted ecclesiastics as preachers on these occasions, but no excitement was ever aroused like that which attended the appearance of Canon Body.[3] Then hundreds were turned away while the

[1] Rowland E. Prothero, *Life and Correspondence of A. P. Stanley*, vol. i, pp. 288–94.
[2] From a manuscript in the Chapter Library by the Rev. H. E. B. Arnold, O.W., sometime Vicar of the Church of St. Matthew, Oakley Square, N.W.
[3] The Rev. George Body, Canon Missioner of Durham, the noted mission preacher.

Abbey was packed with masses standing anywhere they could.'

It is difficult for twentieth-century folk to realize the extraordinary prejudice which existed down to compara- tively recent years against the performance of sacred music in consecrated buildings. In the reign of William IV a Musical Festival was organized at the Abbey on a large scale, a precursor of the Handel Festivals at the Crystal Palace, under the conductorship of Sir George Smart.[1] The early Tractarians, and not they only, were rendered furious. There was serious talk of organizing a petition to William IV against the desecration of the Abbey by 'music meetings'.[2] Things were not a great deal better thirty-seven years later when Bach's *Passion according to St. Matthew* was performed for the first time in an English church. Dean Stanley, though by no means musical, sup- ported the scheme heart and soul and made himself respon- sible for the heavy expenses. He was violently attacked, not least by members of the High Church party. However, the Dean carried all before him and the hostile critics were silenced. Thus, the Abbey became the pioneer of a prac- tice universal today throughout the Anglican Com- munion.

During the second half of the nineteenth century the Chapter were strong in preachers and a powerful influence radiated from the Abbey Pulpit. The names of Milman, Wordsworth, Trench, Stanley, Kingsley, Farrar, West- cott, and at the close Charles Gore and Basil Wilberforce, speak for themselves. The institution of the Sunday even- ing service, too, made it possible for the Dean to invite leading preachers of the Anglican Communion, not least some from outside the homeland, to occupy the Pulpit. People are still living who can recall the eloquence of such

[1] Bertram Cox & C. L. E. Cox, *Leaves from the Journal of Sir George Smart*, pp. 277–81.
[2] G. Faber, *Oxford Apostles*, p. 363.

famous divines as Philips Brooks, Bishop of Massachusetts, and 'Primate Alexander' of Armagh.

Stanley, both by the written and the spoken word, magnificently impressed upon the public mind the significance of the Abbey from a national and historical standpoint. His great book will remain a classic, so long as the Abbey endures.

More than one important work of construction was successfully carried out during these years. The restoration of the western face of the Altar screen, though not beyond criticism, transformed the Sanctuary, while the two splendid organ cases designed by John Loughborough Pearson twenty years later were equally effective in the choir.

The arrival of Sir Frederick Bridge in 1875 effected a veritable revolution in the musical rendering of the services. The organ was wholly reconstructed in 1884 (and on a lesser scale in 1910). The choir, up to that time far from efficient, was enriched by a number of renowned singers and in his day had but few rivals. The needs of the Choristers, too, were not forgotten, for new and more spacious quarters were provided for their accommodation in 1894 and again in 1915.

9. A HALF-CENTURY OF ADVANCE

No one can deny that a veritable resurrection was accomplished at Westminster Abbey during the period bounded by the installation of Dean Buckland in 1845 and that of Dean Bradley in 1881. These volumes make no claim to be fully comprehensive or to include every department of the rich and varied life of this wonderful Church, but even within these circumscribed limits the evidence fully justifies that description. The torpor which for generations had clogged every movement was by degrees sloughed off. People began to realize that the

Abbey was not simply a venerable relic from a distant past, but that it also possessed a vital message for a new age. The Church dear to the hearts of the down-trodden Saxons during the stern days of Norman and Angevin domination commenced to play a part no less beneficent, in the face of the complex problems with which the Victorian age was so plentifully strewn.

At the same time, it must be admitted that at the end of the nineteenth century much still remained to be done. Thousands of people went away strengthened by the spiritual truths proclaimed from the Pulpit, or uplifted by worshipping in a church of such surpassing beauty, or inspired by the splendid rendering of the music; but the forward movement, uplifting though it was, left on one side those departments of the life of the Abbey with which these volumes are so largely concerned, its treasures, its order, its decency. In certain respects there was little to choose between 1845 and 1895, for the Abbey was still lagging behind in a manner which to the present generation seems incredible. The plucky and laudable attempt of the Restoration Chapter and their immediate successors to make good the cruel losses of the past, to infuse a measure of beauty and dignity into the worship of God's House, instead of going on from strength to strength had gradually succumbed to the numbing atmosphere of the eighteenth century and was followed by generations of inertia, not wholly dispelled till the close of that century's successor.

Gifts for the service of the sanctuary disappeared altogether. From 1710, when Mrs. Helen Sprat on leaving the Deanery presented the Dean and Chapter with her husband's cope of blue silk,[1] our records preserve an almost unbroken silence as regards such offerings. Some slabs of Egyptian purple porphyry used for the paving of the steps of the High Altar, the gift in 1869 of the ninth Earl of Elgin, and a couple of fine pieces of tapestry from the

[1] Chapter Book.

THE BLUE SILK COPE OF DEAN SPRAT
Worn by the Rev. Lord John Thynne, Sub-Dean at the Coronation of Queen Victoria

THE CLERGY AT THE THANKSGIVING SERVICE FOR THE GOLDEN JUBILEE OF QUEEN VICTORIA

(*From left to right*) The Rev. T. J. ROWSELL, Canon; The Ven. F. W. FARRAR, Archdeacon and Canon of Westminster; The Rev. GEORGE PROTHERO, Sub-Dean and Canon; The Most Rev. W. THOMSON, Archbishop of York; The Rev. Dr. JOHN TROUTBECK, Custodian and Minor Canon; The Most Rev. E. W. BENSON, Archbishop of Canterbury; Rev. H. ALDRICH COTTON, Minor Canon and Librarian; The Very Rev. Dr. BRADLEY, Dean of

collection at Hawnes Park near Bedford, the country seat
of the Sub-Dean, Lord John Thynne, alone served to
relieve the darkness.

The Victorian Chapter appear to have felt no qualms
about this barren state of things. A fine Persian carpet in
front of the High Altar, two pairs of unworthy silver gilt
patens and chalices, four equally unworthy metal candlesticks together with a miserable altar in Henry VII's
Chapel form the sum total of their official additions to the
instrumenta of worship for the best part of two centuries.
They were even content to use coconut matting for the
protection of Abbot Richard de Ware's famous pavement
in the Sanctuary. A piece of violet cloth used in Lent was
the sole apology for a frontal. The chapels, where they
had not been stacked with monuments commemorating
departed worthies and other people not so worthy, were
in more than one case treated as so many lumber rooms.
The use of the cassock still in force in the time of Dean
Wilcocks disappeared at some date unknown. The ancient
custom of making a reverence to the Altar, although
definitely enjoined by Chapter Order, was allowed to fall
into disuse. The oft-quoted story of the Verger who conceived it his duty to veto private devotions within the walls
of the Abbey is probably apocryphal; but it must be
admitted that there was little to suggest that the primary
function of the Abbey was to be a house of prayer. Such
ceremonial as existed was slovenly in the extreme. Even
at so relatively late a date as 1889 the Funeral of Robert
Browning produced a furious outburst from a great artist,
Edward Burne-Jones.

'I broke off work and went to Browning's funeral under
protest—for I hate that beautiful heaven to be turned into a
stonemason's yard for any one. . . . It wasn't impressive—no,
not a bit—it was stupid. No candles, no incense, no copes, no
nothing that was nice. Now they have got these churches, they
don't know what to do with them.

'And the procession—so poor and sorry! A canon four feet high next one of nine feet high—surplice, red hood like trousers down the back—You know them all. I would have given something for a banner or two, and much I would have given if a chorister had come out of the triforium and rent the air with a trumpet; How flat these English are.'[1]

With the arrival of Dean Bradley who was installed on All Saints' Day, 1881, a number of welcome developments began to take place.

This Dean was most emphatically a member of the Arnold and Stanley school of thought, and to this theological outlook he remained consistently loyal. He combined it, however, with a most beautiful piety and a broad-minded tolerance. Not once but many times did he say that he was prepared to permit the introduction of various practices which he had reason to believe were helpful to others, though to himself, personally, they made no appeal. Another chief might well have imposed his stern veto at the bare suggestion of such things. It will never be known in this world how much the Abbey owed to the work and example of this much-loved Dean.

Before many months had elapsed a Celebration at 8 a.m. became the rule on *all* Sundays, and soon this practice was extended to the late Celebration. Dean Bradley was also responsible for the introduction of Celebrations on Saints' Days, and at a later date a regular Thursday Celebration. The latter development took place during the time when the late Bishop Gore was a Canon.

The Daily Celebration was introduced with some misgiving, as an experiment, from Ash Wednesday to Low Sunday in the year 1901. It met with a considerable measure of appreciation, and accordingly it was resumed the following Advent. Since then it has continued without a break save for two periods in 1902 and 1911 when the

[1] Mrs. Drew, *Some Hawarden Letters*, 1918, p. 234.

Abbey was of necessity closed during the preparations for the Coronations.

Not until the end of the nineteenth century did the slovenly custom known as a 'surplice and legs' receive its congé. People can still remember the sight of the Abbey Choir advancing up the church, Lay-vicars and Choristers alike, and even some of the Clergy, thus habited or rather semi-habited, the colour of their trousers displaying an amazing variety below their surplices.

It was at length decided about the year 1897 to array the Choristers in red cassocks, a practice subsequently extended to the Lay-vicars and Clergy. Dean Bradley was fully justified when he inaugurated this innovation, for Westminster Abbey like St. George's Windsor is a Royal Chapel (a very different thing from a Royal foundation), and the use of red in such institutions possesses a certain amount of historical precedent, which is not to be found elsewhere.

The last decade of the nineteenth century witnessed other changes also, which though it could not be realized at the time, represented the opening of a new epoch, analogous to the inauguration of the Early Celebration in 1847.

In 1895 the Chapel of St. Faith was set apart for private devotion. With its meagre and inartistic furnishing, this new Chapel looked almost insignificant; but its influence was quickly felt. It was the first in a long series of developments, great and small, all of which can be summed up in the one word, Worship.

Four years later came the Earl of Rosebery's splendid gift of an Altar Cross for the High Altar, another outstanding event. Looking back it can be seen that the old bad days had come to an end, that a new spirit was being spread abroad, and that people were coming to realize more and more the joy and happiness of offering to the House of God 'precious things simply because they are precious, not as being necessary to the building, but as an offering, surrendering and sacrifice of what is to ourselves desirable'. Since 1899 four hundred additions, if not more, exclusive of minor items have been made to the instrumenta of worship possessed by the Abbey. In this good work nearly one hundred individual donors have taken part, exclusive of the immense number of those who have contributed to the corporate gifts offered by Societies. The Dean and Chapter, too, despite the many calls upon their resources, have striven their utmost towards the same end. We can at least claim that the poverty-stricken condition of (let us say) the year 1890 has vanished, it may be hoped for ever.

In the year 1916 an Inventory of these various treasures was drawn up, the first for several generations. New editions have followed every few years, each of them an advance upon its predecessor. A comparison of some of the items in the Inventory drawn up in 1540 at the time of the Dissolution of the Monastery, with the state of things existing today will be found full of interest and by no means devoid of encouragement.

	Inventory of 1540[1]	*Inventory of 1948*
Copes	330	52
Stoles	92	47
Corporas Cases	10	18
Frontals	85	78
Banners	6	6
Falls and Hangings	30	13
Carpets	50	14
Albs and Amices	288	66
Crosses	9	5
Patens and Chalices	13	38
Candlesticks	34	40
Basons	8	11
Cushions	53	56

[1] 'The Inventories of Westminster Abbey at the Dissolution.' Edited by Mackenzie Walcott. *London & Middlesex Archaeological Society Transactions*, vol. iv, part iii (Aug. 1873).

Although we can hardly vie with the full glory of Pre-Reformation days (for there are many gaps still to be made good), it is not unreasonable to express the belief that were some of our great medieval benefactors such as Henry III or Henry VII, Simon de Langham or Nicholas Litlington, with us today, they would acclaim us as fellow workers with them in our zeal for the honour of God's House and would admit that we are not wholly unworthy of our great heritage.

Considerations of space render any detailed description of the numerous modern additions to the Sacristy impossible, but certain special items can scarcely be passed over in silence.

The great Cross on the High Altar, one hundred and eighty-four ounces in weight, stands on a par with some of the costly offerings of Pre-Reformation days. It was the gift of the Right Hon. the Earl of Rosebery and commemorates the marriage of his daughter the Lady Margaret Primrose with the Right Hon. the Earl (afterwards Marquis) of Crewe on April 20th, 1899.

Three years after Lord Rosebery's notable gift the Dean and Chapter became the possessors of another Cross in circumstances so historic that the story must be told at length. For centuries to come this ornament will occupy a high rank among the more interesting of the Abbey treasures.

Today there survives only a small and dwindling band of those present in the Abbey on the brilliant summer morning of the twenty-sixth day of June in the year 1902. None of them will forget that overwhelming moment. The east end of the Church was full of bustle and excitement. Members of the staff of the Abbey, the College of Heralds, and the Office of Works were busily engaged in adding finishing touches to the preparations for the Sacring of our seventh Edward. The last and most important of the long succession of rehearsals for the great event was about to start. The King's Band on the screen were already at work rehearsing the instrumental music under the unexpected conductorship of Sir Walter Parratt: for the Director of the Music, Sir Frederick Bridge, was not in his place. The large choir, four hundred strong, were streaming into the galleries on the north and south sides expecting in a few moments to find themselves singing Sir Hubert Parry's glorious Processional Anthem, 'I was glad when they said unto me', then on the eve of being given to the world.

Everyone was filled with a sense of happy and joyous expectation; but a moment before a mounted messenger from Buckingham Palace had dashed up to the Abbey in hot haste with a letter for the Right Hon. Viscount Esher, who, as Secretary to the Office of Works, had played a major part in the preparation of the Abbey. People were far too busy and excited to notice the anxious faces of a group of Abbey clergy, Heralds and others, who had hastily drawn together near the High Altar, every one of them struck with consternation.

The brilliant march drew to a close. Its concluding bars seemed all of a sudden to have become invested with a strange sense of inappropriateness. A hush fell over the whole Abbey, and an announcement, painful in its brevity, was made by the Bishop of London. 'The Coronation will not take place. An operation is to be performed upon His Majesty at twelve o'clock.' No pen can describe the poignancy of that moment. It soon came home with a shock to every man, woman and child in the land, but to those standing in the Abbey that morning in the presence of the gorgeous trappings of the approaching solemnity the ground seemed to be giving way beneath their feet.

Everyone then fell upon their knees and in another moment all were joining in an extemporized service. It may be doubted whether the Abbey walls have ever witnessed anything more impressive. The Bishop of Bath and Wells, one of the two prelates appointed to sing the Litany in the Coronation Service, passed to the Litany Stool and, Sir Frederick Bridge having now returned to his place, the offering of this great act of intercession commenced. By this time, about one-half of the singers had reached their places and were able to join in the noble music of Thomas Tallis. The familiar hymn 'O God our help in ages past' followed with Walter Alcock accompanying it on the organ, and then the venerable Dean came forward and in awestruck tones pronounced the Benediction. 'I felt', he afterwards exclaimed to some of those standing near, 'as though my tongue clave to the very roof of my mouth.' All then, save one or two persons, passed out of the Abbey into the bright June sunshine, into the streets crowded with people who had poured into the metropolis from every part of the British Empire, in order to take their part in celebrating a great and historic event.

But the day was not yet over. Before the sun had set another missive reached the Precincts of the Abbey, directly inspired by the overwhelming events of a few hours before. It was a communication to the Dean from the late Ras Makunan, official Envoy to the Coronation from the Court of Abyssinia, who was staying at the old-fashioned establishment in Victoria Street formerly known as the Westminster Palace Hotel. In this letter the Ras preferred the request that the Dean would grant him the privilege of making a votive offering to Westminster Abbey, coupled with his own fervent prayers, for the restoration to health of the stricken monarch. The proposal was gladly accepted, and before long the offering arrived, a silver gilt Cross of curious Abyssinian workmanship, weighing forty-five ounces, overlaid at the back with an elaborate net of wire-work soldered and gilt, and inscribed back and front with a brief inscription in Amharic characters.

In the course of the next few weeks, this notable and welcome gift was mounted upon a staff of ebony, to which was affixed a top of metal gilt, engraved with the following words: 'Pro Salute Regis Edvardi Dedit Ras Makunan VIII Kal Jul. MCMII.'

Before long anxiety gave place to joy, the prayers of his subjects were answered, and on August 9th King Edward was seen passing up the Abbey greeted by the traditional 'Vivats' of the King's Scholars of Westminster School. The new Cross was used for the first time in the Procession of the Regalia, the interesting ceremony which immediately precedes the great Solemnity of the day.

As the years rolled on, the Abyssinian Cross became a prominent feature in the worship of the Abbey, but it failed to escape criticism. At the head of a procession in a building so vast it looked far too small in spite of its undoubted though unusual beauty.

In the year 1922 the Dean and Chapter became the recipients of the munificent offering of a warm friend of this country, the Honourable Rodman Wanamaker, who occupied the important position of Chief Commissioner of Police in New York. This distinguished citizen of the United States had long devoted himself to the development of 'brotherly union and concord' between the British Empire and the great Republic of the West. This ideal was touchingly manifested in the sumptuous design of a new treasure, a great Processional Cross designed, by his express orders, regardless of expense. Not one square inch of wood, much less of any base metal, is to be found in its composition. It is built up out of three materials only, viz. ivory, silver gilt, and gold, adorned with a number of plaques or small panels of beaten gold and embellished by sapphires. Both the obverse and the reverse sides are decorated with large plaques of eighteen carat gold depicting the Ministry and the Majesty of our Blessed Lord.

A series of canopied niches runs round the base of the Cross, each niche occupied by the figure of an historical personage connected with the story of the Church of

Westminster. The Apostle St. Peter occupies the place of honour by virtue of his patronal position. He is flanked by the three royal founders and builders: Sebert, King of the East Saxons, St. Edward the Confessor, and Henry III. The series is completed by the two Tudor sovereigns, Henry VII, the founder of the Chapel which bears his name, and his granddaughter Queen Elizabeth, wearing period costume, in whose reign the existing Collegiate establishment was set up. The base of the Cross springs from a highly decorated boss surrounded by coloured enamels blazoned with the Royal Arms of Great Britain and Ireland, the Arms of the Pre-Reformation Monastery and those of the Collegiate Church, impaled according to custom with those of Dean Ryle.

The Cross is attached to a massive staff of silver gilt, where the wealth of decoration comes to an end, save for two inscriptions, the first of which records the fact and date of the presentation.

The second inscription sets forth the noble ideal which inspired this magnificent gift, beautifully summed up by Isaiah's great prophecy in the Vulgate translation, viz.: 'Non Levavit Gens Contra Gentem Nec Exercebuntur Ultra Ad Proelium.'[1]

The Cross was officially presented to the Dean and Chapter of Westminster by the representatives of Mr. Rodman Wanamaker on Christmas Eve of the year 1922. By a happy coincidence that day happened to fall upon a Sunday, which fact lent additional interest to a great occasion. Those present are unlikely ever to forget it; the Abbey crowded from one end to the other: the Christmas hymns, heard for the first time that year: the stately Procession in which the Cross, carried for the moment slant-wise, was escorted through the Nave and Choir to the steps of the Presbytery: the graceful words in which Dean Ryle

---

[1] 'Nation shall not lift up sword against nation, neither shall they learn war any more.'

signified the acceptance by the Dean and Chapter of this notable gift, before laying it for dedication upon the High Altar and lastly the beautiful excerpt, 'Be peace on earth', from William Crotch's well-known anthem 'Lo star-led chiefs, Assyrian odours bring.'

The Abbey possesses a splendid memorial of the Coronation of King George V and Queen Mary in 1911. Unlike most of their predecessors who contented themselves with offering at the Oblation a piece of cloth of gold or other precious material, they strictly conformed to the letter of the rubric in the Order of Coronation and each provided 'a pall or altar cloth' based upon the pair of beautiful medieval frontals of white satin damask belonging to the Church of St. James, Chipping Campden in Gloucestershire—the only complete pair of Pre-Reformation frontals surviving in England today. These Royal gifts were designed by Professor Lethaby and carried out by the students of the Royal College of Art, every effort being made to reproduce the archaic character and general feeling of the work at Chipping Campden. The damask silk, creamy white in colour, woven by the St. Edmundsbury silk weavers on their looms at Letchworth, forms the general groundwork of the frontal, while the major portion of the embroidery has been executed in pure gold and silver thread. The frontal is embroidered with a representation of the Crucifixion with the customary figures of the Blessed Virgin and St. John the Evangelist on either side. This centre-piece is flanked by half-length angel-figures holding shields and surrounded by clouds. The dexter shield bears the Royal Arms of Great Britain and Ireland and the sinister the familiar cross patence and martlets of St. Edward the Confessor. The groundwork of both frontal and frontlet, like that at Chipping Campden, is powdered with conventional motifs of bold floral spray work executed in coloured silks and gold. The dorsal of similar material is powdered with the same floral motif and embroidered with the figures of St. Edward the Confessor and the Pilgrim together with the kneeling figures of the two pious donors.

A word must also be said about the four Ryle almsdishes. During the sixteen years of his decanate this distinguished Dean greatly endeared himself to Westminster citizens of every rank and class. An earnest desire was expressed after his death in August, 1925, to perpetuate his memory in some permanent manner and a civic memorial was the result, to which a large number of people contributed. After long consideration it was decided that it should take the form of a set of four silver-gilt almsdishes, and this magnificent offering was officially presented to the Dean and Chapter by the Mayor of Westminster (Councillor Jacques Abady) at the City Hall on Wednesday, December 21st, 1927.

Each dish is 17 inches in diameter and 60 ounces in weight. All four are similar in shape and are richly decorated with repoussé and hammer work. They are stoutly ribbed in view of the heavy weight to which they are constantly subjected. In the centre of each dish is a large representation of the Arms of the City of Westminster, while the rim is adorned with four other shields, each surrounded by a wreath. The bottom of each dish is engraved with the following inscription:

'In Piam Memoriam Herberti Edwardi Ryle, K.C.V.O., D.D., Olim Ecclesiae Collegiatae Beati Petri Westmonastẽr et Honoratissimi Ordinis de Balneo Decani, DD. Cives Westmonastẽr Amico Dilectissimo Amici A.D.MCMXXVII.'

The Chapel of St. Edward the Confessor plays an important part on those comparatively rare occasions when Holy Matrimony is solemnized at the High Altar. At the conclusion of the ceremony the bridal party passes through the King's Door on the north side of the sanctuary into the Chapel, where, while vocal or instrumental music is being rendered, the Registers are duly signed.

Hence it was a happy thought on the part of our present beloved King and Queen to make an offering to this Chapel in memory of their marriage on April 26th, 1923. It took the form of a fine pair of Altar candlesticks of wrought silver of Renaissance character which had the effect of completely transforming the Altar and its surroundings.[1] They also marked their Coronation by the joint gift of a splendid white frontal.

Prominent among the modern fabrics belonging to the Dean and Chapter is the festal Tunicle of blue silk worn by the Cross Bearer. Donor and artist were one and the same, viz.: the late Mrs. Walter Sickert (née Angus). This wonderfully beautiful vestment occupied three years in working. It was seen to be a work of supreme excellence and was at once accepted by the Hanging Committee of the International Exhibitions which took place at Ghent in 1913 and Paris in 1914. It was also exhibited at Burlington House during the First World War. On leaving England for a new home at Dieppe in 1920 Mrs. Sickert offered her beautiful work to the Dean and Chapter and it was used for the first time at the Feast of the Dedication in that year.

The bulk of the decoration is concentrated upon a large medallion on the upper portion of the back and a large oblong panel at the foot, back and front. In the centre of the former is a representation of the Eternal Child wearing a crown of thorns, surrounded by children. The two panels consist of fascinating groups of children together with masses of clouds, trees, flowers, and foliage. The figures have all been worked from life. One of them is Peter Scott, son of the distinguished Antarctic Explorer.

For many years no alteration took place in the old-fashioned ceremonial inherited by the Abbey from a distant past. The 'north-end' position continued to be the official use until after the Installation of Dean Armitage

[1] See vol. ii, illustration facing p. 114.

Robinson on the Festival of St. Simon and St. Jude, 1902. Dean Bradley made no variation from his accustomed practice throughout his decanate and his example was scrupulously followed by his Sub-Dean. It must, however, be stated in this connexion that during the closing years of the nineteenth century the Eastward Position was permitted to such individual members of the Chapter as desired to use it, notably the Ven. Archdeacon Furse, whose installation as Canon went back to the year 1883, and Charles Gore.

Down to 1903 the two candles on the High Altar were never lit at all, save at the Early Celebration on some winter morning when they were supposed to be required for the purpose of giving light. Even at Evensong the High Altar remained in unillumined dignity. At the commencement of the present century a curious tradition was current among the older Vergers to the effect that this unhappy darkness was in itself an innovation upon the custom of former times, when the altar candles had been lit at Evensong, during a considerable portion of the year. Furthermore, the credit of this unsatisfactory 'innovation' was assigned to Dean Stanley, who, so it was stated, had abolished the ancient custom and ordered the Altar candles to remain unlighted on the ground that they would mar the general effect of the new Reredos! For some unknown reason, however, it was the custom at the end of the nineteenth century to light the two standard candlesticks at Evensong every day from the Festival of All Saints to that of the Purification. Possibly this curious and unexplained practice may have been due to some 'Stanleyan' compromise made in former years, but it is impossible to speak positively.

Altar lights at all Celebrations of the Holy Communion, both early and late, became the regular practice by order of Dean Armitage Robinson on Easter Day 1903. Evensong was also included in the Dean's order and some ten or twelve years later the custom was extended to Matins when rendered chorally.

To this Dean, who rendered such valuable service to the Abbey by his research work in the Muniment Room and by many literary contributions, we owe the restoration in 1905 of the interesting Sequence of Colours which is coeval with the existing Church. Simultaneously with the opening of Henry III's choir Abbot Richard de Ware compiled an important Consuetudinary or Book of Customs at that time observed in the monastery. The said customs include the Westminster Use as regards Colours. Supplemented by the later evidence of the Inventories, we possess, therefore, a complete record of the practice of our Pre-Reformation forefathers, and it is loyally followed today.

The remarkable decanate of Dean Ryle commenced in April 1911, a few weeks before the Coronation of King George V and Queen Mary. He gave of his best to the Abbey for fourteen years. He was dogged by uncertain health throughout his decanate; but he served our historic Church with a devotion which has rarely, if ever, been equalled. As a result of his leadership the Abbey rose to a height in popular estimation and general prestige which it had never before attained.

His name will always be associated with three outstanding events in which he bore a prominent part—the Re-inauguration of the Most Honourable Order of the Bath in 1913, the Burial of the Unknown Warrior in 1920, and the raising of the great Restoration Fund administered today under his name.

But these events were far from being the end of his work. He was a real pastor and he strove heart and soul to emphasize the spiritual witness of his Church. The Sunday Evening Service was his special care. He always regarded it as representing a mine of spiritual possibilities. Under his rule this Service was invariably thronged with a vast congregation who came to regard the Dean almost in the light of a personal friend. It has been said with truth that he held that congregation in the hollow of his hand. The following touching letter speaks for itself:

'I am only a common working man. But I should like to convey to you my great sympathy on the great loss of the late Dean, Dr. Ryle—Socially there is a great space between him and myself but I always loved him *very, very much*. What I liked best was the "silent prayer" of a Sunday night. I feel sure many a soul has been in touch with God whom we all like to call "Our Father".'[1]

Again, he deeply cared for the public worship of the Abbey and strove his utmost both from a spiritual and an aesthetic point of view to make it representative of the Church of England at its best. Thus at the first Easter after his Installation, he reverted to the custom of our fore-fathers by reviving the Procession. It was the day of small things, for the six magnificent Banners, to mention nothing else, were still a thing of the future, but it was to Dean Ryle that we owe the start of this revival.

In Pre-Reformation times a Procession took place every Sunday morning in many great Churches both in Eng-land and France. It still survives in old-fashioned places such as Rouen and Bayeux, where the ancient customs have not been wholly submerged beneath the flowing tide of Ultramontanism. The Sunday Procession at West-minster, Durham, and other great Benedictine founda-tions must have been of the most imposing character.[2] The entire Convent took part, arrayed in copes, and every altar in the place was visited and censed.

How dear this custom was to the hearts of many people is indicated by a pathetic clause in the will of one Thomas Elfryd, Prebendary of the Ninth Stall, who died in 1546.

[1] M. H. Fitzgerald, *Life of Herbert Edward Ryle*, p. 372.
[2] *Customary of the Benedictine Monasteries of Saint Augustine Canterbury and Saint Peter Westminster*. Edited by Sir E. M. Thompson, Henry Bradshaw Society, vol. ii, pp. 60–1.

Elfryd had entered the monastery at the close of the fifteenth century when the Abbot's stall was occupied by John Estney. He took his part in the great doings associated with the magnificent Islip, and after the crash he was appointed by Henry VIII to a prebendal stall in the new Collegiate Church. He survived the tragedy of the Dissolution six years, and then as he passed away, looking back wistfully to the old days, he gave utterance to the wish that he might be buried near the south door of the church where was 'sometime the procession waye'.[1] Thus a liturgical Procession became a dead letter until the days of Dean Ryle.

On the Feast of the Dedication in the year 1920 the cope was used for the first time at one of the regular Services and on Whitsunday of the following year it was extended to Processions on Sunday evenings. Today the Procession forming a glorious band of colour passing down the aisles of the great church is one of the most impressive and uplifting features of the worship of the Church of Westminster.

At this point it may not be inappropriate to quote two recent appreciations of the Abbey ceremonial from worshippers at a recent Christmas. The first comes from the pen of a certain noble Lord who was present on the morning of Christmas Day at the High Celebration and the Procession which preceded it; the second from a well-known artist, who attended one of the Carol Services during the same Festival:

'I was more than impressed by the utter dignity, without fussiness, of the whole ceremony. The wonderful dramatic beauty, so full of awe, almost left me without words to express myself. Yet beneath all this lovely pageantry one sensed the real, unaffected personal religion of the English Church.'

'I have never seen anything so truly beautiful as the slow moving drama of the Procession—a dignified progress of

[1] Westlake, *Westminster Abbey*, vol. i, p. 203.

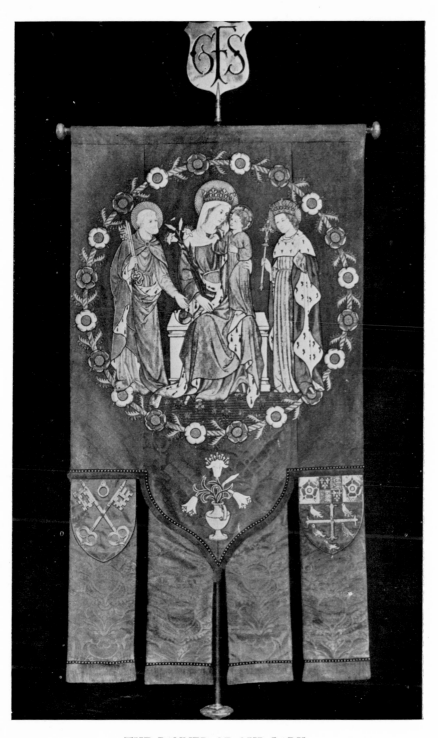

THE BANNER OF OUR LADY

A BODY OF SERVERS

wonderful colour, suddenly being frozen into stillness and forming a living picture out of a Thirteenth Century Missal. I was more than moved; but remembered to thank God that such things could be.'

The three Sacred Ministers were arrayed in copes at a Celebration of the Holy Communion for the first time in the year 1921, a practice which was permanently established during the decanate of Dean Foxley Norris on all Sundays and Red Letter Days, in Processions, at the Occasional Offices, and on special occasions. The traditional ceremonial, sometimes designated the 'English Use', has from the first been undeviatingly followed. It includes today the Procession of the Gospel and the Great Entrance of the Elements at the Offertory.

Another outstanding feature of the great Ryle decanate was the immense increase of Special Services of every sort and kind. The staff of the Abbey had long been familiar with such events as Consecrations of Bishops and a Funeral or Memorial Service of some outstanding personality. During the First World War, however, the public mind seemed to wake up to the significance of the Abbey and its mission to the English-speaking world in a manner and to an extent unknown before. Apart from such hardy annuals as the Distribution of the Royal Maundy, the Annual Service for the Lord Chancellor, Judges and members of the Bar at the Reopening of the Law Courts in October, and the immensely popular Carol Services in Christmas week, no less than eighty-six Special Services took place in those fourteen years (all of them involving an immense amount of preliminary staff work) with the Abbey crammed to its fullest capacity.

The walls of Henry III's choir were white and fresh from the mason's hands when Edmund Crouchback, Henry III's second son, plighted his troth to the beautiful Aveline, daughter of the wealthy Earl of Albemarle.[1] It

---

[1] Stanley, *Historical Memorials of Westminster Abbey*, p. 117.

was the first of the many thousands of public events which those walls were destined to witness and the only Royal Wedding, with the doubtful exception of that of Richard II and Anne of Bohemia, till our own day.

History constantly repeats itself, but it sometimes takes a long time about it. Upwards of six and a half centuries came and went after this historic Plantagenet marriage till there came a grey winter day in the February of 1919 when the Abbey was once more crammed for a Royal Wedding, this time including many khaki-clad figures (for the First World War was barely over) when Princess Patricia of Connaught was united in holy wedlock to the Honourable Alexander Ramsay amid an intense outburst of popular enthusiasm.

Two other Royal Weddings, equally popular and even more splendid, followed at no great distance of time, those of Princess Mary and Viscount Lascelles on February 28th, 1922, and of our present beloved King and Queen on April 26th, 1923. That of Prince George, Duke of Kent and the Princess Marina of Greece took place on November 29th, 1934.

The bare enumeration of the Special Services which characterized the decanate of Dean Ryle is impossible; but two among them were of such overwhelming and outstanding importance that they cannot be passed over.

During the summer holidays of 1920 a novel suggestion found its way from two wholly independent sources into the Dean's extremely varied postbag. The suggestion made a great impression upon his mind and after consulting with others on the spot he decided to lay his splendid proposal before the Government; who cordially approved the burial of an Unknown Warrior.

In all its history 'the Abbey can have witnessed no such moving spectacle' as that which took place a few weeks later.

'The congregation of nearly one thousand of those bereaved in the War and one hundred nurses, wounded or blinded in the discharge of their duty; the lines of soldiers, sailors and airmen who had won the Victoria Cross "for Valour", stretching down the centre of the nave on either hand; the long procession from the north transept to the west end of the nave in which, as chief mourners, the King and the Princes of the Blood followed the coffin with its nameless burden,—a procession, blessed it might seem at its entry by the effigy of the great Earl of Chatham and greeted as it reached the graveside by the figure of his famous son, all this was such as might have made the very stones cry out. The popular feeling matched the occasion. Outside the Abbey for a distance of a mile or more stretched a long line of people eager to enter and pay their tribute to the heroic dead. For over ten hours, till it was necessary to close the doors at 11.0 p.m. they passed through the Abbey in a ceaseless stream; and day by day throughout the following week the grave was visited by thousands of those whom the Unknown Warrior and his comrades had died to save.'[1]

Five years later a congregation, no less vast, assisted at a Solemn Eucharist in the presence of our own Primate supported by a number of English Bishops and five distinguished representatives of the Holy Orthodox Church of the East. Well might Archbishop Davidson say in his sermon 'these old walls have never seen the like' as the successor of St. Athanasius advanced to the centre of the Sanctuary and solemnly recited the Nicene Creed in the Greek tongue. For a moment the gap between East and West was bridged, the harbinger, all must hope, of a closer union to come.

When building operations on the Abbey ceased with the death of Abbot Islip in 1532, the two towers were left incomplete, but some, if not all, of the bells were transferred from Henry III's old campanile on the north side of the Abbey (destroyed in the eighteenth century) and hung in the north-west tower which at that time had progressed somewhat farther towards completion than its companion. It proved an unsatisfactory arrangement. The bells were

[1] Rev. M. H. Fitzgerald, *Memoir of Herbert Edward Ryle*, pp. 311–12.

suspended in a position so low and boxed up that their
sound could travel but a short distance, as Wren forcibly
complained to Dean Atterbury.[1] His words were doubtless taken to heart but thirty years passed by before his
suggested remedy materialized. With the completion of
the north-west tower it was decided not only to raise the
bells to a higher level, but also to provide the Abbey with
a ring full worthy of such august surroundings. Some of
the existing bells were recast from older bells, one of which
went back to the distant reign of Edward IV. Two others,
the gift of Dean Goodman, one of which must have helped
to swell the triumph over the Invincible Armada of Spain,
were also available and in good condition. Six were now
suspended in the newly built tower but for some reason
unexplained the Dean and Chapter never completed the
octave. Two places in the new oak frame remained permanently vacant. It was the heaviest ring of six in the
country, it is true, but its inadequacy was painfully
obvious.

For at least three centuries it has been customary to
reserve the ringing of the full peal for certain special occasions only, mainly national and political. The faithful were
and are summoned to the Daily Offices by a five minutes
ding-dong half an hour before the hour of Service followed
by the chiming of one of the other bells for a quarter of an
hour. Sermons are announced by the chiming of forty
strokes on the tenor. The origin of this, the 'Sermon Bell',
is not very clear, but it almost certainly goes back to the
sixteenth century.

As time went on the full ring was heard less and less. Its
condition became increasingly unsatisfactory. Even the
historic custom of ringing on 'Foundation Day', i.e. the
Anniversary of the Accession of Queen Elizabeth on
November 17th, 1558, was dropped. The Coronations in
1902 and 1911 and the return of King George V and

[1] *Parentalia: Life and Works of Sir Christopher Wren,* by his Son, p. 166.

Queen Mary from India in 1912 were the sole occasions on which they were heard for many years, for they had become almost unringable. Only for a few minutes were they able to make their contribution to the great outburst of rejoicing over the signing of the Armistice on November 11th, 1918.

Fortunately, a generous benefactor came forward and put an end to this scandalous state of things. The belfry was brought up to date by the completion of the octave. One of the old bells was recast, another was replaced, and the entire eight were hung in a new steel frame. The renovated peal was dedicated by Dean Ryle on June 3rd, 1919, and its music now plays an important part among the 'laudable customs' of the Abbey. Some twenty-two days in the year are marked as Abbey Ringing Days. The full ring is usually heard between the hours of twelve and one on the great Festivals of the Church, on all days associated with the Sovereign, who is the official Visitor of the Abbey, and on various occasions of local importance. Its beauty is specially manifest when the bells are rung half-muffled.

Two other important changes, both of them in the nature of revivals, must also be placed to the credit of Dean Ryle.

On Ash Wednesday, 1921, the Abbey reverted to a time-honoured custom of the English Church. For the first time for many generations were the Altars vested in white linen. The beauty of the change was quickly realized and widely appreciated.

That the Lenten Array was customary at the Abbey in Pre-Reformation times is definitely settled by the evidence of our Inventories. Thus, in the Suppression Inventory of 1540, there occurs among others the following entry: 'a whyte clothe of sylk wyth a red cross serving for Lent'.[1]

---

[1] *Transactions of the London and Middlesex Archaeological Society*, Aug. 1873, p. 345.

More important still is the evidence furnished by a still earlier Inventory, that of 1388, drawn up by the Sacrist of that day, Ralph Tonneworth, which describes in full detail the Lenten hangings presented by him to the Abbey.

'Quintum decimum frontellum pro tempore quadragesimali magno altari de panno de bawdekyn coloris de tawny cum frontilecto et uno Reredos attingente ad celaturam predicti altaris unius secte in quibus continentur ymago crucifixi Marie et Johannis, Agnus Dei cum Evangelistis et unum par ridellarum ejusdem coloris de tartaryn ex dono N.L. Abbatis.'[1]

The Lenten frontal and upper frontal of the High Altar with its representation of the Crucifixion, the Agnus Dei, and the Evangelistic symbols recall the fourteenth-century hangings bestowed by Ralph Tonneworth. The conjunction of the two sets of initials, viz. N.L. and H.E.R., likewise preserves the memory of two distinguished men who presided over the Church of Westminster during the reigns of Richard II and George V respectively. The lettering is derived from a boss in the Cloisters on which are sculptured Abbot Litlyngton's initials.

In Lent, 1935, a further development took place with the introduction of a Lenten Veil of white linen covering the entire altar screen, save of course that portion over which the dorsal is suspended. The decoration designed by the late Sir Walter Tapper has been carried out in dark blue stencilling which emphasizes most effectively the red emblems on the upper and lower frontals of the Altar. The simple dignity of the east end completely draped in these Lenten hangings is most striking. In the opinion of many people the Abbey Sanctuary looks more impressive in Lent than at any other time of the year.[2]

Funeral Reform was another subject to which Dean Ryle devoted close attention. In Pre-Reformation days,

---

[1] J. Wickham Legg, Inventory of the Vestry in Westminster Abbey taken in 1388: *Archaeologia*, vol. iii.
[2] See vol. i: illustration facing p. 118.

a comely Hearse-cloth formed part of the furniture of almost every parish church. Our forefathers never dreamt of allowing their dear ones to be borne to the grave sur-rounded by the trappings of woe with which subsequent generations became familiar. Bright colours alone were in their eyes appropriate at seasons of mourning. Some of the ancient City Companies have fortunately preserved the noble Hearse-cloths which used to enshroud the remains of their departed brethren during the last Offices of the Church. Few, however, if any, parochial Hearse-cloths survive. They long ago disappeared, largely as a result of the troubles of the sixteenth and seventeenth centuries. Henceforth the idea of gloom came to be inseparably associated with death, and the undertaker, with his hideous palls, remained in possession of the field, though Hearse-cloths of considerable magnificence continued to be used in the seventeenth century on great occasions such as a Royal Funeral.

That the Abbey was not without a Hearse-cloth of its own during the eighteenth century is clearly proved by evidence contained both in the Precentor's Book and the Burials Book, in fact it was the custom to charge a fee of ten shillings for the use of the 'Church Pall'. The date and reason for the cessation of its use are unknown. We can only suppose that it wore out and that in an age of general laxity the Dean and Chapter did not trouble to replace it.

The reaction against the sombre paraphernalia of the average funeral in this country was long in coming; and it took an unfortunate form. The horrible black velvet, beyond which the mind of the undertaker seemed unable to rise, gave place to the practice of bedecking a coffin with a multitude of wreaths and crosses, till at last the wanton expenditure upon flowers attained scandalous pro-portions. There was no alternative save a return to the old ways.

The first symptom of a desire for something more fully

in keeping with the spirit and traditions of the Christian Church manifested itself at the Funeral of the Right Honourable W. E. Gladstone in 1898 followed by that of Mrs. Gladstone in 1900. On both occasions the coffin was draped in a white pall of great beauty, the gift of the Armenian Christians for whose welfare the departed statesman had laboured so strenuously.

This admirable precedent was followed a few months later at the Funeral of Queen Victoria in January 1901, when, to the surprise of many, a white pall, embroidered with the Royal Arms, was thrown over the coffin.

About twenty years later a noble gift enabled the Church of Westminster to be equipped once more with this beautiful adjunct of Divine Worship. It was decided to make good the gap created by the disappearance of the eighteenth-century Hearse-cloth. Immense pains were taken to follow the comely practice of pre-Reformation days, Dean Ryle being particularly insistent upon the selection of white as the foundation colour.

This welcome addition to the treasures of the Abbey, designed by the late Mr. W. D. Caroe, was offered by the members of the Actors' Church Union, as a memorial of the numerous members of that profession who gave their lives during the First World War. The presentation was made on May 7th, 1920, by the Right Rev. W. W. Perrin, Lord Bishop of Willesden, Chairman of the Actors' Church Union, supported by Sir John Hare, Sir Ben Greet, and other prominent representatives of the stage. No one present will ever forget the touching way in which the Dean accepted this splendid gift and expressed the hope that it might be the privilege of the Abbey to lead the way in the adoption of customs and practices at once more beautiful and more historical in themselves and more closely in accord with Christian teaching. The Hearse-cloth was first used at the Burial of the Unknown Warrior on November 11, 1920, when it lay for many days beneath the Union Flag spread over the unfilled grave. At a later date the coffin of the beloved King George V lay enwrapped in its folds during the solemn Lying-in-State in Westminster Hall.

The improvement in the Funeral ceremonial of the Abbey was by no means confined to the addition of the Hearse-cloth. The unworthy altar-hangings were replaced by a magnificent frontal and dorsal designed by Mr. W. H. Randoll Blacking.[1] Massive oak candlesticks took the place of brass horrors borrowed for the occasion. The ancient Restoration copes were employed as a model for six additional companions of rich purple velvet from designs by the late Mr. F. E. Howard. The conclusion of the Service with a muffled peal, which first took place at the Funeral of Admiral Lord Fisher in 1919, became another regular addition to our 'laudable customs', while the Abbey staff took over the entire management of such functions from the moment the coffin entered the Precinct until its departure. The cumulative result of these numerous changes was complete transformation.

All through the sixteen years of his decanate Dean Ryle was the victim of frail and uncertain health. More than once was he compelled to take a prolonged rest. When he was at last overtaken by the final collapse, it was difficult to believe that the end was in sight. His great recuperative powers had served him so well in the past that people took for granted that they would see him reappear before long in his familiar place. But it was not to be, and after nearly a year of increasing weakness, borne with wonderful fortitude, the tenor bell rang out one August evening and proclaimed that another great chapter in the story of Westminster Abbey had closed.

It was an astonishing congregation which assembled a few days later to pay their last tribute. Although it was the depth of the holiday season, when official London is

[1] See illustration facing p. 71.

scattered to the four winds, numbers of people rushed back in order that they might be with the beloved Dean for the last time. The Abbey was crowded out. It might have been some great occasion of state, when this good man was 'buried among the Kings because he had done good both towards God and towards his house'. Surely it was hardly surprising that in the minds of some present there uprose the thought of the high priest, Simon the son of Onias, 'who in his life repaired the house again' and 'took care of the temple that it should not fall', who 'when he went up to the holy altar made the garment of holiness honourable' and 'lifted up his hands to give the blessing of the Lord with his lips and to rejoice in his name'.

The good work was continued under his successor Dean Foxley Norris. The canopies of the stalls and the wrought-iron gates of the choir were gilded, with fine effect, introducing a much needed element of colour. The clumsy early Victorian benches in the transepts were replaced by chairs; and the seventeenth-century pulpit was beautifully renovated. An increased dignity and spaciousness was conferred upon the overcrowded choir by the removal of certain unsightly kneelers and benches. Additional furniture was added to what is now the Chapel of St. George. Above all, the Chapel of King Henry VII was scientifically cleansed, with magnificent effect, a renovation fittingly crowned by the erection of the new altar and baldacchino after the model of Torrigiano's splendid sixteenth-century masterpiece—a generous offering on the part of the members of the Most Honourable Order of the Bath.

10. THE ABBEY UNDER FIRE

Since the publication of the preceding volumes of this work the Church of Westminster has had to sustain the shock of War once more. The continuity of its life was maintained without a break, but it was a life lived at high pressure, full to overflowing with difficulties surmounted and blessings received in the providence of God. The story of these overwhelming years will always be associated with the decanate of Dean de Labillière.

The latter was installed on the Feast of the Purification, February 2nd, 1938. No Dean in the whole history of this Collegiate Church has ever been subjected to a heavier burden. Six out of the eight years of his short decanate were spent in time of War. The ultimate responsibility for the protection of the Abbey and its Precincts, so far as such a thing was humanly possible, rested upon him, and likewise the maintenance of the daily life and organization of the Church under the stress of unique and almost impossible conditions. He saw the major portion of the historic Deanery go up in flames (together with his own possessions), also a number of the official houses in the Little Cloister together with the Dormitory and the Great Schoolroom of Westminster School. The roof of the Lantern came crashing down; the Choir School was heavily bombed. Masses of stained glass were destroyed and many other lesser injuries inflicted. The Dean did not flinch for a moment. His determination to maintain the spiritual witness of the Abbey (needed more than ever in those years) without one iota of abatement was never relaxed. It was a terrific burden and, as subsequent events proved, it was beyond his strength, for he was called away at an age when many more years of useful activity seemed to lie ahead of him. His was another great decanate, in spite of its comparative brevity, and the immense congregation representing the manifold interests of his life which

c c

gathered within the Abbey at his Funeral showed that he had told.

During the eight years of Dean de Labillière's rule, despite the hampering conditions imposed by the War, the stream of gifts continued unabated. They included the Great Candelabra of the Old and New Testaments; a Lectern of wrought-iron work with a richly embroidered Fall of White Silk, which has enabled the Procession of the Gospel to be rendered with becoming dignity; the anonymous gift of a set of figures for the Christmas Crib and two Banners of exceptional beauty. The use of Wafer Bread at the Holy Eucharist was introduced and a host of other improvements, great and small, in the general rendering of the Services.

The Choir, although grievously maimed by the disbanding of the Choristers' School early in the War, continued to officiate without a break. The Lay-vicars who had joined the Forces were temporarily replaced by older singers and from 1943 onwards a body of Choristers living at their own homes in divers parts of London rendered admirable service on Sundays and the more important weekday occasions.

In spite of the difficulties associated with the 'blackout' and war conditions generally, the number of Special Services reached enormous dimensions, surpassing even the record number which characterized the longer decanate of Dean Ryle. They included five Consecrations of Bishops, nine Funerals of outstanding public men, twenty-six Marriages and a host of Memorial Services. Throughout the War an annual Service took place in connexion with the British Red Cross and the Venerable Order of the Hospital of St. John of Jerusalem. The Centenary of the Diocese of Gibraltar was solemnly celebrated, likewise the Seventy-fifth Anniversary of the Foundation of the Dominion of Canada and the Annual Thanksgiving Day of the United States of America. Solemn Services of

Intercession and Thanksgiving were organized on behalf of Greece, Ethiopia, Yugoslavia, Belgium, Norway, and Denmark; while the W.V.S., the W.R.N.S., the A.T.S., the Home Guard, and the Civil Defence Organizations, all occupied prominent positions in the lengthy record running into three figures.

To Dean de Labillière we also owe the revival of the historic connexion between the Abbey and the House of Lords which for some unexplained reason had been allowed to fall into abeyance. Twice over in the year 1945 did the members of the Upper House with the Lord Chancellor at their head take part in a great Service of Thanksgiving for Victory.

The Dean, who had enjoyed the personal experience of work in the Church overseas, also laboured incessantly throughout his decanate in the forging of fresh links between the Abbey and the various countries comprised in the British Commonwealth of Nations. His efforts culminated in the assignment of Stalls in the choir to Canada, Australia, New Zealand, and South Africa, and on June 10th, 1945, he installed their respective High Commissioners therein.

Last, but assuredly by no means least, must be recorded the impressive Service of Welcome given by the Dean and Chapter to the Metropolitan Krutitsky and the Patriarchal Delegation of the Holy Orthodox Church of Russia when for a brief and blessed moment East and West joined hands.

As time goes on the details of a particular Dean's work tend to be obscured and ultimately even forgotten, but in the case of many who have held this office, one or more outstanding features remain, inseparably linked with a particular name. Atterbury will always be associated with the Dormitory, Wilcocks with the completion of the two Towers, Stanley with his monumental History, Ryle with the Burial of the Unknown Warrior and the raising of the great Restoration Fund. Posterity will recall Dean de

Labillière in connexion with the great and far-reaching developments in the nave which have formed such a prominent feature in the fifth decade of the twentieth century. Here he has left his deepest mark and here his mortal remains appropriately lie.

From time immemorial the north door had formed the main entrance to the Abbey. The vast elaboration of the great cliff of carved stone which rises above proclaims such to have been the intention of Henry III. The building operations on the nave, extending over several generations, must have made the west entrance unsuitable, if not impossible, anyway for purposes of ceremony. Thus, for generations the hosts of pilgrims and visitors were invariably received at the north door and carefully shepherded by the monks (for pilgrims were an extremely mixed crowd) and conducted by a definite route round the Abbey to the Shrine of the Confessor.[1]

The disappearance of the monastic régime made no difference. The north porch continued to be used alike by royalty and by the general public. Later on it became customary to open the western doors on important occasions of ceremonial, such as an Installation of Knights of the Bath and, of course, the Coronation, but such events were few and far between. Even at the funeral of George II in 1760 the traditional arrangement was followed.

During the nineteenth century, however, a state of things grew up which could only be termed intolerable. Worshippers and visitors alike found their way in growing numbers to the Abbey, as a result of the increased population of London, the development of railway travel, and later the motor-car, as well as the constant arrival, notably in the summer months, of crowds of Britons from overseas. The Abbey ceased to be the church of a country town two miles distant from the metropolis, the quiet regularity of its life only interrupted by some comparatively rare

[1] Francis Bond, *Westminster Abbey*, pp. 71, 72.

ceremony of State. Crowds of people now poured into the church, all of whom entered the building by the north door in obedience to time-honoured custom.

A more unsatisfactory state of things can hardly be imagined. To the devout worshipper the sight of the vast mountains of masonry, some of them downright pagan in feeling, with which the north transept has been crowded during the last two centuries, formed a sorry introduction to Divine Service. As for the average sightseer he found himself struggling to push his way along a narrow and crowded thoroughfare. He was hopelessly precluded from realizing the perfect proportions and the full beauty of the great church. Many came and went without ever finding their way westward at all, while in the nave itself there was little to suggest that its primary function was the worship of Almighty God. As the hour of Service drew near, people were hastily evicted from this particular part of the Abbey which became, for the time being, a great empty space, except on certain occasions such as the popular Carol Services at Christmas when the enormous crowds overflowed and made its use imperative. During those years not a few people both regretted and resented the non-use of the western entrance. Custom made hoary by centuries, however, takes a long time to dislodge, and the closed doors at the west end continued year after year to impose their veto. In 1899 a reform was attempted, but evil tradition once more asserted itself and gained the upper hand. Even the forceful personality of Charles Gore failed to effect any permanent change.

Reform came at last and it came with a rush. Dean de Labillière had not long been in the saddle, when he determined to overthrow the bad old tradition for ever. The great west doors by his orders were thrown open, while the former entrances in the north and south transepts henceforth remained closed save at the time of Service. In one moment the centre of gravity was shifted. Today people automatically enter by the west door and at once receive an overwhelming and probably lifelong impression from the glorious full-length view extending right up to the graceful lines of the apse (one of the purest gems of Gothic art) with the High Altar in the distance. In former times this uplifting experience was enjoyed by a bare handful of people at the most.

But this is not the last word by any means. During the night of Friday, October 4th, 1940, a huge bomb fell but a few yards from the east end of Henry VII's Chapel. The Abbey escaped major damage, but masses of glass were destroyed, fortunately much of it thoroughly bad, while from the organ screen eastwards the place was swamped in such dirt and litter as to render the choir unusable for weeks.

Fortunately, the nave had suffered to a slight extent only, and the Dean at once gave orders that the Services of the following day, which was Sunday, should be transferred thither from the choir. A makeshift altar composed of two tables was hastily set up. Some disused ornamenta were placed thereon and in a few hours' time an extemporized sanctuary had been brought into being, by no means undignified in appearance, on the exact site of the Pre-Reformation Altar of the Holy Cross. The result was amazing. The most casual observer could not fail to realize that the general feeling and atmosphere of the nave had in those few hours undergone a complete transformation.

There was no question about the future. A brief experience indicated clearly enough that a return to the practice of our forefathers was the only right policy to pursue. Accordingly, a permanent altar was placed here which has by degrees been habited and made full worthy of its surroundings. A magnificent carpet was given by our Canadian brethren. A pair of carved and richly gilded candlesticks was dedicated on February 10th, 1943, at a Service, overwhelming in its pathos, as a memorial to

Captain Cooke and the Officers, Warrant Officers, Petty Officers, and men of H.M.S. *Barham* who went down in the Mediterranean on November 25th, 1941. A pair of altar candlesticks followed, while a careful process of scientific cleaning has revealed the delicate colour of the surrounding pavement. Much work still remains to be done, notably the replacement of the great Rood which for many generations looked down on the worshippers from above the Altar of the Holy Cross in silent majesty. A nobler opportunity for some generous benefactor can hardly be imagined.

The setting up of this new Altar was productive, however, of certain complications. On November 11th, 1925, the newly established Chapel beneath the south-west tower had been brought into being. It was decided to dedicate it to the Holy Cross, on the ground that an Altar bearing that title used to stand in the nave in Pre-Reformation times. It was an unfortunate choice and could only be justified by the belief of many at the time that an altar at the east end of the nave on the actual site of this medieval predecessor could hardly be regarded as practical politics. Thus, a wholly anomalous state of things had come into being. There was only one possible solution of the problem, and on the evening of Low Sunday 1945 Dean de Labillière officially rededicated the small chapel, assigning to it the title of Saint George. A more appropriate designation could hardly have been found for a chapel containing more than one War Memorial and the graves of Field-Marshals Plumer and Allenby. At the same time he conferred upon the new Altar, with equal appropriateness, the title of the Holy Cross, thus reverting to the former time-honoured practice after a lapse of nearly four centuries.

Never let it be forgotten, then, that Dean de Labillière was responsible both for throwing open the west doors and for bringing the nave *permanently* within the orbit of the regular worship offered in the Abbey. Outward and visible signs manifested during the last few years proclaim that the value of his wise and sympathetic policy can never be over-estimated.

The medieval builders of the Abbey, it must be remembered, never desired, much less did they anticipate, the vast congregations of modern times; indeed, in planning their church they gave no heed whatsoever to the needs of the general public. The latter hardly came into the picture at all. Such people could repair to St. Margaret's, the Parish Church of Westminster; indeed, it had been built for their special benefit. They could steal into the nave, if they so desired, and hear Mass at one of the altars standing there: but they were entirely shut off from the worship constantly offered by the monastic brethren in the enclosed inner chapel of the choir, save for such fragments as happened to float westwards over the two screens. The replacement of the monks by the Dean and Chapter made not the slightest difference. The time-honoured conditions continued to prevail unchanged.

Today a large number of people are invariably present in the nave while Service is taking place. It frequently happens on a Sunday that every seat is filled, and many people are perforce standing. The gates of the choir are always left open. The High Altar is visible in the distance to nearly all. The amplifiers convey every word that is uttered, while on high days when the Procession passes round the nave people are able to assist in the fullest manner.

As already stated, the number of Special Services in the time of Dean de Labillière reached a total as varied as it was unique. Probably he would say that the most outstanding of them all was that which first took place on Christmas Eve 1941 and has been continued ever since.

During the closing weeks of that year the Dean came to learn that a large number of people would be working throughout the night in Government Offices in Whitehall and the neighbourhood. Consequently they would be precluded from making their Christmas Communion. He therefore announced that the Holy Communion would be celebrated at midnight in the Abbey. It was not altogether a simple matter. London was in the grip of the 'blackout'. Many of the depleted staff lived at a distance and the authorities insisted that the lighting of the Abbey should be reduced to the barest minimum, viz. the four candles at the newly-set-up altar in the nave. A disappointing response to the invitation was quite possible. The Dean's action was rewarded, however, by a success almost phenomenal in its magnitude and to which no pen can render adequate justice. The nave was literally crammed with people from end to end, many, of necessity, standing. Upwards of seven hundred persons received the Blessed Sacrament that night, probably a record in Abbey history. None who were present could have failed to carry away lifelong impressions—the unearthly beauty of the church, the mysterious shadows cast by the four twinkling candles; the great volume of sound as people uplifted their voices in singing from memory the Christmas hymns, and the sense of the abiding presence of God over all. On that night the Abbey indeed came into its own.

At this uplifting and hallowed moment this survey of one aspect, but only one, of the varied and complex story of Westminster Abbey may well close. We look back over an eventful century, since, in the distant days of Dean Buckland, the first tentative efforts were inaugurated, having for their object the stressing of the primary reason for which the Abbey was founded. The story of the past shows that under God's providence blessings have been poured forth upon this place in rich abundance, far exceeding the wildest dreams of any of our grandparents or great-grandparents. Less than a score of years have to run before the time arrives for celebrating the long story and the manifold blessings spread over nine hundred years of history, since this church was founded by Saint Edward the Confessor. May the great ideals ever present to that King's mind as he watched the walls of his beloved Abbey rising above the Isle of Thorns, so beautifully described by a fifteenth-century historian, ever remain a living inspiration as generation gives place to generation:

Haec Domus Aula Dei Decus Urbis Janua Coeli;
Angelicas Hominumque Preces Haec Scala Sonabit[1]

[1] 'This house is the Hall of God, the Jewel of the City, the Gate of Heaven and a Ladder in the Prayers of Angels and Men.' These two hexameters are taken from a fifteenth-century manuscript in the Bodleian Library usually entitled *The Oxford Life of Edward the Confessor*. It is said to have been composed as a present to King Henry VI.

THE INVENTORY OF ST. EDWARD'S CHAPEL
NOVEMBER 1520

THIS Indenture Trypartyte made the Xth day of the moneth of Novembr in the xijth yere of the Reigne of Kyng henry the viijth wyttenessyth yt Dan Wyllyam Grene late kepar of Saynt Edwardys shryne And of the relykys of saynt Peters chyrch of Westm. hath delyueryd unto Dan Henry Wynchester successour of ye sayde Dan William Grene ffyrst iij longe chestys for to putte in the vestymentys and the other clothes belongyng to the sayde shryne, Item ij clothes to couer the ymagys of saynt Edward and saynt John Euangalyste in lent; Itm a cloth to couer the tombe of Kynge Edwarde with the long Shankys; Itm a Canvas cloth steyned blacke with a whyte Harte to couer the tome of Kyng Rycharde the second, Itm ij whyte tapettes, ij tapettes of blewe and iij redde tapettes, All these to serve for the longe coffre byfore the Relykys; Itm xj quysshyns of clothe of gold and one of them a longe quysshyn; Itm ij quysshyns of blew clothe of sylver; Itm iiij quysshyns of grene velvett fygury; Itm vj payr of curtayns for saynt Edwardys Awter, ffyrste one payere redde, the second blewe, the thyrde whyte, the iiijth blacke, the vth Tawney, and the vjth grene; Itm Another payer of Curteyns of whyte tarterne for lent; Itm iiij quysshyns of blewe velvett; Itm viij Awtar-clothys with frountellys A fore them, the ffyrste redde the grounde with Braunches and honysocles of grene velvett And flowers of golde, the seconde of redde bawdekyn dyaper with levys of golde, the iijde blewe with braunches of whyte And byrdys of golde; the iiijth of blew coloure with fawcons and other byrdys of gold, the vth whyte with byrdys and braunches of gold, the vjth whyte vynes and butterflyes of grene, The vijth blacke, and the viijth whyte tarterne with a redde crosse for lente; Itm v corporas and v Corporas casys, the fyrste Case redde saten with grene braunches of velvet with flouers of gold, The seconde velvett with an ymage of saynt Edwarde, The thirde blew with the letter E and starrys of gold, the iiijth purple with garters, And the vth velvett; Itm iiij olde chesybles, The ffyrste redde with grene velvett and flowris of golde with stole, fanon, Awbe and Amytte, The seconde redde braunches with flowris of gold lackyng the Awbe wt the Apparell, The iij de blew wt rosys of golde lackyng all hys Apparell, the iiijth Chesyble of whyte damaske with Awbe, stole and fanon, embroderyd with flowers of golde; Itm the parelles off A awbe of blewe damaske with flouris of golde; Itm ij newe Chesybles with stolys, fanons, Aulbys and Amyttys, The firste redde damaske with flouris of sylke and golde and seconde blew saten with flouris and chalicys of golde; Itm one masboke; Itm vj bokys of saynt Edwardys masse on the sondays to syng uppon; Itm a Chalyce of sylver and gilte weying xliij unces, ij Cruettes of tynne; Itm ij Auter clothes of blew damaske wt ij curteyns of the lady hungerfordys gifte; Itm an awter clothe of whyte damaske with flouris [of] golde and the Armes of saynt Edwarde in the myddys, of the gyfte of Sir Richarde Caston; Itm a olde Chesyble with stole, fanon, and awbe of blewe damaske embroderyd with flowrys of gold, of John ffeytte's gyfte: Itm An Awter cloth of pourpyll and whyte velvett to ha ve afore the Auter Tabble, embroderyd with flouris of gold and been coddys within the same flouris, of my lady of Bedfordys gyfte; Itm a valaunce of blew velvett embroderyd with flouris of golde with the ymages of saynt Edwarde and saynt John Euangelyste, with another valaunce of blew damaske to hange the shryne and a creiste of tymber and of bron golde, of Dan Thomas lyn's gyfte; Itm iiij other valaunces of Crynsyn Bawdekyn embroderyd with blew garters and flouris of gold; Itm ij longe Candylstekkys in either syde of the Awter with a latyn standerd to sett over the cruettes. Itm iiij small latyn Candylstycks; Itm ij surplyces, the one old, the other newe; Itm a payer of Curteyns of purple sarcenett; Itm on corporas and j case of blewe tyssue, of Dan John holandys gyfte; Itm iiij new tapettes to laye before saynt Edwardys Awter, ij the fyrste redde, the second whyte, And the iiijth blewe; Itm a paper masseboke of Salisbury's use, of William Caxton gyfte; Itm a cloth hangyng abowte the shryne of the lyff of saynt Edward; Itm iij longe stoolys with feete to sett over the shrynes with the relykys; Itm a cheyn of yron to fasten over the shrynes at the foresayd ffeeste; Itm a cloth steynede with the Xij Apostles to hang abowte the sayde relykys at the sayde feste; Itm an olde sawterboke of parchement.[1]

[1] W. A. M., quoted by H. F. Westlake, *Westminster Abbey, 1923*, vol. ii, pp. 504–5.

APPENDIX II

THE INVENTORY OF DEAN NEILE
W.A.M. 6612

THIS valuable document never before published throws no small amount of light on various happenings at the Abbey during the later sixteenth and early seventeenth centuries. The publication of the document in its entirety is unfortunately impossible for lack of space, hence those portions which deal with subjects unconnected with these volumes have been omitted.

Richard Neile was installed on November 5th, 1605, at the moment when Westminster was seething with the excitement produced by the discovery of the Gunpowder Plot. He was fortunate in that he had secured the friendship of the great Cecil family while still a boy. This powerful patronage proved invaluable, for Neile owed nothing to his birth, which was of the humblest. At the same time he possessed an industry and a force of character calculated to carry him far. He was Dean for a relatively short time; but the five years of his administration were crowded with activity which left an enduring mark upon the place. The story of the building and repairs, the increase of the revenue and furniture of the church, the over-hauling of the charters and registers together with works of charity and hospitality is almost incredible. Already become Bishop of Rochester, Neile left Westminster in 1610, ultimately reaching the Archbishopric of York by way of Lichfield, Lincoln, and Durham. His immediate successor at the Abbey was George Monteigne, who anticipated Neile in the Primacy of the Northern Province.

An Inventory of the College Plate, &c., in 1617

[Endorsed] [fol. 1 is blank]

[fol. 1d] Things necessary to bee provided for the Communion table:

One Carpett of purple or greene Kersey broade cloth or perpetuary.

One white holland cloth to laye upon the carpett.

One basin, 2 flaggons, 2 cupps, 2 plates for the bread.[1]

[fol. 2] An Inventorie of all such Plate as belongeth to the Colledge of Westminster, and of all such thyngs as are in H. 7 chapple and in the body of the Churche, the Vestry and Treasury and in the Colledge as it was taken by Richarde B. of Rochester and Deane of Westminster and delyvered to George Mountaigne Dr. of Divinity at the entrance into this Deanery. Whereunto is annexed a Breviat of all such things as were wantinge at the departure of the said George to the Bishopricke of Lyncolne and at the entrance of Robert Tounson Dr. of Dyvinitie now Deane. December 20 anno domini 1617.

Plate in the Churche

	li.	s.	d.
In primis two great flagon Pottes for wine all guilte weighinge 102 ozs. ½ at 6s. 10d. the oz.	35	00	5
Item a Bason and two Pattens all guilt weighinge 77½ oz. at 6s.10d. oz.	26	09	07
Item two Challices and Covers of guilt weighinge 69 ozs. ¾ at 6s.10. ozs.	23	16	07

Plate in the Colledge[2]

	li.	s.	d.
Item one Bason and Ewer parcell guilt weighinge 89 ozs. ¾ at 6s. the ozs.	26	18	06
Item one Salte with a Cover all guilt weighinge 16 ozs. at 6s.8d. ye ozs.	05	16	08
Item one fayre Salt with a cover all guilt of the Countesse of Rutlandes gifte weighinge 27 ozs. ¼ at 6s. 8d. the oz.	09	01	08

[1] The items of fol. 1 are in a different hand from that of the actual Inventory.

[2] The common life was still being maintained at the Abbey during the first part of the seventeenth century. King's Scholars, Choristers, and to a considerable extent the Chapter also, used to take their meals in the Dean's Hall or College Hall as it is termed today—a custom maintained until the great break due to the Civil War and the rule of the Commonwealth. This fact explains the vast accumulation of silver gilt plate.

	li.	s.	d.	

Item one trencher Salte new made to it all guilt weighinge 8 ozs. jd. weighte 6 graines at 6s.8d. the oz. — 02 13 09

Item one midlinge salte all guilte new made to it weighinge 18 ozs. at 6s. 10d. ye oz. — 06 03 00

At the makinge of which two salts was chaunged an olde broken salt a cover of a Boole and an olde great spoone with a lattine posye.

Item one salte with a vice without a cover all guilt weighinge 12 ozs. halfe quarter at 6s.8d. the ozs. — 04 00 10

Item one Nutt Cuppe with a Cover all guilt weighinge 16 ozs. ¼ at 6s.8d. the oz. — 05 08 04

Item one other Cuppe with a Cover all guilt weighinge 11 ozs. at 6s.8d. ye oz. — 03 13 04

Item one little Pott with eares and cover all guilt weighinge 9 ozs. ½ jd. waighte 12 graines at 6s. 8d. ye ozs. — 03 03 08

Item one Nest of Bolles all guilt weighinge 66 ozs. ½ at 6s. 8d. ye oz. — 22 03 04

Item one standing Cuppe with a cover all guilt de dono Com' Northumb' weighinge 19 oz. ½ at 6s. 8d. the oz. — 6 10 00

Item one standinge Cuppe with a cover all guilt with the L. Burghleys Armes weighinge 30 ozs. ⅛ at 6s. 8d. the oz. — 10 00 10

Item one great silver Pott of the L. Cranbornes guifte with his armes weighinge 36 ozs. at 5s. 6d. the oz. — 10 00 09

Item one great silver Pott of the L. Rosse his guifte with his Armes weighinge 40 ozs. ¼ at 5s. 6d. ye oz. — 11 01 04

Item one great silver Pott of the L. Vauxe his guifte waighinge 39 ozs. ¾ at 5s. 6d. ye oz. — 10 18 01 ob

Item one ffrenche Bolle of Mr. Bellots[1] guifte weighinge 10 ozs. at 5s. 6d. ye oz. — 02 12 03

---

[1] Prebendary from 1594 to 1613.

	li.	*s.*	*d.*

[fol. 2 d] Item two great flagon Potts white weighinge 130¾ ozs. at 5s. 6d. ye oz. — 35 19 00

Item one chaffinge dishe white weighinge handle and sylver 27½ ozs. at 5s. 6d. the oz. — 7 11 03

Item one Bason and Ewer of Mr. Camdens[1] guifte white weighing 104¾ ozs. at 5s. 6d. ye oz. — 28 16 01

Item two sponte Potte white weighinge 73½ ozs. at 5s. 6d. ye oz. — 20 04 03

Item a Bason and Ewer of Mr. Pickeringes guifte parcell guilte weighinge 96 ozs. ½ at 6s. ye oz. — 28 13 00

Item one great double Bell Salt white weighinge 22 ozs. ¼ and ⅛ at 5s. 6d. the oz. — 06 05 01

Item one silver Pott with a cover parcell guilt with the Colledge Armes and a Bill thereon weighinge 20 ozs. ¼ at 5s. 8d. ye oz. — 05 14 09

Item sixe silver Potts with eares of the same worke weighinge 106 oz. ¾ at 5s. 6d. the ozs. — 29 07 01

Item a silver Pott of Mr. Middletons guifte weighing 18 ozs. ¾ jd. waighte at 5s. 6d. the oz. — 05 03 05

Item one guilt Bolle with the Colledge armes on it weighing 18 ozs. 2d. waighte 12 graines at 6s. the oz. — 05 08 09

Item three broade silver Bolles white weighinge 61 ozs. ½ wt. at 5s. 6d. the oz. — 16 18 03

Item one little ffrench Bolle for wine weighinge 5 oz. ½ 2d. wt. at 5s. 6d. the oz. — 01 10 09

Item 18 silver spoones parcell guilt weighinge 24 ozs. ¾ at 5s. 6d. the oz. — 06 16 01

Item one ffrenche Bolle with the Colledge Armes de dono Mri. Doctoris Butler weighinge 8 oz. at 5s. 6d. the oz. — 02 04 00

Item ffower spoones bought by Mr. Foxe weighinge 5 ozs. 3d. wt. — 01 10 00

Item two small Colledge Potts white weighinge 28 ozs. whereof one hath Mr. Curlles Armes at 5s. 6d. ye oz. — 07 14 00

[1] The famous historian who was Headmaster of the School from 1593 to 1598.

li.   s.   d.

Item one single Bell Salte with a cover
weighinge 7 ozs. ¼ at 5s. 6d. the oz.   01 19 10
    Item one dozen of spoones more weighing
13 ozs. ¾ ⅛ at 5s. 6d. the oz.   03 16 09
    [li. s. d.] The whole valew is
    [441. 5. 5] 441 li. 05s. 05d.[1]

In H. 7 Chapple and in the body of the Churche

In primis one new orgaine sett up in H. 7 Chapple.
    Item one great Carpett of Peniston of two breadthes con-
teyninge five yardes in length.
    Item in the body of the Churche 10 large strong wainscott
Pewes[2] in and aboute the Preachinge place with Lockes and
keys to every of them.
    Item a great stricking Clocke.
    Item olde formes in the prechinge place and at ye Com-
munion Table.

In the Vestry

In primis one olde Cope of blew Cloth of golde with ye
Salutacion in ye Cape.
    Item one other Cope of blew Cloth of golde with the
Resurrection in ye Cape.
    Item one other Cope of blew cloth of golde with God the
ffather and the Crucifixe in ye Cape.
    Item one other Cope of blew Cloth of golde with St. Paul
in ye Cape.
    Item one other Cope of cloth of golde with blew velvet with
a border of beaten golde and a Cape to the same.
    Six Copes receaved of Mr. Standen, viz. fower of them
with borders of flower deluces and are thus distinguished,
viz.
    In the first with the Salutacion in ye Cape.

---

[1] This figure must be multiplied many times in order to reach its twentieth-
century equivalent.
[2] These must be the unsightly pews which sadly marred the beauty of the
crossing (see illustrations, vol. i, facing pp. 64, 86, and 101). They were erected
by Dean Neile, doubtless for the families of the married members of the Chapter
who had by this time become a permanent feature in the buildings once occupied
by the celibate monks.

[fol. 3 d] Item the second with God the father and Christe dead in his armes.

Item the third with the Salutacion in ye cape being of Cloth of beaten golde.

Item the fowrth with the death of our Lady in ye cape.

Item the other two of red cloth of golde, viz. the one with the Epiphanie in ye Cape, th'other with the Nativitie in ye cape.[1]

Item two olde Pulpitt clothes fringed, whereof the one is with red greene and white silke fringe of blew Cloth of golde, th'other is of red cloth of golde, fringed with red green and yellow fringe.

Item two olde Cushions of blew cloth with short tassells of divers collors.

Item two long Cushions, one of red cloth of golde both sides alike without tassells and th'other with crimson cloth of golde mingled with silver with tassells.

Item one rounde crimson velvet Cushion, one the one side, one thother 4 Lyons imbrodered round aboute with golde, and tassells of crimson silke.

Item two olde long Cushions, and one short Chagable silke with birds of golde in thone and flowers in thother.

Item two square Cushions of blew cloth of golde for Mr. Deanes seate in K.H.7 Chappell, one of red cloth of golde for ye same place without tassells.

Item the Pillowe of a Cushion without the case.

Item one verie longe olde Cushion of cloth of golde.

Item fower long Cushions of blew cloth of golde lined with leather.

Item two new Cushions of white and green satten without tassells for Mr. Deanes seate.

Item one Canoopie of green Cloth of golde fringed about with red, greene and white fringe lace of silke.

Item one olde one of blew cloth of golde.

Item one new of blew cloth of golde fringed aboute with crewell fringe of yellow and blacke.

---

[1] These eleven copes are the remains, no doubt, of the large collection, twenty-four in all, handed over by Abbot Feckenham to Dean Goodman. Ordinary wear and tear were not alone responsible for the shrinkage in number. The conversion of several into a canopy for Queen Elizabeth and the loss of at least one, as a result of carelessness, forms an adequate though regrettable explanation. See p. 213.

Item one canapie of blacke velvet imbrodered with 4 Pellicans the Sunne and Moone and bordered with greeke letters uppon cloth of golde and fringed with white silke fringe.

Item one faire great Canapie made for Q. Elizabeths comminge to the Parliament of white and red cloth of tissew lyned with red sarcenet, and fringed with white silver, and red silke fringe with sixe staves pointed with silver, with silk pointes, and white ribbons belonging therunto.

Item one Altar Cloth parte of beaten golde and part of blew cloth of golde fringed with blew, red, and greene.

Item one other of blew cloth of golde without fringe.

Item three olde table clothes, one of Holland, one of Dieper, and one of Damaske.

[fol. 4] Item one herse Cloth of blew cloth of golde intermingled with a border of percullices in the middest of red velvet.[1]

Item one silver Challice with a Cover all guilt.

Item one other silver Challice with a Cover all guilt.

Added heerunto by Richard Neile Doctor in Divinitie.[2]

Deane of the Collegiate Churche of St. Peter of Westminster the 26 Feb. 1605.

Imprimis one new fronte of cloth of golde and blew velvet for ye Communion Table.

Item one pale of cloth of golde fringed at one side and both endes with a gold fringe.

Item one Bason for offerings double guilt with ye Colledge Armes theron.

Item two guilt Potts with the Colledge Armes.

Item two guilt Plates for Communion bread with the Colledge Armes.

Item two crimson velvet Cushions with golde fringe and Tassells suitable.

Item a second pale of willow colloured Cloth of golde for dayly use for the Communion table fringed round aboute with golde and silke.

---

[1] Evidently the practice of carrying the dead to the grave beneath a covering of bright colours had not yet given place to the sombre practice which still prevails in many places today.

[2] It is clear that Dean Neile was by no means satisfied with the appearance of the High Altar for he took good care to provide it with magnificent new hangings.

Item two olde Chaire, one of blew velvet th'other of red velvet.

Item one new Pulpett of wainscott and a Pulpett ladder.[1]

Item two long hangins on both sides of the quire with white and red Roses uppon a wollen Cloth.

Item two other olde hangings for the quire thone side conteyninge the story of Christe, thother side the story of K. Edward ye Confessor.[2]

In the great Chamber called Hiersualem

Imprimis seaven olde peeces of Tapestry hangings about ye Chamber.

Item one great wainscot Chest.

Item one large Turkie carpet.

Item fower cushions of cloth of golde.

Item two other cushions of Imagery woorke of cloth of golde.

Item one standinge Cupborde of wainscott.

Item two longe formes.

Item one short forme for sealinge at Chapter.

Item two great Chaires of cloth of golde.

Item one paire of brasse Andirons.

Item one fire shovell and tongs tipped with brasse.

Item a long Table with drawers.

Item two new large drafte worke Curtaines lined with buckeram with rings and a Curteyne rod for ye great window.

Item twelve Russia red leather Chaires.

Item the olde Chamber wainscotted.

27° die May: 1629:

	li.	s.	d.
Item paid to Mr. Spence upholster for one white ground turkie carpett	02	14	00
Item paid to Adam Browne Joyner for making the Chymneypeice in Jerusalem Chamber[3]	14	17	6

---

[1] Doubtless the beautiful Pulpit which, after generations of neglect, was gilded, renovated, and re-erected in the Lantern in 1935.

[2] These tapestries were clearly those given centuries before by Abbot Berkyng. This Inventory fully confirms statements made by Weever and other historians.

[3] Still *in situ*, having been erected by Dean Williams about 1626.

The document concludes with a Breviat in which is set forth a list of items which had disappeared during the short seven years decanate of Dean Montaigne, and which he failed to hand over to Dean Tounson on his departure to Lincoln. Evidently Montaigne fell far below the standard set up by his energetic predecessor in his zeal for the honour of God's House. One item in particular is deplorable, viz. 'One Coape of cloth of gold with blue with a border of beaten gold and a cape for the same which was lost in the time of Rice Williams being in the country and no sextons attending.'

THE INVENTORY OF 1661
W.A.M. 44026, A and B

THIS Inventory, already quoted in various parts of this work, requires little detailed description. It is a pathetic document, for it represents a grievous falling off from the splendour of former days. There could not be a more damning indictment of the leaders of the Long Parliament and their methods. At the same time one's indignation is somewhat tempered by admiration for the good men who in 1660 embarked, patiently and courageously, upon the task of building the glories of the temple anew.

An Inventory of Plate and other Utensills for ye Altar and Pulpit in ye Sacrist's Custody for Abbey Church in Westminster. January 30, 1661

Imprimis 9 pieces of guilte Plate viz. one bason, 2 flagons, 2 chalices, 2 pattens and two covers for ye chalices.

Item: Tho white damaske Clothes for ye Altar: 2 other narrow damaske clothes for the same and 2 course clothes to make cleane ye Plate:

Item: One large purple cloth for ye Altar, trymed with a deepe silk fringe:

2 large cushions of ye same Cloth, lined with crimson damaske and trymed with silk fringe and tassells.

One fronte behind ye Altar: and a fronte before ye Altar panned with cloth and damaske and trymed with fringe, suitable to ye Altar cloth and cushions.

Item: One other plaine purple Cloth and 2 cushions for ye table in Henry VII's Chapel.

Item: ffour large pieces of tapestree hangings for the Altar, imagery work given by his Majesty at ye Coronation.

Item: 3 lesser pieces of tapestree hangings, lyned with canvice formerly given by Sir Paul Pindar.

Item: One Pulpitt Cloth and Cushion of purple velvett imbroidered with silke and gold:

Item: One other Pulpitt cloth and cushion of purple cloth, trymed with silk fringe; and one purple velvett cushion for ye pulpitt.

Item: 4 brasse candlesticks for ye Altar and 3 brass branches for ye Altar and Quire.

Item: 14 yards of blacke bayse for ye Altar and 12 yards of course blacke bayse for ye foote pace before ye Altar to be used ye 30 of Jan and a pulpitt Cloth and Cushion for ye same day:

and 2 black bayse covers for ye Bible and Book of Common Prayer; and one black cloth and cushion case for ye pulpit.

12 Copes in Mr. Shene's Custody.

Item: five red bayse covers for ye Chaires in ye Harry yᵉ 7th Chappel and Cover for ye Table and afore ye West End of ye Chappel.

Item: one gt needlework cushion with a small silk fringe and 4 green tassels   and a greene bayse cover to it given by Mrs. Maidwell.

The Crowne and other Vestments of ye Regalia worne by ye Kinge at his Coronation, were delivered to Dr. Earle the then deane, the same evening the Kinge was crowned and also ye Cloth of gold that covered the Coronation Chair.

APPENDIX IV

THE INVENTORY OF 1750
W.A.M. 6613

THE brevity of this document speaks for itself. We are nearing the end of the decanate of Dean Wilcocks and the commencement of an era of stagnation.

It is noteworthy, however, that the High Altar is equipped with a change of frontals, and the mention of 'four candlesticks at the altar' suggests the existence of a pair of standards.

An Inventory of the Furniture belonging to the Sacrists of
St. Peter's, Westminster (1750)

For the Chappell.

Pulpit Cloath and Cushions and the Cloath for the Altar Table and two Cushions.

The Altar in the Quire.

The Best Furniture and the Book of the Altar; the Cloath for the Altar Table and the Two Cushions and the Pulpit Cloath and Cushion for the same.

Twelve Cushions belonging to the Altar for kneeling on.

The common Altar Cloath and two Cushions for the Common Pulpit Cloath and Cushion.

The Black Furniture for the Altar and Pulpit.

For Sacrament Days.

Two Table Cloaths and two Napkins Twenty-nine belonging to the Altar. The three Brass Branches, and the four Candlesticks at the Altar, and the Candlestick for the Pulpit.

The two white Candles for the Altar.

A Silver Spoon Gilt.

Sam[ll] Steen Sacrist.

A LETTER FROM DEAN GABRIEL GOODMAN TO LORD TREASURER BURGHLEY

November 15th, 1577

GABRIEL GOODMAN was the second of the Deans appointed under the Elizabethan foundation. His rule over the Church of Westminster covered no less than forty-one years. To his predecessor, William Bill, had fallen the responsibility of organizing the new Collegiate Church, which started upon its career on May 21st, 1560. In less than a year, however, that Dean passed away. He had accomplished an immense amount of work in those short months, but the work of consolidation and systematization fell to the lot of Goodman and it took a long time to complete.

In a letter, a portion of which follows, the Dean makes an appeal to Lord Burghley with the object of procuring the Royal Assent to the Statutes of the Collegiate Church, a request which, for some unexplained reason, was never granted. He also enclosed a statement setting forth the Order of Government drawn up by Dean Bill, which he himself had maintained, much of which survives to this day.

'That he was bold to send his honour a brief declaration of the orders used in the government of the college by Dr. Bill, and him, since the last erection: that it might please him to confer the same with the statutes, and to consider thereof, as he should think good. He prayed God that might be done which might be to God's glory, the Queen's honour and the good example of the church. He wished a convenient residence of both dean and prebendaries. First, that every one might sometime preach in their own persons. Secondly, that they (both dean and prebendaries) might be present in the church to pray, as their most bounden duty was, for Her Majesty, being their founder. And thirdly, for the better order and government of the church. That unless there were daily commodity for residence in the church, as it was at Windsor and such like places (which he was sorry to speak) the residence would not be so well kept. I beseke your honour, that there may be that moderation used which shall be most convenient for all respects. Hitherto I and the company, I thank God, have agreed very brotherly, and with great quietness as any such company, I hope; I would be sorry, if by seeking to better things, dissension should grow, or unquietness. My special trust is in God, that as he hath done under Her Majesty, with motherly care to his church, and your honour, with godly zeal to virtue and learning, so he will work some good effect of this travail. Thus with my continual prayer for you and all yours, I humbly take my leave. From Westminster College this 15th of November, 1577.

Your honour's most bounden,
Gabriel Goodman.'

The Order of the Government of the College of Westminster, syns the last Erection, begonne by D. Byll, and contynued by me (Dr. Goodman) with the Assent of the Chapiter: as appeareth by Divers Decrees, Recorded in the Chapiter Book[1]

Daily prayer in King Henry the Sevenths chappel at six of the clock in the morning; and a lecture there read upon the Wednesday and Friday.

Dayly service song in the chancel of the great church, according to the order of her majesties chappel, at the usual hours; that is, upon Sundays, from eight to eleven in the forenoon. Upon Wednesdays and Fridays, and other holy days, from nine to eleven. And on other days, to begin at nine until almost eleven. Or in the afternoon, service to begin at four, and to continue until five, or after five.

A sermon every Sunday in the year, either by the dean, or one of the prebendaries, or some other for them. The dean to preach four times in the year in his own person, unless there be cause to the contrary: that is, upon Christmas-day, Easter-day, Whit-sunday, and Allhallown-day. Every prebendary to preach in their own persons upon the Sundays in their course of residence; or else some other for them.

A solemne communion ministered upon the great feasts, and every first Sunday of every month. Where by order there do communicate the dean and prebendaries present: the ministers and four of the clarks, and four of the almesmen.

Upon those days that the dean is bound to preach, either he himself doth minister the communion, or some one of the prebendaries.

[1] Strype's *Annals of the Reformation*, vol. ii, part III, App. X.

Twelve almesmen of her majesties foundation are bound to be resident; and in the church daily at service, according to her majesties order.

Every Sunday in the year, there is 40 mess of meat, for 40 poor householders of the parish, by the oversight of the chaunter of the church. Every mess being allowed there in flesh, or fish, a peny loaf in bread, and a peny in money.

Every Saturday the dean, or one of the prebendaries, whose course is to be resident, after the service, morning prayers being ended, they do call before them the ministers of their church, and the clarks, the twelve almesmen; and whom other they see cause. And there the chaunter of the church, in the book of Perditions, doth show the default of such as were absent or negligent in the week before.

Dr. Byll did appoint two square tables, and one mess to either of them: the one for himself, or whom he would call unto him. The ordinary allowance of the same for himself and six of his men, was 28s. The extraordinary as occasion served, he did further allow.

The other table, to serve the four prebendaries, whose course it was to be resident. And they bear each one for himself, and his man, 7s a week. But shortly after, by decree in chapiter, it is encreased, so that every prebendary was to allow for himself and his man, in his course of residence weekly 10s in toto. For four 40s.

In my time, for ease of charge, I and the four prebendaries have joyned together at one table, having one full mess, and sometimes more, as occasion serveth, I allowing thereto my ordinary portion, and the residentiaries theirs. The detriments are born by the college; unless there be some special occasion of some special allowance.

The school-master, and such as be officers, are allowed all the same table. The scholars do dine and sup in the hall, by the dean and prebendaries; and be allowed according to their rates: having a several buttry or pantry, and cellar by themselves.

The servants in likewise in the hall, having the reversion of the masters, and special allowance for those that are the college servants, and necessary officers, according to a necessary proportion.

Every week, commonly upon the Saturday after dinner, the charges of the week past is cast by the weekly charges of masters and servants in one book. The scholars charges in a several book by themselves.

The dean hath the general charge of all. The sub-dean under the dean to oversee the good order of the church and house. The archdeacon hath to do with the ecclesiastical jurisdiction, and such causes, either by himself, or by his official. The treasurer, one in like wise of the prebendaries, receiveth of the receit what is convenient for all charges. The steward of household who is also a prebendary, receiveth of the treasurer, or general receiver; and layeth out for the necessary charges of the house in diet and other provisions. Under him is an understeward, and the clark of the kitchen, and other officers.

Once a year the general receiver, treasurer, stewards, and all other accomptants and under-officers, make their accounts unto the auditor.

There be two teachers, the schoolmaster and the usher of the school. The scholars of the grammar be in number fourty: elected both into the house, and from the house to the universities, according to a special statute from her highness.

The scholars for their prayers in church, school, and chamber, for their teaching, for their diet in the hall, and lodging in one chamber, and for all other orders, they are served as they were in Dr. Byll's time and was appointed, by him in special statutes; very like the orders used in Eton and Winchester schools.

The master of the singing-boys hath his house, and other due allowances for himself and ten children. Whom he is charged to bring up in song, for the daily service of the church.

PARTICULARS OF MONEYS EXPENDED BY THE DEAN AND CHAPTER IN 1660 AND 1661 AMOUNTING TO £24,763. 15. 4

W.A.M. 44024

		£	s.	d.
Expenditure upon the Church.	Repairs of the Church.	2,313	9	4
	Repairs of ( ) Chapel.	295	0	0
	Copes and Vestments.	1,031	7	2
	Organ.	120	0	0
	Choir Books.	29	8	0
	Communion Plate & Silver Verge.	41	0	0
		3,930	4	6
	Repairs of the College Deanery and Prebends' Houses.	975	10	10
	Prexit to the King's Majesty Dean and Prebends' free consent.	2,000	0	0
	Redemption of Captives.	500	0	0
	Augmentation of Vicarages after the rate of eight years' purchase.	3,480	0	0
	Allowances to the purchasers.	12,705	0	0
	Allowances to Tenants for increase of rents towards maintenance of the quire and officers according to the rate of ten years purchase or thereabouts.	1,173	0	0
		£24,763	15	4

APPENDIX VII

W.A.M. 44216

THE WAX CHANDLER'S BILL FOR 1690

October 17. 1690.

Henry Preedy
Wax Chandler
in ye Strand.

Delivered to Mr. Tinker for the use of Westminster Abbey.

	£	s	d
100 pound of sixes, twelf in the pound for the use of the branches.	1	1	8
18 pound of sixteens in the pound for the use of the prebends.	5	10	6
84 pound of twenty in the pound for the use of the choir and ladys.	5	19	0
36 pound of thirty in ye pound for the use of Henry VII Chapel.	2	11	0
36 pounds of sixes lights for the use of the Dean & Sub-Dean.		17	0
12 pound of fouers for the pulpit: 7 dozen and a half for to light the Dean and Sub-Dean from Church	2	12	6
4 dozen of links for to shut up the Church dores every night		10	0
2 Whit Tapers for the Alter		10	0
8 yelow Tapers for the use of the Alter every day	1	2	8
	29	5	4
Received back 12p of 6s		17	0

April 21. 1690.   28 8 4

Received of this bill twenty pounds
by me Henry Preedy.

N.B.—This interesting document seems to indicate that during the period following the Restoration the altar candles were regularly lighted, whatever may have been the custom later on.

A new Precentor was appointed at the Restoration, Philip Tynchar or Tinker, who started the Abbey Registers. Three years later a Minor Canonry fell vacant, and John his son, though only in Deacon's Orders, was appointed to fill it. He served the Abbey as Minor Canon for nearly forty years and as Sacrist from 1673 to 1694.

THE SURVEYORS OF WESTMINSTER ABBEY

Fabric Surveyor	*College Surveyor*	*Deputy Fabric Surveyor*
	Drew Sterrill (1660–1662)	
	Robert Woodroffe (1662–1675)	
	Thomas Plucknett (1675–1690)	
	Robert Hooke (1690–1696)	
	James Broughton (1696–1710)	
Christopher Wren (March 11, 1698– Feb. 25th, 1722/3)		James Broughton (1698–1710)
	William Dickenson Feb. 19th, 1710/11– Jan. 24th, 1724/5	W.D.
Nicholas Hawksmoor March 21st, 1722/3– March 25th, 1736		Thomas Hinton Feb. 17th, 1724
John James March 27th, 1736– May 8th, 1746	John James Jan. 29th, 1724/5– May 15th, 1746	
	Thomas Hinton May 29th, 1746– Aug. 12th, 1746	
James Horne May 29th, 1746– Oct. 24th, 1752		
Henry Keene Sept. 29th, 1752– Jan. 1776	Henry Keene Oct. 31st, 1746	

James Wyatt, Jan. 22nd, 1776–Sept. 5th, 1813
Benjamin Deane Wyatt, 1813–1827
Edward Blore, 1827–1849
G. G. Scott, 1849–1878
J. L. Pearson, 1878–1897
J. T. Micklethwaite, 1897–1906
W. R. Lethaby, 1906–1928
Walter Tapper, 1928–1935
Charles Peers, 1935–1951
Stephen Dykes Bower, 1951

[I am much indebted to my friend Mr. Lawrence E. Tanner, M.V.O., F.S.A., for his help in the compilation of this list. *J.P.*]

INDEX

Page references to vol. i appear thus: **125**; *vol. ii thus: 125*; *vol. iii thus:* 125

Abady, Jacques, Mayor of West-
    minster, 177
Abbot, Peter, *130*
Abbot's Pew, 27
Abbott, Archbishop, *166*
Abyssinian Church Relic, *198*
Abyssinian Envoy, 173
Actors' Church Union, 190
Adam (King's Workman), *119*
Addison, Joseph, *130*, 146
Agincourt, Battle of, *72*
Albemarle, Earl of, 183
Albemarle, Monk, Duke of, Funeral,
    125
Alcock, Sir Walter, 173
Alexander William, Archbishop of
    Armagh, 165
Alexander III, Pope, *31*
Alfonso, *57*, *117*
Alfred, King, *32*
Allen, Prebendary, 81
Allenby, F. M. Lord, Grave, 199
Allestree, 138
Alms Dishes, **105**, 56, 58, 177
Almsmen, King's, 128
Altar Cross, **48**, **49**, 169, 171
Altarpiece, Classical, **36**, **45**, **65 ff.**,
    88 ff., 49, 136, 142
Altar Rail, **81**, **82**, **104**, **112**, 101, 105
Altar Screen, **42 ff.**, **73**, **94**, 165
Altar Steps, **28**, **73**
Amiens Cathedral, **11**, **131**, *170*
Ancaster, Earl of, Manuscripts, 90
Andrewes, Lancelot, Dean, *146*, 57, 95
Angelo, Michel, *161*
Angerstein Collection, *215*
Angoulême, Duc d', 151
Anne of Bohemia, Tomb, *63*
Anne of Cleves, Tomb, **12**, **85**, **87**, **98**,
    99, 46, 65
Anne, Queen, **65**, **69**, **73**
Annunciation and All Saints, Altar of,
    144 ff.

Annunciation depicted, **32**
Applebee, Dorothy, 121
Arbuthnot, Captain, *198*
Archdeacon of Westminster, 20
Argyll and Greenwich, Duke of,
    Tomb, 27, 128
Armil, *129*
Arms on Stalls, **193**
Armstead, H. H., Sculptor, **108**
Arnold, Matthew, Memorial, 22
Arnold, Samuel, 145
Arras Tapestries, **41**, **58**, 108; *see also*
    Tapestries
Ascension Relic, 57
Ashby, Nicholas, Bishop of Llandaff,
    144
Ashmolean Museum, *200*
Ash Wednesday Sermon, 134
Atterbury, Francis, Dean, **81**, 22, *189*,
    62, 67, 77, 138, 146, 186
Austin, Bishop of Guiana, **100**
Ayloffe, Sir Joseph, **36 ff.**, **85**

Bacon, Francis, Viscount St. Albans,
    133
Bailey, Dr. Anselm, Precentor, 65
Baker and Baylis, 63
Bancroft, Richard, Prebendary, 95
Bangorian Controversy, *189*
Baptist Denomination, 48
Baptistery, 22, 42
Barbados, Bishop of, *100*, 157
Barham, H.M.S., 199
Barlow, William, Prebendary, 89
Barlowe, William, Prebendary, 97
Barrow, Dr. Isaac, 35, 127
Basire, **37**
Basset, Lord Philip, *41*
Bath, Earl of, 10, 18, 148
Bath, Order of the, **135**, *172*, *189 ff.*,
    70, 180, 192, 196
Battell, William, Precentor, 140
Batterby, Receiver-General, 63

Bayeux Cathedral, 48, 181
Bayne, Captain William, Memorial, 41
Beaconsfield, Earl of, **191**
Beadle, 67
Beaufort, Lady Margaret, *139*, *210*, 142, 153
Becket, Thomas, Archbishop, *31*
Belfast Cathedral, 40
Bell, Edward, 79
Bell, Prebendary, **139**, *193*
Bells, 185 ff.
Belton, **67**
Bendigo Cathedral, 39
Benedictine Abbeys, **159**
Benedictine Rule, **5**
Benedictine Monks, *80*, *89*, 87, 88
Bennett, Mrs. Julian, Mayoress of Westminster, 25
Benson, E. W., Archbishop, *191*, *128*, 82
Benson, Richard, Abbot and Dean, *76*, *78*
Berkeley, Gilbert, Bishop of Bath and Wells, 88
Bernasconi, **50**, **94** ff., **152**, 37, 72
Berri, Duc de, 151
Bill, William, Dean, **115**, *89*, 89
Birch, Peter, Prebendary, 59, 65, 133, 135
Bishops, Consecration of, **100**, **167**, *188*, 156 ff., *see also under names of Bishops concerned*
Black Rood of Scotland, 26
Blacking, W. H. Randoll, *114*, 191
Blair, Dr. John, Prebendary, **139**, 144
Blair, Captain William, Memorial, 41
Blake, William, **37**, **38**
Blessed Virgin, Altar of, 2
Blomberg, F. W., Prebendary, 81
Blood, Precious; Relic, *56*
Blore, Edward, **13**, **14**, **101**, **102**, **124**, **156**, **158** ff., **169**, **174**, **182**, *13*, *15*, *16*, *139*, 38, 47, 50
Blount, George L., Funeral, 145
Blow, Detmar, *211*
Blow, John, *10*
Blück, B., picture by, 34, 36
Body, Canon George, 163
Bohemian Visitors, *72*

Bond, Francis, quoted, **4**, *4*, *160*, 1, 14, 17, 23, 196
Bosworth Field, Battle of, *214*
Bouchier, Lord, Tomb, 18, 53
Boughton Tapestries, 85
Bourges Cathedral, **11**
Bradley, Dean, 165, 168, 179
Brayley, E. H., *140*
Brayley, G. W., 27
Bridge, Sir Frederick, **184**, *16*, *129*, 165, 172
Bridgwater, **93**
Brighton, St. Paul's Church, 160
Broadway Chapel, Westminster, 149
Bromle, William, 19
Bromley, Widows' College, 148
Brooks, Bishop Philips, 165
Broughton, James, **72**
Brown, H., *49*
Browning, Robert, Funeral, 167
Bruges, Sir W., Bequest, 64
Buckeridge, Bishop, 96
Buckingham Palace Chapel Plate, 65
Buckinghamshire, Duke of, Funeral, 80
Buckland, Dean, **102**, **157**, **166**, **167**, **173**, **182**, 155
Bulkeley, Dr., Prebendary, 100
Burges, William, **2**, **40**, *34*, *60*, *120*, *136*
Burglary, *92*, *180*
Burgundy, Duke of, *145*
Burleigh, Lord, *164*, *165*, 90, 94
Burne-Jones, Sir Edward, 167
Burnham-on-Sea, St. Andrew's Church, **91**
Bury St. Edmunds Abbey, **58**
Bury St. Edmunds, Abbot of, **47**
Busby, Dr., Prebendary, **60**, **127**, **172**, 58, 108, 111, 117, 130, 138
Butler, Bishop, 137, 144
Butterfield, William, 73

Calais, Church of Our Lady, **79**
Caldecote, Jonas, Minor Canon, 115
Cambridge Camden Society, **165**, **166**, **173**, **181**
Cambridge, King's College Chapel, *158*, *184*

Page references to vol. i appear thus: **125**;

Cambridge, Life of St. Edward the Confessor, *52*
Camden, William, **20**, *167*
Campan de Cavelli, Marquise, *104*
Canada, Dominion of, 194
Canaletto, Picture by, *205*
Candelabra, 194; *see also* Chandeliers
Candlesticks, **49**, **54**, **61**, **128**, 59 ff., 119, 121, 167, 178
Canonization of St. Edward the Confessor, *31*
Canterbury Cathedral, **11**, *1*, *45*, *198*, 47
Carey, Henry, Baron Hunsdon, **59**
Carey, William, 48
Carleton, George, Precentor, 65
Carnegie, W. H., Sub-dean, *24*
Caroë, W. D., 70, 190
Carol Services, 183, 197
Caroline, Princess, 148
Carpets, Sanctuary, **97**, **111**, **117**, 72, 167
Cartulary, 24
Cary, Mr., 122
Cassocks, 129, 167, 169
Catafalque, **48**
Catherine of Aragon, Queen, 45
Catherine of Valois, Queen, *144 ff.*
Catling, George, Verger, 42, 65
Causton, Dr., Prebendary, 81
Cavallini, **14**
Cawagium Regis, **12**
Cellini, Benvenuto, **163**
Cementarius, **25**
Cerdic, House of, *28*
Chair of King Edward, *see* Edward I
Chair of State, *129*
Chalices, 55, 57, 63
Champneys, Weldon, Precentor, 65
Chandeliers, **60**, **130**, **188**, 61, 121; *see also* Candelabra
Chantrey, Sir Francis, **8**, *2*, *138*, **103**, **122**, **136 ff.**
Chantries, Royal, *154*
Chantry of Henry V, **42**, 65
Chapel of the Pyx, 51
Chapel Royal, **185**, 116; *see also* Buckingham Palace and St. James's Palace

Chapels: Henry VII's, *4*, *149 ff.*, 141
Holy Cross, *see* Holy Cross Altar, and Chapel of St. George
Islip, **13**, *169*
Lady, *2*, *33*, *146*, *158*
My Lady Margaret's, 60, 70, 86
St. Benedict, 52
St. Blaise, 128
St. Catherine, 52
St. Edmund, **56**
St. Edward, *3*, *28 ff.*, 53, 177
St. Faith, **81**, **99**, **131**, *141*, 52, 69, 83, 85, 86, 104, 128, 169
St. George, 42, 192, 199
St. Helena, *3*
St. John Baptist, *68*, 53
St. John Evangelist, 8
St. Nicholas, 19
St. Paul, 132
St. Saviour, *150*, *158*
Chapman, Christopher, Lay-vicar, 113
Chapter House, 51, 53
Charing Cross, *182*
Charles I, *187*, 102
Charles II, **63**, *147*
Charles II, Coronation, **61**, *191*, 33, 64, 74, 83, 119
Charles VI of France, *144*
Charles X, 151
Cheapside Cross, *182*
Cheney, Richard, Prebendary, 89
Chertsey Abbey, *156*
Chester, Sir William Dawes, Bishop of, *188*
Chester Cathedral, *45*
Chichester, Simon Patrick, Prebendary and Bishop of, 99
Chipping Campden, Church of St. James, 176
Choir, **121 ff.**, **183**, *1*, 131, 150, 154
Choir, Destruction of, **81**, **131 ff.**
Choir Dinner, 140
Choir School, 193
Choir Stalls, **121**, **123 ff.**, **160**, **173 ff.**, **193**
Choristers, **175**, **187**, 116, 126, 165
Christchurch Priory, Screen, **44**, 67
Christmas Decorations, 131

vol. ii thus: 125; *vol. iii thus:* 125

Christmas, *see* Carol Service, Midnight Communion, Crib
Cifaccio, **68**
Clare, Arms of, 52
Clarke, Kenneth, quoted, **166**
Clayton and Bell, **107**
Clayton, Rev. P. B., 51
Clement IV, Pope, *51*
Clement XIII, Pope, *21*
Close, Francis, Dean of Carlisle, **165**
Close Rolls, *2*
Coffin of St. Edward the Confessor, *105*
Colchester, Abbot, 19
Coldwell, Elizabeth, 79
Cole, T., Picture by, *8*
Coleridge, Edward, 157
Collection Box, *11*
College Garden, **78**
Colobium Sindonis, *129*
Colour Sequence, 180
Comper, Sir J. Ninian, 25, 26
Congreve, William, 133
Consecration of Bishops, **100**, **167**, *188*, 156 ff.
Consistory Court, *20*, 42
Constantine, Emperor, 26
Consuetudines of Abbot Ware, **7**, *2*, 180
Convocation, *166*, *189*, 3
Cooke, Captain, 199
Cooke, Dr. Benjamin, **145**, 145
Cooperculum, *45*, *55*
Cooptarium, *55*
Cope, Sir John, Sub-dean, **139**
Copes, *31*, 74 ff., 119, 182
Copley, John, 90
Cornets, use of, 116
Cornwall, Captain, Memorial, *21*
Cornwall, Earl of, *43*, 52
Cornwallis, James, Prebendary, **139**
Corona, **11**, 121
Coronation Chair, *see* Edward I
Coronations, **104**, *90*, 44, 65, 71, 74, 186, 196; *see also under names of Sovereigns*
Cosin, John, Bishop, 34, 78, 99
Cosmati School, **18**
Covent Garden, St. Paul's Church, 98

Cowper, William, Memorial, *22*
Cox, James Bell, 82
Cox, Richard, Dean, *78*
Coysevox, 26
Craggs, James, Monument, *21*, *23*, *25*
Crane, Dr., Prebendary, **139**
Cranmer, Archbishop, 33, 45
Creighton, Mandell, Bishop of London, 83
Crespion, Stephen, Precentor, *100*, *188*
Cretton, Roger, 3
Crewe, Earl (afterwards Marquess) of, **49**, 171
Crib, Christmas, 194
Croft, Dr. William, *10*
Cross, Processional, 173 ff.
Crown of Thorns, Relic, 57
Cromwell, Oliver, *126*
Cromwell, Thomas, 75
Cromwellians, **51**
Crouchback, Edmund, Tomb, **17**, **29**, **36**, **74**, **79**, **114**, 183
Crozier, Legend of St. Wulfstan's, 29
Crucifix, 4
Crucifixion depicted in mural painting, 31
Crusaders, Order of, *114*
Cundy, Dr. H. G., **185**
Cures at the Shrine, **54**
Curtys, Sir Thomas, Alderman, 91
Customary of Abbot Ware, 45
Czar Nicholas of Russia, Coronation, 83

Dakins, Dr. W. W., Precentor, 42, 65, 144
Damascus Church Relic, 198
Danegeld, 69
Danes, Skins of, 28
Danish Church, Wellclose Square, **69**
Dante, 43
Dart, John, **26**, **38**, **58**, **74**, *8*, *9*, *168*, *24*, *104*, *142*
Davidson, Randall T., Archbishop of Canterbury, 185
Dawes, Sir William, Bishop, *188*, 156
Deanery, 86, 193
Decian Persecution, 70

Declaration of Indulgence, *99*
De Grasse, Admiral, 41
Deist Controversy, 5
de Labillière, Bishop, Dean, 156, 193
Delahay Street Chapel, 149
Demons' Door, *4*, 23
de Montpensier, Albert, Duc, 150
de Saravia, Adrian, Prebendary, 97
Descent from the Cross depicted, 86
de Ware, Richard, Abbot, **25**
Dickson, W. E., 153
Dirge, **50**
Dolben, John, Dean, **63**, 137
Dolben, Katherine, 122
Dolben, William, 132
Dominicans, 57
Don, Alan Campbell, Dean, 12
Doughty, John, Prebendary, 132
Doughty, Katherine, 132
Downham, William, Bishop, Pre-
  bendary, 89
Dryden, John, Monument, 22
Dunstaffnage Castle, *117*
Dunstan, St., **58**
Dupe, Cyril, 64
Dürer, Albert, *170*
Durham Cathedral, **172**, *45*, 9, 78,
  130, 181

Earles, John, Dean, **60**, 74, 113, 118,
  126
East Herling, Norfolk, *214*
Easton, Hugh, 12
Ecclesiological Society, **165**
Edgar, King, **58**
Edgson, Walter S., 68
Edinburgh, St. Giles', 202
Edith, Queen, *14*, *42*
Edmund, King, *39*
Edward the Confessor, **3**, **32**, **58**, *14*,
  29 ff., *145*, 202
Edward the Confessor's Chapel, **75**,
  28 ff.
Edward the Confessor's Shrine, **86**,
  119, **137**, *32 ff.*
Edward I, **31**, *14*, *74*, *116 ff.*
— Chair of, **17**, *116 ff.*
— Tomb, 11
Edward II, 47, 58

Edward III, *58*, *123*, 21
Edward IV, **30**, 67, *178*, 15
Edward V, 15
Edward VI, 5, *167*, *181*, 33, 45,
  64
Edward VII, **113**, *111*, *198*, 202, 40,
  44, 72, *172*
Edward, son of Otho, clerk, *34*
Edward of Westminster, *2*
Edwards, Howell Holland, Prebend-
  ary, 73, 81
Eleanor of Castile, Tomb, **8**, **103**, *139*,
  29, 50, 53
Eleanor of Provence, *52*
Eldon, Viscount, 145
Elfride or Elfryd, Thomas, *210*, 181
Elgin, 7th Earl of, **28**
Elgin, 9th Earl of, **28**, 166
Elizabeth, Queen, 5, *87*, *153*, 23, 87,
  142
— Tomb, 139
Elizabeth (Windsor), Queen, *114*
Elizabeth Wydville, **68**
Elizabeth of York, Queen, *150*
Ely, Thomas Turton, Dean, Bishop
  of, **157**
Emma, Queen, 69
Empire Stalls, 195
Ephesus, Seven Sleepers of, 70
Esher, Viscount, 172
Essex, James, *135*
Estney, Abbot, 5, 182
— Tomb, **83**, 7
Ethelgoda, Queen, **29**
Ethelred the Unready, 69
Evelyn, John, **65**, **67**, **76**, *98*
Evreux, *55*, 48

Farmer and Brindley, *109*, 43
Farrar, F. W., Canon, **191**, 164
Fascet, George, Abbot, 12
Feckenham, John Howman of, Abbot,
  55, *50*, *24*, *80 ff.*, *106*, *108*, 68, 87,
  91
Fell, Dr., 138
Feretory, *44*, *85*
Ferrer, Nicholas, *181*
Fife, Earls of, *117*
Fisher, Admiral Lord, Funeral, 191

vol. ii thus: *125*; *vol. iii thus:* 125

Fisher, Thomas, Bishop of Rochester, *150*

Fitzroy, Lord Henry, Prebendary, 81

Flagons, 55, 58

Flower, Barnard, *184*

Font, *22*

Foundation Day, 186

Franklin, Sir John, Monument, 4

Frederick II, Emperor, 52

Fredericton Cathedral, New Brunswick, 73

French Sermon, 162

Friend, Dr., Prebendary, 26

Froissart, 14

Frontals, 68, 191

Funerals, 145, 188

Furse, Archdeacon, 179

Fynes-Clinton, Dr., Prebendary, 81

Garter, Order of the, *190, 202*

Gastaway, Thomas, *182*

Gates, Choir, *12*, 48

Gayfere (Clerk of Works), **99**

George I, *173, 191,* 79

George II, Coronation, **81,** 72

— Funeral, **86,** 23, 80, 147, 196

George III, *147,* 73

— Coronation, **132,** 72

George IV, Coronation, **88, 143** n., **155,** *131,* 29, 36, 76, 77, 80

George V, *205,* 63

— Coronation, 34, 62, 176

George VI, *114,* 178, 184

George of Denmark, Prince, 69

George, Duke of Kent, 184

Gethin, Dame Grace, 133

Gethin, Sir Richard, 133

Gibbons, Christopher, 116

Gibbons, Grinling, **26, 66, 68, 69, 70, 71, 76**

Gibbons, Orlando, 101

Gibbs, James, 2, 26

Gibraltar, Diocese of, Centenary, 194

Gifford, Dr. Bonaventura, **67**

Gilbert, Archbishop of York, 47

Girdle of Our Lady, *67*

Gladstone, William Ewart, 148, 153, 190

Gloucester, Thomas Duke of, Tomb, 61

Gluckstein, Sir Samuel, Alderman, **193**

Goddard, Guilon, 35

Godfree, Richard, **87**

Godolphin, Earl, Lord Treasurer, **71**

Godwin, Earl, **169**

Goodenough, Dr., **155**

Goodman, Gabriel, Dean, **56, 153,** 65, 68, 90, 134, 186

Gore, Charles, Canon, **178,** *113,* 134, 164, 168, 179, 197

Gospel Lectern, **50,** 45, 194

Goss, 62

Gough's 'Sepulchral Monuments', **34**

Gowns, 129

Gray, George Kruger, 68

Gray, Robert, Bishop of Cape Town, 47, 157

Great Exhibition, 162

Greatorex, Thomas, 145

Green, Dan William (or Wyllyam), *56, 73, 75*

Greenwich, 88

Greet, Sir Philip Ben, 190

Grey, Lord, **154**

Grey, Lady Jane, *79,* 88

Grimes, Sir John, 100

Grindal, Archbishop, *6,* 79

Grosvenor, Countess, *211*

Gunton, Symon, *99, 122*

Hacket, John, Bishop, 96

Hackett, Maria, 154

Hacombleyn, Dr. Robert, *184*

Haddon Hall Tapestries, 85

Hakewill, John, **84**

Hakluyt, Richard, Prebendary, 97

Hampton Court, **70,** 64, 84

Handel, George Frederic, 25

Harding, John, Lay-vicar, 113

Hardyman, John, Prebendary, **56,** *89, 167, 211,* 89

Hare, Sir John, 190

Harley, Sir Robert, *182, 210,* 104, 109, 117

Harley, Robert, Earl of Oxford, **26**

Harpedon, Sir John, Tomb, 7

Harris, Renatus, **66**

Page references to vol. i appear thus: **125;**

Hart, Charles, *115*
Harvey, Miss Mary, **22**
Hatton, Sir Christopher, Tomb, 10
Havering-atte-Bower, *70*
Haveus, Theodore, **98**
Hawksmoor, Nicholas, *5, 10,* 50
Hay-Drummond, Hon. Robert, Prebendary, **52**
Hayter, Dr. Thomas, Bishop of London, **133, ʳ34**
Hearse-cloth, 189, 190
Heath, Nicholas, Archbishop of York, *88*
Heath, Sir Thomas, 133
Heber, Richard, Bishop, 157
Heisonbittle, John, **66**
Henry II, **54**
Henry III, **3, 7, 12, 28, 43, 177,** *2, 4, 14, 32 ff.,* *61,* 32, 53, 171
Henry IV, *124*
Henry V, *63*
Henry V's Chantry, **42, 103, 122, 136 ff.,** *65*
Henry VI, **1,** *62, 146, 151, 171*
Henry VII, **122,** *58, 145, 149 ff.,* *158, 160, 184, 209,* 16, 171
Henry VIII, **54,** *77, 149 ff.,* *168,* 45
Henry of Winchester, or Wynchester, *73*
Herbert, George, Memorial, **22**
Hertford, Frances, Countess of, 22, 52
Hervey, Lord, *179*
Heylin, Peter, Prebendary, 35, 102, 103, 112
Heynes, Simon, Treasurer, **54,** 45, 47
Heywood, Thomas, Lay-vicar, 113
Heywood, William, Prebendary, 113
High Altar, **10 ff., 48, 63, 98, 108, 122,** *1,* 64, 119, 121
High Commissioners' Stalls, 195
Hill, John, Cornet player, 116
Hills, George, Bishop of British Columbia, **103**
Hoadley, Bishop, *179*
Hoare, Dr., Prebendary, **139**
Holbein, **22,** 47
Hollar, Wenceslaus, **35, 61,** *33,* 64, 119
Hollingbourne, All Saints' Church, 134

vol. ii thus: 125; vol. iii thus: 125

Holy Cross Altar, **5,** *1, 3, 4,* 6, *25,* 42, 53, 192, 198
— Relic, *169*
Holy Saviour, Altar of the, *150*
Holy Trinity, Altar of the, *2, 19,* 56
Hook, Dr., 154
Hooper, William, Minor Canon, 113
Hope, Alexander J. B. Beresford, 125
Hope, Sir William St. John, 48
Horsley, Samuel, Bishop and Dean, 37
Howard, F. E., 191
Howley, William, Archbishop of Canterbury, *128*
Hughes, Sarah, 58, 124
Hugolin, **58,** 69
Hunsdon, Henry Carey, Baron, Funeral, **59**
— Tomb, 53
Hutton, William, Minor Canon, 106, 108

Imperial Mantle, *129*
Inglis, Charles, Bishop, 156
Innocent II, Pope, *30*
Iowa, Bishop of, 27
Ireland, John, Dean, **100,** *103,* **153,** *156, 138, 139,* 77, 144, *150,* 152, 155
Isabella, Queen, *123*
Islip Chapel, **13,** *169*
Islip, John, Abbot, **122,** *20, 27, 150, 156, 160,* 4, 7, 16, 42, 185
Islip Roll, **57, 107, 123,** 8, 45

Jack, George, **115**
James I, Coronation, *125,* 71, 98
— Coffin, *195*
James II, **65, 69**
— Coronation, **61, 64, 126,** *90, 98,* 83, 119
James, John, 50
James, Dr. Montagu Rhodes, **15,** *52,* 68
James, Sir Walter, 40
Jeffries, Lord, 112
Jericho Parlour, *90,* 96, 109
Jerusalem Chamber, **35, 87, 199,** *83,* 128, 160
Jesus Anthems and Masses, 9

Jeune, Francis, Bishop of Peter-borough, 162
John of Eltham, Prince, Tomb, 21
John of St. Omer, 32
John of Thirske, *62, 65*
John of Waltham, Bishop of Salisbury, *61*
Johnson, Roger, *137*
Jones, Inigo, **92**
Jones, Dr. Walter, Prebendary, 55
Jubilee of Queen Victoria, *128*, 80, 81, 83
Julius III, Pope, *125*

Kahn, Peter, **116**
Katherine of Aragon, Queen, 45
Katherine de Valois, Queen, *144 ff.*
Keble, John, 163
— Memorial, *22*
Kedyngton, Richard de, Abbot, **31**
Keene, Henry, **84, 87, 132, 145, 173**, *13, 18*, 36, 142, 160
Keeper of the Clock, *115*
Keeper of the Shrine, *47*
Kenneth II, King of Scotland, *117*
Kennion, Bishop of Bath and Wells, 44
Kent, Duke and Duchess of, *113*, 184
Kent, William, *12*
Kettlewell, Thomas, 66
Killigrew, Dr. Henry, Prebendary, *185*, 138
Kimber, S. G., sculptor, *22*
King, Walker, Bishop of Rochester, **90**
King's Door, **44, 51, 96**, 67
King's Evil, *47*
King's Scholars, **175**
Kingsley, Charles, Canon, 164
Kinnoul, Lord, **52**
Kipling, Rudyard, *26*
Kirton, Edward, Abbot, 2
Kitchener, Earl, Memorial, *212*
Kneller, Sir Godfrey, Monument, *3*
Knight, Dr. Samuel, Archdeacon, *100*
Knight, F. W., *26*
Knights of the Bath, *see* Order of the Bath
Knipe, Dr., Prebendary, 58
Königsstuhl, *118*
Krutitsky, Metropolitan, 195

Lamb, James, Prebendary, 114
Lambeth Conference, 1908, **113**
Lambeth Palace Chapel, **104,** 156
Lancaster, Aveline Countess of, Tomb, **87**
Laney, William, Prebendary, 113
Lanfranc, Archbishop of Canterbury, *29*
Lang, Cosmo Gordon, Archbishop of Canterbury, 34
Langham, Simon, Tomb, 53
Langley, Thomas, 59
Langres Cathedral, **52**
Lantern, **148,** 193
Lascelles, Viscount, 184
Laud, William, Archbishop of Canterbury and Prebendary, **59,** 90, *181*, 100
Laurentius, Abbot, *30*
Lay-vicars, **175,** 126, 194
Lectern, Gospel, 194
Lecterns, Medieval, **54, 122, 123**
Lee of Fareham, Viscount, *209*
Legrix, John, 67
Le Keux, Picture, 36
Lent Lectures, 134
Lenten Hangings, 187
Lia-Fail, *117 ff.*
Lichfield Cathedral, 2
Liddon, Dr. H. P., Canon of St. Paul's, 163
Linsell, Augustine, *181*
Litany Cloth, 43
Litany Desk, **129,** 43, 130
Litlington (or Litlyngton), Nicholas, Abbot, 24, 171, 188
Little Cloister, *98*, 193
Little Gidding, *182*
Littlemore, Oxon., **99**
Liverpool Cathedral, **3**
Liverpool, St. Margaret's Church, 82
Llewellyn, Prince of Wales, 57
Lloyd, Edward, Precentor, 65
London, John, 12
Lords, House of, **161**, 144, 195
Lottery, 93
Louis XIV, 26
Louis XVI, 37
Louis XVIII, 151

Page references to vol. i appear thus: **125**;

Lovell, Gregory, *214*
Lovell, Sir Thomas, *213*
Lyons, Dan Thomas, *74*

Mace, 67
McIlvaine, C. P., Bishop, 28
Maclagan, Archbishop, 83
Magdala, *198*
Makunan, Ras, Abyssinian Envoy, 173
Manners, Lord Robert, Memorial, 41
Margaret, Statue of St., *153*
Marie Josephine Louise de Savoie et de Lille, Queen, Funeral, 151
Marina, Princess, 184
Marlborough, Duchess of, *190*
Marlborough, Duke of, Funeral, *189*
Marriott, Prebendary, **139**
Marshall, Stephen, Presbyterian Minister, 107
Mary of Modena (Maria Beatrice d'Este), Queen, **65**, *105*
Mary, Princess, 184
Mary, Queen, *54*, *78*, *87*, *125*, *153*, 87
Mary, Queen of Scots, Tomb, *139*
Mass, Daily, 7
Mathon, 59
Matilda, Queen, Grave, *42*
Maundy, Royal, 183
May, William, Dean of St. Paul's, 89
Mayor of Westminster, **193**, 177
Medley, John, Bishop of Fredericton, 73
Mensa, *see* Annunciation and All Saints
Merrill, Thomas, Verger, 66
Michelangelo, *161*
Micklethwaite, J. T., **112**, *4*, *76*, *103*, *111*, 16, 44
Middleton, Dr. Conyers, 5
Middleton, Dr. J. H., *200*
Middleton, Thomas F., Bishop of Calcutta, 156
Midnight Communion, 201
Milan, *169*
Milman, Rev., Prebendary, **155**, *139*, *152*, *161*, 164
Millyng, Abbot, 15
Misericordes, *174*
Monk, James H., Bishop, **158**, 158
Monk, General, Funeral, 189

Montague, Captain, Monument, **3**
Montaigne, George, Dean, 99
Montfort, Simon de, *43*
Montpensier, Duc de, 151
Morley, Thomas, 111
Morris Looms, **41**
Mortimer's Cross, Battle of, **30**
Mosaic, **18**, **107**, **59**, *82*, *85*; *see also* Pavement
Mothers' Union, 25
Moulton, John, 91
Muniment Room, **12** n., 51, 55
Mural Paintings, 13, 31
Murrimouth, John, 22
Muscovy, Duke of, *81*
Music Festivals, 164

Napoleon, *118*
National Society's Training College, 154
Nativity, Picture of, *165*
Needham, John, Receiver-General, 59
Neile, Richard, Dean, **57**, **98**, **127**, **129**, **148**, 8, 22 n., *111*, *71*, *97*, *100*, *109*
Nelham, Edmund, Minor Canon, 106
Newcastle, Duke of, Monument, 2
Newman, John H., **99**
Newton, Sir Isaac, Monument, *4*, *12*
Newton, Thomas, Bishop of Bristol, **85**
New Westminster, British Columbia, *201*
Neyt, **47**
Nicene Celebrations, 185
Nicholas II, Czar, 82, 83
Nicholas, Matthew, Prebendary, 113
Nightingale, Lady Elizabeth, Monument, 3
Nixon, Bishop of Van Diemen's Land, *100*
Nollekens, Joseph, Sculptor, *22*, 41
Norman Undercroft, *11*
Norris, Dr. William F., Dean, *211*, 183, 192
North Transept Door, **8**, 196
Northampton, John, Monk, *12*
Northampton, Treaty of, *123*
Northumberland, Duchess of, Funeral, *147*

vol. ii thus: 125; vol. iii thus: 125

Nowell, Alexander, Prebendary, 79, 89

Nye, Philip, Presbyterian Minister, 107

Odoricus, Master Workman, **20**, *38*, *50*, *60*

Ogilby, John, 83, 119

Oglethorpe, Bishop of Carlisle, *88*

Oil, Consecrated, *124*

Opus Alexandrinum, **122**, *59*

Organ, **125**, **129**, **140**, **184**, *2*, *9 ff.*, *36*, *49*, *95*, *105*, *115*, *125*, *129*, *140*, *145*, *155*, *160*, *165*

Organ Loft, 108, 129

Organists' place in Quire, 129

Orthodox Church, 185, 195

Osbaldstone, Lambert, Prebendary, 107 ff., 110

Ostia Presbyterii, **121**, *1*

Owen, John, Dean of Christ Church, 112

Oxford, All Souls College, 67

Oxford, Christ Church, 130

Oxford, Magdalen College, 126

Oxford, Lord, **26**

Oxford Movement, **154**, *111*

Paget, Francis, Bishop, 44

Pall over Shrine, *112*

— Funeral, 189, 190

Palm Sunday Procession, 27

Palmer, James, 2

Palmer, Samuel, **38**

Pannemaker, William, 84

Paris, Matthew, *33*, *52*, *54*, *57*

Parker, Archbishop, 6, 7, 88

Parkes, Lord Chancellor, 5

Parliament Robe, *129*

Parratt, Sir Walter, 172

Parry, Bishop of Barbados, **100**

Parry, Sir Hubert, 172

Parry, Sir Thomas, 92

Passion Music, 164

Patricia of Connaught, Princess, 184

Patrick, Symon or Simon, Bishop, Prebendary, *98*, *99*, 130, 134

Pavement, **11**, **18 ff.**, **73**, **101**, **112**, **156**, *38*, *59*, *102*, *172*, 22, 51, 139, 167

Pawning of Jewels, *40*

Pead, Duell, 41

Pearce, Zachary, Dean, **10**, **82**, **83**, **86**, **133**, **134**, **158**, *5*, *10*, 147, 156

Pearson, J. L., **103**, *17*, 166

Pecksall, Sir Robert, **56**, **59**

Peculiar, *20*

Peel, Sir Robert, 155

Pegram, Bertram, *26*

Pelling, Prebendary, 59, 79

Pembroke, Mary Countess of, 13

Pembroke, Earl of, Tomb, **83**

Pepys, Samuel, *147*, 34, 114

Percy, Lady Charlotte, Funeral, 21

Percy, Elizabeth, Duchess of Northumberland, Tomb, *147*

Perkins, Humphrey, Prebendary, 89

Perrin, W. W., Bishop, 190

Perry, C., Bishop, 157

Persano, Giovanni de, 46

Persano, Marquis, 46

Peter, St., depicted, **33**

Peter of Hispania, 32

Peter the Roman Citizen, *38*, *50*, *60*

Pew, Royal, **12**

Pews, **127**

Philip de Lewesham, Abbot, 36

Philippa of Hainault, Queen, Tomb, **17**

Piccadilly, St. James's Church, **70**

Pierce, Dr., Precentor, 106

Pilgrims, **43**, *1*

Pindar, Sir Paul, **63**, 86

Pipe Roll, *61*

Pitt, William, Statue of, **169**

Plague, *88*

Plucknett, Thomas, 62, 66

Plumer, Field-Marshal Lord, 199

Pole, Cardinal, *80*, *88*

Poole, Henry, *106*, *52*

Pope, Alexander, *21*, 127

Porphyry, *38*, *85*

Porter's Staff, 67

Portman, Richard, Organist, 113

Prayer-Books for Altar, **101**

Primrose, Lady Margaret, **49**

Prince Regent, *see* Regent

Page references to vol. i appear thus: **125**;

Princess Royal, 115
Prior, Matthew, 26
— Monument, 24
Privy Council, *156, 199*
Procession, Sunday, 90, 181 ff.
Public Worship Regulation Act, 82
Pugin, A. W., **101**
Pulpit, 33
Pulpit Cloth, **82**
Pulpitum, **4, 121, 123** ff., **140, 159,**
  164, 169
Pulteney, William, M.P., 10
Purbeck Marble, **23,** *107,* 2
Purcell, Henry, Organist, *10, 17*
— Monument, *130*
Purcell, Henry, the Elder, 116
Pusey, Dr. E. B., 163
Pyx, Hanging, **52**

Quebec Cathedral, 73
Queen Anne's Gate Chapel, 149
Queen's Door, **45, 51, 96,** *68*
Quellin, Arnold, **66**

Ragged Regiment, **13**
Ramsay, the Hon. Alexander, 184
Receiver-General, **80**
Red Cross Society, British, 194
Redying, John, *3*
Reeve, Thomas N., 42
Refectory, 52
Reform Movement, 154
Reformers, **120**
Regalia, **90,** 103, 105
Regent, Prince, **88,** *195*
Relics, Altar of, *56*
Renaissance work, **160,** *51, 84,* 9
Rennell, Rev. Dr., 157
Repton, Rev. Edward, Prebendary, 39
Reredos, **10,** *46*
Restoration, The, **60**
Retabulum, **11, 13** ff., **51**
Revisers of the Bible, *199*
Rheims Cathedral, 130
Ricasoli, Rinaldo de', Florentine Con-
  sul, *162*
Richard II, **12** (portrait), **87, 126, 145,**
  58, 74, 14, 184
— Sarcophagus, *63*

vol. ii thus: 125; vol. iii thus: 125

Richard III, *124*
Richard of Berkyng, Abbot, **57,** 108
Richard de Crockesley, Abbot, **36**
Richard of Cirencester, *3*
Richard de Merston, Prior, 24
Richard de Ware, Abbot, *37, 48, 55,*
  60, 180
Richardson, John, Bishop, *73*
Richelieu, Cardinal, 86
Richmond, Duchess of, *187*
Richmond, Duke of, *187*
Richmond, George, **103**
Riddels, **11,** *46*
Robert, Bishop of Bath and Wells,
  121
Robert, Patriarch of Jerusalem, *56*
Robessart, Ludovic, Tomb, 18
Robinson, Dr. J. Armitage, Dean, **40,**
  53, 113, *128, 14, 26, 96,* 128, 134,
  179
Robinson, Sir J. C., *215*
Rochester, Thomas Fisher, Bishop of,
  150
Rodney, Sir George, 41
Rome, Church of St. Prassede, *60*
Rood, **12, 51, 54, 120, 121,** *19, 67*
Rood Screen, **5, 123,** *1 ff.*
Rosebery, Earl of, **49,** 169, 171
Roubilliac, 3, 27
Rouen Cathedral, **11, 124,** 48, 181
Rovezzano, Benedetto da, *163*
Rowe, John, Independent Minister,
  114
Royal Robe of Purple Velvet, *129*
Rundell and Bridge, Goldsmiths, *140*
Ruff, 81
Russian Church, 195
Rusticus, Mercurius, *see* Ryves
Ruthall, Thomas, Bishop, 12, 14
Ruthin, 90
Rutland, John, 184
Ryle, Dr. H. E., Dean, **115, 187, 193,**
  113, 202, 36, 63, 130, 177, 180,
  187, 191
Rysbrack, *12,* 26
Ryves, Bruno, *181,* 105

Sacristy Doorway, *4,* 23
St. Albans Abbey, Screen, **44,** *1, 67*

St. Albans Shrine, *45, 58*
St. Andrew, Statue of, 13
St. Athanasius' Tooth, 57
St. Bartholomew's, Smithfield, *184*
St. Benedict, 70
— Head, 21
— Skull, *58*
St. Candida, *87*
St. Catherine of Alexandria, Statue of, *212*
St. Christopher's Chapel, *3*
— Depicted, 25
St. Columba, *117*
St. Cuthbert, Shrine of, *45*
St. Denys, *153*
St. Edmund's Chapel, **56**
— Statue, **39**
St. Edward's Chapel, *3*
St. Erasmus, 15, 16
St. Etheldreda, Shrine of, *45*
St. Faith's Chapel, **81, 99, 131**
St. George, Relic of, *169*
St. Giles, *153*
St. Helena depicted, *26*
— Altar, *3*
St. James's, Piccadilly, **70**
St. James's Palace, **185**, 65, 84, 141
St. John's Westminster, 20, 149
St. John Evangelist, Statue of, *47, 53*
— Depicted, **32**, *85*
St. John of Jerusalem, Order of, 194
St. Margaret depicted, *26*
— Statue of, *153, 210, 212*
St. Margaret's Westminster, *4, 20, 205, 7, 51,* 100, 106, *149,* 152, 200
St. Margaret and St. John Volunteers, 151
St. Martin-in-the-Fields, 10
St. Mary, Altar of, *19*
St. Mary's, Vincent Square, Westminster, **155**
St. Mary Hawnes, 73
St. Michael, Figure of, *25*
St. Michael and St. George, Order of, *202*
St. Ouen of Rouen, 48
St. Paul's Cathedral, London, **3**, *85,* **185,** *202,* 48, 152
St. Paul's Ecclesiological Society, 64

St. Peter, depicted, 85
— Statue of, 13
St. Saviour, Chapel of, *158*
St. Stephen's Church, *15*
— Palace of, *205*
St. Swithun, Shrine of, *45*
St. Sylvester, Arm of, 57
St. Taurin, Shrine of, *55*
St. Thomas, 57
— Painting, 25
St. Thomas of Canterbury, *31, 124*
St. Ursula, *153*
St. Werburga, Shrine of, *45*
St. Wulfstan, *29*
Saints, Cultus of, **6**
Salviati, **107**
Sancroft, Archbishop William, *99,* 34, 135
Sandford, **61,** *85,* **125, 126,** *7, 164, 22, 49, 81, 83, 119*
Savery, John, *3*
Scambler, Edmund, Prebendary, 89
Sceptre, *58*
Schrider, Christopher, **160,** *10,* **39**
Scone, *117*
Scott, Sir Gilbert, **24, 28, 50, 81, 95, 102 ff., 182, 186,** *11, 49, 71, 76, 106 ff., 140, 197, 207, 4, 27, 29, 39, 40, 43, 49*
Screens, Choir, **4,** *84,* **147, 158, 160**
— Altar, *67, 165*
— Henry VII's Chapel, *156*
— Western, Chapels, *31*
— Wrought-iron, **104, 117**
Scrope, Lady, 15
Seager, James L., 38
Seating, in Presbytery, **156, 162**
Sebert, King, Figure of, **33**
— Tomb, **29,** *67*
Secker, Archbishop, 137, 147
Sedilia, **17, 29 ff.,** *74, 78, 85, 87,* **113**
Selwyn, George A., Bishop, 157
Sermon Bell, 186
Shene, 88
Shene, Sacrist, 74, 79, 88
Shepherd, C. W., 38
Shoreditch, Nunnery of Holywell, *214*
Shoreham (Kent) Church, 39
Short, A., Bishop, **167,** 157

Shrine of St. Edward the Confessor, **18, 42, 43, 122,** *31* **ff.**
Shroud of Edward the Confessor, *101*
Sickert, Mrs. Walter, 178
Sidney, Lady Francis, 132
Sillitoe, A. W., Bishop of New Westminster, *201*
Simon de Langham, 171
Skidmore, Messrs., 49
Skilbeck, Clement O., *112*
Smart, Sir George, 164
Smith, Mr. and Mrs. A. Murray, **41**
Society of Antiquaries, **36, 53,** *49, 50, 56, 77, 82, 84, 100, 104*
Society for the Propagation of the Gospel in Foreign Parts, *189*
Solemn League and Covenant, 106
Somerset, Duchess of, 3
Somerset, Duke of, 20
Sonwell, William, 7
South, Robert, Prebendary, 35, 112, 114, 130
Southey, Robert, Monument, *22*
Southwark Cathedral, Screen, **44,** 67
Spoon, Straining, 60
Sporley, Richard, Monk, **20, 22,** 49
Sprat, Mrs. Helen, 77, 166
Sprat, Thomas, Bishop of Rochester, Dean, **26, 36, 63, 71, 78, 80,** 76, 130, 137
Stalls, Canons', **127,** *18*
Stamford, St. George's Church, 64
Stanhope, Earl, Monument, **4,** *12*
Stanley, Lady Augusta, **28, 191**
Stanley, Dr. A. P., Dean, **40, 74, 80, 106, 109, 190,** *106, 180, 183, 192, 199, 207,* 4, 35, 42, 101, 134, 151, 163, 164, 179
— Funeral, 148
— Sermon quoted, **95**
Stanton, Edward (mason), *10*
Stead, John, 43
Stevens, John, 108
Stevens, Thomas, 108
Steward, Richard, Dean, 112
Stockwood, Prebendary, **139**
Stone of Destiny, *166 ff.*
Strype, **56**
Sudbury, John, Prebendary, **60,** 57, 114

Suffolk, Duchess of, 88
Suffragettes, *132*
Sulcardus (historian), **29**
Sumner, Archbishop, **104**
Supertunica, *129*
Suppression Inventory, *2,* 77, 187
Surplices, 129
Sutton, Charles Manners, Archbishop of Canterbury, 145
Sutton, Rev. Christopher, Prebendary, 97
Sutton, John, 18
Syon, Monastery, 88

Taine, M. Hippolyte, **186**
Tait, Archbishop, **103**
Tanner, Laurence, Keeper of Muniments, *105*
Tansley, Samuel, *139*
Tapestries, **41, 61, 62, 63, 82, 144,** *212,* 30, 83 ff., 108, 119
Tapper, Sir Walter, **192, 208,** 36, 188
Taylor, Alexander, *100,* 135
Taylor, Charles, Lay-vicar, *93, 100*
Taylor, James, Minor Canon, 106
Taylor, Dr., Prebendary, **139**
Taylor, Surveyor to Office of Works, *134*
Templars' Badge, 52
Temple, Frederick, Archbishop of Canterbury, 83
Thistle, Order of the, *191*
Thomas, Dean, **53, 64, 85, 123, 131, 134, 139,** *18,* 20, 36
Thompson, H. Yates, **41**
Thomson, William, Archbishop, 82
Thoresby, Ralph, antiquary, **77,** *102, 104,* 137
Thorn, Sacred, Relic, 57
Thorndike, or Thorndyke, Herbert, Prebendary, **77,** 41, 114, 137
Thorndyke, Paul, 41
Three Captains, Monument, **22**
Throne, Royal, *129*
Thursby, John, Silversmith, 59
Thynne, Lord John, Sub-dean, **106, 154, 157, 161, 174,** *139,* 22, 47, 73, 77, 86, 152, 156, 167
Tijou, Jean, 48

vol. ii thus: **125**; *vol. iii thus:* *125*

Tiles, Ancient, 30
Tingle, or Tingles, Anthony (Verger), 55, 61, 120
Tinker, John, Precentor, 120, 135
Tinker, Philip, Precentor, 115
Tomlinson, Bishop of Gibraltar, 100
Tonneworth, Ralph, Sacrist, 188
Torrigiano, 56, *160 ff.*, *200*, *123*, *9*, *71*
Torrisany, *see* Torrigiano
Tosti, *69*
Tothill Fields, 132
Toulon, Battle of, *21*
Towers, Western, *21*
Town Boys, **175**
Tractarianism, **184**
Transept Screens, **166**, **168**
Translation of St. Edward the Confessor, *31*, *81*
Trap Doors in Choir, **185**
Trench, Very Rev. R. C., Dean, 39, 160, 162, 164
Trevisano, *72*
Trinity College, Cambridge, *68*
Tristram, Professor, **18**, **32**, **46**, **114**, *23*, *120*, *25*
Trottiscliffe Church, 37
Truro, Bishop Benson of, **191**
Tucker, William, Minor Canon, 115
Tudor Dynasty, *178*
Tudor, Owen, *145*
Tuffnell, Captain (Clerk of Works), **72**
Turle, James, **184**
Turner, Lawrence, *208*
Turton, Dean, **156**, 155
Tyler, Wat, 14
Tyrell, F., Bishop, 157

United States of America Thanksgiving Day, 194
Unknown Soldier, 184
Upton, Dame Joan, 134

Valence, Aymer de, Tomb, **10**, **174**, *7*, 13, 53
Van Orley, Bernard, 84
Venables, Edmund, Precentor of Lincoln, **165**, **171**
Verdun, Trophy, *25*
Verges, 57, 63, 66 ff., 128

Vergers, 128, 143
Verrio, Painter, **66**, **68**
Victoria Cathedral, British Columbia, **118**, 49
Victoria, Queen, *111*, *128*, 73, 77, 80, 190
Villiers, Monument, *147*
Vincent, Dean, **153**, 143, 144, 150, 151
Visitation Articles, *6*
Viterbo Cathedral, *43*
Vivarini, Bartolomeo, *209*
Voluntaries, **184**

Wafer Bread, *100*, *194*
Wagner, Arthur, 160
Wake, Dr., Prebendary, **139**
Walmisley, T. A., 153
Walpole, Horace, **82**, **131**
Walpole, Sir John, *10*, *173*
Walsall, Francis, Prebendary, 113
Walsingham, *122*
Walter, de Suffield, Bishop of Norwich, 57
Walter of Durham, Painter, **15**, *119*, 25
Walters, Ivy, 131
Wanamaker, Rodman, 174
Wanders, Pieter, 185
War Memorial of Abbey staff, 24
War Precautions, *114*
Warburton, William, Bishop of Gloucester, 78
Wardrobe Accounts, *119*
Ware, Abbot, **7**, **11**, **18**
— Tomb, **25**
Warrenne, Earl of, *41*
Waterloo Place, St. Philip's Church, 39
Wax Effigies, **13**, 127
Weare, T. W., **167**
Wellclose Square, **69**
Welldon, J. E. C., Bishop, *113*
Wellesley, Sir Henry, *195*
Wellington, Duke of, *195*
Wells Cathedral, 47
Wenlock, Walter de, Abbot, **25**, **31**
West, William, *115*
Westlake, F. H., **43**, *72*

Page references to vol. i appear thus: **125**;

Westminster, Archdeacon of, *20*
Westminster City, **154**, 148, 177
— Council, **193**
Westminster, Duke of, *163*
Westminster, Mayor of, 177
Westminster School (buildings), *107*, 155, 193
Westminster Schoolboys, **37**, **101**, **125**, **129**, **148**, **155**, **167**, 141, 144, 161, 163
Westcott, Rev. Canon B. F., *164*
Westmacott, Richard, 150
Weston, Hugh, Dean, *79*
Weston-super-Mare, **93**
Whitchurch Canonicorum, *87*
White, Robert, Minor Canon, 106, 108
Whitehall Palace, **65** ff.
Whitgift, Archbishop, *126*
Wilberforce, Basil, 12, 164
Wilberforce, Samuel, Bishop, **103**, **157**, **185**, 12, 155
Wilberforce, William, 12
Wilcocks or Wilcox, Joseph, Dean, *21*, *179*, 139, 146
Wilford, **91**
Will of Henry VII, *35*.
William I (the Conqueror), *29*
— Coronation, *29*
William and Mary, *4*, *127*, 71
William IV, *111*, 80
William of Colchester, Abbot, 12
William of Florence, 32
William of Gloucester, Goldsmith, *43*
William de Valence, Tomb, *61*,
William of Westminster, 32
William 'the beloved painter', 32
Williams, John, Dean, 35, 99, 101, 103
Wilmington, Lord, *179*
Wilson, Henry, 'ffreemason', *183*
Wilson, Prebendary, **139**
Wilson, Thomas, Sub-dean, 105
Wilton, Joseph, Sculptor, **10**, **83**, 6

Winchester Cathedral, **102**, **124**, *45*, *125*, 117
— Screen, **44**, *67*
Wingham, William, M.P., **150**
Windsor, 47
Windsor, St. George's, *152*, *156*, *202*, 169
— Choir, **174**
— Stalls, **131**
Wine Accounts, 135
Wisbech Castle, *89*
Wiseman, Sir Richard, 103
Wiveliscombe, **93**
Wolfe, General, burial, 6
— Monument of, **10**, **83**
Wolsey, Cardinal, *162*, 84
Wood, Seth, Independent Minister, 114
Woodford, James, Bishop of Ely, **49**
Woodstock, **35**
Woolcombers, Patron Saint of, 24
Woolcott and Browning, Wood-workers, **96**
Wootton (of Bloomsbury), *102*
Worcester, 9
Wordsworth, Christopher, Canon, **163**, **166** ff., **174**, *22*, 152, 161, 164
Wordsworth, William, Monument, *22*
Wren, Sir Christopher, **26**, **27**, **65**, **70**, **79**, **148**, **151**, *4*, *56*, *101*, 49, 186
Wren, Matthew, Bishop, **49**
Wulfstan, Bishop of Worcester, *29*
Wurtemburg, Dukes of, 95
Wyatt, Benjamin, **13**, **45**, **50**, **90**, **94** ff., *13*, *139*, 37, 72
Wyatt, James, **135**, **145**, **152**
Wydville, Elizabeth, 15
Wynchester, Henry, *73*

York, James, Duke of, 116
Young, Prebendary, **139**

Zouch, Thomas, 58

PRINTED IN
GREAT BRITAIN
AT THE
UNIVERSITY PRESS
OXFORD
BY
CHARLES BATEY
PRINTER
TO THE
UNIVERSITY

THE ALCUIN CLUB—of which Dr. Walter Howard Frere was for many years the President—exists for the object of promoting the study of the History and Use of the Book of Common Prayer. It encourages, by publications and other means, the practical study of the English liturgy with its ceremonial, and the arrangement of churches, their furniture, and ornaments, in accordance with the rubrics of the Book of Common Prayer, strict obedience to which is the guiding principle of the work of the Club. During the last half-century the Alcuin Club has issued some eighty publications—Collections, Smaller Books, Pamphlets, and Leaflets—and Members of the Club are entitled to the publications of the current year *gratis*, while Associates are entitled to such of the smaller works *gratis* as the Committee may determine. The subscription for Members is 20s. per annum, and for Associates 5s. per annum. Application for election and for the List of Publications should be sent to the Assistant Secretary, as well as all subscriptions.

President
The Right Rev. the LORD BISHOP OF LONDON

Committee
The Very Rev. A. S. DUNCAN-JONES, B.D., Dean of Chichester, *Chairman*

J. H. ARNOLD, Esq., D.MUS.

W. H. R. BLACKING, Esq., F.R.I.B.A.

F. BRITTAIN, Esq., LITT.D.

The Right Rev. COLIN DUNLOP, M.A., Dean of Lincoln.

F. C. EELES, Esq., D.LITT., O.B.E., F.R.HIST.S., F.S.A.SCOT.

HAROLD C. KING, Esq., M.A.

The Rev. JOCELYN PERKINS, C.V.O., M.A., D.C.L., D.D., F.S.A., Sacrist of Westminster Abbey.

*The Rev. C. E. POCKNEE, A.K.C.

The Rev. J. W. POOLE, M.A.

F. J. E. RABY, Esq., C.B., LITT.D., F.B.A.

The Rev. Canon J. H. SRAWLEY, D.D. (late Chancellor of Lincoln Cathedral).

The Rev. G. B. TIMMS, M.A., Sacrist of Southwark Cathedral.

E. G. P. WYATT, Esq., M.A.

Hon. Secretary
Dr. J. H. ARNOLD
16 Bentley Way, Stanmore, Mddx.

Hon. Treasurer
E. G. P. WYATT, Esq.
Leeholme, St. Winefride's Road, Littlehampton, Sussex.

Assistant Secretary and Assistant Treasurer
The Deanery, Chichester, Sussex.

PUBLICATIONS

(All prices are net)

THE COLLECTIONS

Books not out of print may be obtained from the publishers

SOCIETY FOR PROMOTING CHRISTIAN KNOWLEDGE

9 Northumberland Avenue, W.C. 2

Books out of print are marked thus *

*I. **English Altars.** Sir W. H. ST. JOHN HOPE.

*II. **Exposition de la Messe.** Edited by the Right Rev. W. H. FRERE.

*III and IV. **Pontifical Services,** vols. i and ii. Right Rev. W. H. FRERE.

*V. **Dat Boexken van der Missen** (The Booklet of the Mass). By GHERIT VANDER GOUDE, 1507. The Rev. PERCY DEARMER, D.D.

VI. **The Edwardian Inventories for Bedfordshire.** Edited by F. C. EELES, from transcripts by the Rev. J. E. BROWN. 5s.

VII. **The Edwardian Inventories for Huntingdonshire.** Edited by Mrs. S. C. LOMAS, from transcripts by T. CRAIB. 10s.

VIII. **Pontifical Services,** vol. iii. Descriptive Notes and 143 Illustrations from 16th-century woodcuts. Edited by F. C. EELES. £1 1s.

*IX. **The Edwardian Inventories for Buckinghamshire.** Edited by F. C. EELES.

*X. **Fifty Pictures of Gothic Altars.** Edited by the Rev. PERCY DEARMER.†

*XI. **The Sarum Missal in English.** By the Rev. F. E. WARREN.

*XII. **Pontifical Services,** vol. iv. Edited by ATHELSTAN RILEY.

XIII. **A History of the Use of Incense in Divine Worship.** By E. G. CUTHBERT F. ATCHLEY. £3.

*XIV. **Visitation Articles and Injunctions of the Period of the Reformation,** vol. i. (Theory, history, and practice.) By the Right Rev. W. H. FRERE.

*XV. **The Same,** vol. ii (1536–58). Edited by the Right Rev. W. H. FRERE, and W. M. KENNEDY.

*XVI. **The Same,** vol. iii (1558–75). Edited by the Right Rev. W. H. FRERE. [See also XXV–XXVII.]

*XVII. **Traditional Ceremonial and Customs connected with the Scottish Liturgy.** By F. C. EELES. £1.

*XVIII. **The Rationale of Ceremonial,** 1540–3. By Sir C. S. COBB.

*XIX. **Illustrations of the Liturgy.** By CLEMENT O. SKILBECK, and the Rev. PERCY DEARMER.

† This work has been reprinted by A. R. Mowbray and Co. Ltd.

XX. The Edwardian Inventories for the City and County of Exeter. Edited by Miss B. CRESSWELL. 10s.

*XXI. The Sacrament Reserved: being a History of the Practice of Reserving the Eucharist up to the IVth Lateran Council. By the Rev. W. H. FREESTONE.

XXII. The Ornaments of the Ministers as shown on English Monumental Brasses. By the Rev. H. J. CLAYTON. £1 5s.

*XXIII. The Chantry Certificates for Oxfordshire, and The Edwardian Inventories of Church Goods for Oxfordshire. Edited by ROSE GRAHAM.

XXIV. Illustrations of the Occasional Offices of the Church. (Medieval pictures and miniatures.) Edited by H. S. KINGSFORD. £1 5s.

XXV–XXVII. Elizabethan Episcopal Administration. An Essay introductory to a further Collection of Visitation Articles, by W. M. KENNEDY. Vol. i: The Essay. Vol. ii: Articles, &c., 1575–83. Vol. iii: Articles, &c., 1583–1603; £3 3s. the set. Vol. i separately; £1 5s.

XXVIII. Studies in the Early Roman Liturgy. I. The Kalendar. By the Right Rev. W. H. FRERE. £1 1s.

XXIX. Historical Survey of Holy Week: its Services and Ceremonial. By the Rev. JOHN WALTON TYRER. £1 5s.

XXX. Studies in the Early Roman Liturgy. II. The Roman Gospel-Lectionary. By the Right Rev. W. H. FRERE. £1 5s.

XXXI. On the Epiclesis of the Eucharistic Liturgy and in the Consecration of the Font. By E. G. CUTHBERT F. ATCHLEY. £1 1s.

XXXII. Studies in the Early Roman Liturgy. III. The Roman Epistle-Lectionary. By the Right Rev. W. H. FRERE. £1 1s.

XXXIII. Westminster Abbey, its Worship and Ornaments. By the Rev. JOCELYN PERKINS. Vol. i. £1 5s.

XXXIV. The Same, vol. ii. £1 5s.

*XXXV. Walter Howard Frere. Vol. i: A Collection of his Papers on Liturgical and Historical subjects. Edited by J. H. ARNOLD and E. G. P. WYATT.

XXXVI. The Chichester Customary. By the Very Rev. A. S. DUNCAN-JONES. 10s. 6d.

XXXVII. The Booke of Common Prayer of the Churche of England: its making and revisions, 1549–1661. By the Rev. Professor E. C. RATCLIFF. 10s.

XXXVIII. Westminster Abbey, its Worship and Ornaments. By the Rev. JOCELYN PERKINS. Vol. iii. £1 15s.

XXXIX. Walter Howard Frere. Vol. ii: Letters on Liturgical Revision and Construction. Edited by the Rev. RONALD C. D. JASPER.
[*In preparation*]

The Carthusian Rite. [*In preparation*]

THE TRACTS (i.e., SMALLER BOOKS)

Books not out of print may be obtained from the publishers

A. R. MOWBRAY & CO. LTD.

28 Margaret Street, W. 1

*I. **Ornaments of the Rubric.** By J. T. MICKLETHWAITE.

*II. **Consolidation.** By the Rev. W. C. E. NEWBOLT.

*III. **Liturgical Interpolations.** By the Rev. T. A. LACEY.

*IV. **The Parish Clerk and his right to read the Liturgical Epistle.** By E. G. CUTHBERT F. ATCHLEY.

*V. **A First English Ordo: A Celebration of the Lord's Supper with one Minister, described and discussed by some members of the Alcuin Club.**

*VI. **The People's Prayers: considerations on the use of the Litany in Public Worship.** By E. G. CUTHBERT F. ATCHLEY.

*VII. **The Sign of the Cross in the Western Liturgies.** By the Rev. E. E. BERESFORD COOKE.

*VIII. **The 'Interpretations' of the Bishops and their Influence on Elizabethan Policy.** By W. M. KENNEDY.

*IX. **Prayer Book Revision: The 'Irreducible Minimum'.** Edited by ATHELSTAN RILEY.

*X. **The Bread of the Eucharist.** By the Rev. R. MAXWELL WOOLLEY.

*XI. **English or Roman Use?** By E. G. P. WYATT.

*XII. **Russian Observations upon the American Prayer Book.** Translated by WILFRID J. BARNES, and Edited with Notes by the Right Rev. W. H. FRERE.

XIII. **A Directory of Ceremonial.** Part I. Fourth edition (revised, with illustrations). 5s. [*See also* XIX.]

*XIV. **Ceremonial Pictured in Photographs.**

*XV. **The Mozarabic and Ambrosian Rites.** Essays in Comparative Liturgiology. By the Rev. W. C. BISHOP.

*XVI. **The Uniats and their Rites.** By Sir STEPHEN GASELEE.

XVII. **Linen Ornaments of the Church.** By the Rev. PERCY DEARMER. 3s. 6d.

*XVIII. **Cassock and Gown.** By the Rev. H. J. CLAYTON.

XIX. **A Directory of Ceremonial.** Part II, for services (of the Seasons) not included in Tract XIII. Second edition (revised with illustrations). 5s.

XX. **Processions.** By the Rev. COLIN DUNLOP. A dissertation, with practical suggestions. 5s.

XXI. **A Server's Manual.** Directions for one server at the Holy Communion (1662 and 1928). 2s. 6d.

*XXII. Anglican Liturgies. Texts of the English Eucharistic Rites of 1662 and 1928, the Scottish, American, South African, Indian, and Ceylon Liturgies, &c.; and 'An Essay in Liturgical Construction' by the Right Rev. W. H. FRERE. Edited by J. H. ARNOLD.

*XXIII. English Prayer Books. By STANLEY MORISON.

XXIV. Thoughts on the Shape of the Liturgy. Essays by the Very Rev. H. N. BATE and F. C. EELES. 3s.

XXV. Notes on Episcopal Ornaments and Ceremonial. By F. C. EELES. 3s. 6d.

XXVI. A Plea for the Prayer of Oblation. By C. LEO BERRY. 2s.

XXVII. How to celebrate the Holy Eucharist, for the information of Deacons, Ordinands, and others. [*In preparation*]

THE PAMPHLETS
Publishers:
A. R. MOWBRAY & CO. LTD.

*I. Liturgical Interpolations and Prayer Book Revision. By the Rev. T. A. LACEY.

*II. The Liturgical Gospels. By the Right Rev. W. H. FRERE.

*III. A Century of Collects. Selected and translated by the Rev. ATWELL M. Y. BAYLAY.

*IV. The Manual Acts. By the Rev. VERNON STALEY.

*V. The Eucharistic Prayer. By E. G. P. WYATT.

*VI. Memorial Services. Extracted by permission from 'A Prayer Book Revised', as issued in 1913 with a Preface by the Right Rev. CHARLES GORE.

*VII. The Burial Service. By E. G. P. WYATT.

*VIII. The Primitive Consecration Prayer. A Lecture given at the Annual Meeting of the Club, 7 June 1922, by the Right Rev. W. H. FRERE. *Dr. Frere's development of this thesis will be found in* 'The Anaphora' (S.P.C.K. for the Church Historical Society. 12s. 6d.).

X. Reservation: its Purpose and Method. By D. L. MURRAY. 1s. 6d.

XI. What is the English Use? An inquiry into the principles underlying the conduct of public worship in the Church of England. By the Rev. COLIN DUNLOP. 1s. 6d.

*XII. A Survey of the Proposals for the Alternative Prayer Book. (The 'Orange Book'.) By a group of members of the Alcuin Club. Part I: The Order of Holy Communion.

*XIII. The Same. Part II: Occasional Offices.

*XIV. The Same. Part III: The Calendar, &c., The Collects, Epistles, and Gospels, and The Ordination Services.

OCCASIONAL PAPERS, LEAFLETS, ETC.

Why Change the Communion Service? By the Very Rev. A. S. DUNCAN-JONES, Dean of Chichester. A paper upon the content of the Eucharistic Prayer of Consecration, with special reference to that of 1928. S.P.C.K. 6d.

Liturgy in the Parish. Six cheap tracts for popular use, by members of the Club, bound in a single volume. Mowbrays. 2s.

This comprises the following:

Praying with the Church.

The Consecration of the Eucharist.

'English Use.'

The Parish Eucharist.

The Catholic Altar.

Processions.

The next series has opened with:

Simple Eucharistic Ceremonial. 2d.

Eucharistic Ceremonial in One-priest Parishes. 2d.

Clerical Members of the Club who find themselves in agreement with these leaflets are asked to keep their parish tract-cases stocked with them. By so doing they will help forward the cause which the Club is designed to serve.

Dixit Cranmer (A Reply to Dom Gregory). By the Rev. G. B. TIMMS. A paper on Cranmer's eucharistic doctrine. Mowbrays. 1s. 6d.

The New Canons and Obedience to the Book of Common Prayer. By the Rev. Canon A. F. SMETHURST. Synodical Secretary of the Convocation of Canterbury. Mowbrays. 1s.

A plain guide to the Consecration of the Holy Communion (1928) —in card form. Mowbrays. *[In preparation]*

PRINTED IN
GREAT BRITAIN
AT THE
UNIVERSITY PRESS
OXFORD
BY
CHARLES BATEY
PRINTER
TO THE
UNIVERSITY